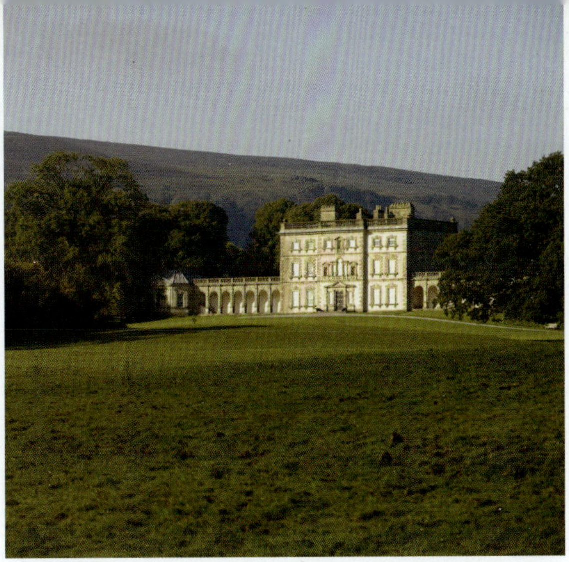

The Big House Library in Ireland

Books in Ulster Country Houses · Mark Purcell

National Trust

Front cover
Lady Londonderry's Sitting Room, Mount Stewart

Back Cover
Plate from William Chambers, *Designs of Chinese Buildings, Furniture, Dresses, Machines and Utensils* (London, 1757) (Springhill)

Frontispiece
Florence Court, County Fermanagh

Endpapers
Marbled endpaper from John Ray, *L'Histoire Naturelle* (Paris, 1767) (Florence Court)

Below
Bookplate of the 3rd Earl of Enniskillen (Florence Court)

Illustrations

The photographs are all National Trust Images/John Hammond, with the following exceptions: British Library p.56; Alec Cobbe p. 76; Country Life Picture Library pp. 8, 73; Irish Architectural Archive pp. 14 (right), 17, 19; National Museum of Ireland p.10; National Trust pp. 12, 87, 91, 99; National Trust Images pp. 22, 71; NT Images/Peter Aprahamian front cover; NT Images/Derek Croucher p. 15 (top), 69, 75; NT Images/Andreas von Einsiedel pp. 13 (bottom), 40 (bottom), 62, 65, 90, 93; NT Images/Angelo Hornak p. 66; NT Images/Christopher Hurst p. 70; NT Images/David Levenson p. 68 (left); NT Images/John Millar p. 1; NT Images/Robert Morris pp. 67, 68 (right); NT Images/Peter Muhly p. 13 (top); NT Images/Derrick E. Witty pp. 39, 54 (top), 55, 64 (bottom), 89; Sir John Soane's Museum p. 97 (bottom).

Published in 2011 in the United Kingdom by:

The National Trust
Heelis
Kemble Drive
Swindon
Wiltshire SN2 2NA
Registered charity no. 205846

ISBN 978-0-7078-0416-3

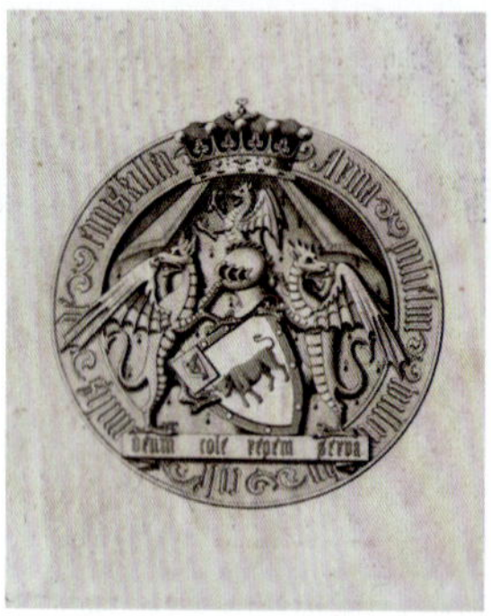

A CIP catalogue record for this book is available from the British Library.

For more information about the work of the National Trust, the properties in its care, membership or other publications, please visit: www.nationaltrust.org.uk

This book can be ordered directly from the National Trust Shop www.nationaltrust.org.uk/shop and all good bookshops.

Design LEVEL
Printing Butler Tanner & Dennis Fine Art Services

Contents

Acknowledgements

Research always depends to a great extent on the support of others. Until 1999 I had never been to Northern Ireland, and it is a pleasure to thank those who have helped me on numerous visits since then. At the National Trust I am particularly grateful to Frances Bailey, the Trust's Curator in Northern Ireland, and at the various Trust properties to Patricia Law at Springhill, Barbara Muhly at Castle Ward, and Jim Chestnutt at Florence Court. My interest in Ireland was first encouraged by the Trust's then Director of Historic Buildings Simon Jervis (aided and abetted by Peter Marlow, then the Trust's Historic Buildings Representative in Northern Ireland), and has been supported in more recent times by Sarah Staniforth, its Museums and Collections Director. Edith Stafford pointed me to important material on the history of The Argory, Anne Casement kindly read my text on Mount Stewart, and Alec Cobbe kindly provided a photograph of bookbinding tools from Newbridge. Many others, North and South, have been generous in sharing bibliographical expertise, and their knowledge of Irish houses and libraries. I am especially grateful to Charles Benson at Trinity College, Dublin, Professor William McCormack and Elizabethanne Boran at the Edward Worth Library (again in Dublin), to members of the Rare Books Group of the Library Association of Ireland, and to the delegates (and organisers) of successive conferences hosted by Archbishop Marsh's Library in Dublin and by the Centre for the Study of Irish Houses and Estates at Maynooth.

Toby Barnard and Peter Hoare read the entire text in its final form, and I owe a special debt of gratitude to them for their comments and suggestions, though remaining errors of course remain my own. Gordon Wheeler prevented me from falling into a multiplicity of errors, and generously shared with me the contents of many decades of his own research, as well as providing some splendid hospitality in Downpatrick. David Adshead, Caroline Shenton and Oliver Garnett provided every possible support in drawing together the final text, which was published with funds from the National Trust's Specialist Publications programme.

It is customary to thank the staff of archives and libraries, and I have visited many, though I am especially grateful to staff at the Public Record Office of Northern Ireland in Belfast, and to friends and former colleagues in the Bodleian Library in Oxford, where much of what follows was written. This gratitude extends not just to those on the issue counters and those who fetched and carried, but also to those staff – less visible and more easily forgotten – who spend years documenting books and manuscripts so that others can find them. I am equally grateful to staff and contractors working for the National Trust. Though I did some of the work myself, I was not always the principal player, with Ed Potten working formidably hard on the cataloguing of the Trust's Northern Ireland libraries, a rewarding but sometimes exhausting task also shared by John Gandy, William Hale, Peter Hoare and Felicity Stimpson.

Right
The English Irish Dictionary. An Focloir Bearla Gaoidhelige (Paris, 1732) (Springhill)

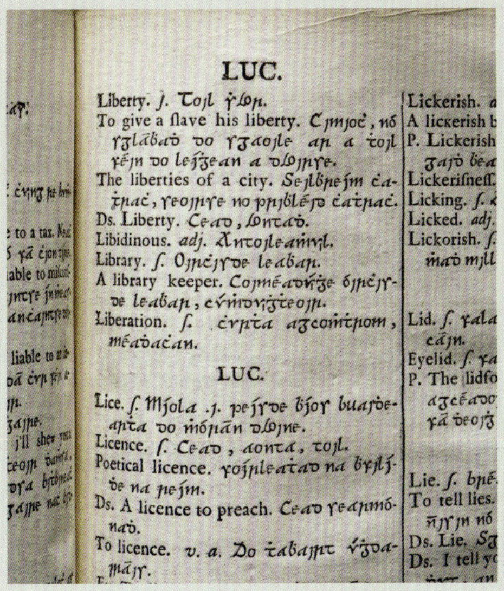
LUC.
Liberty.
To give a slave his liberty.
The liberties of a city.
Ds. Liberty.
Libidinous. adj.
Library. s.
A library keeper.
Liberation. s.
LUC.
Lice. s.
Licence. s.
Poetical licence.
Ds. A licence to preach.
To licence. v. a.
Lickerish.
A lickerish
P. Lickerish
Lickerishness.
Licking. s.
Licked. adj.
Lickorish. s.
Lid. s.
Eyelid. s.
P. The lidfo
Lie. s.
To tell lies.
Ds. Lie.
Ds. I tell y

John Hammond took most of the splendid photographs, a complicated operation organised by Chris Lacey of the National Trust's Photographic Library, with the kind assistance of staff in National Trust properties across Northern Ireland. Gina Murphy and, before her, Becci Shanks helped set up this and many other field trips.

I owe a particular debt of gratitude to the late Lady Mairi Bury. Born at Mount Stewart in 1921, Lady Mairi spent much of her life there, inheriting the estate on the death of her mother, Edith, Marchioness of Londonderry, in 1962, and subsequently presenting the house and many of its contents to the National Trust. Though sadly she died shortly before this book went to press, Lady Mairi warmly encouraged my interests in her parents' library at Mount Stewart. It was a great privilege and pleasure to talk at length with her in the spring of 2009, and her vivid recollections of life at Mount Stewart between the wars – and of family lore reaching back well into the nineteenth century – were fascinating indeed.

Curating an assembly of more then 160 historic libraries of necessity involves constant travel away from home, and in addition to expressing my thanks for the hospitality of many friends and colleagues, I am particular grateful to the staff of the Cuan Hotel in Strangford, which became a regular and extremely welcoming base in the east of Northern Ireland. Hospitality of another kind was dispensed by David Bonar, who allowed me to spend three weeks writing in his apartment in New York, in the process speeding the completion of a book which had already been too long in writing, and provoking some interesting points of comparison with plantation houses of another kind during a weekend driving around Virginia. Finally, mention of America reminds me that my work for the National Trust has ultimately been bank-rolled by its supporter group in the United States, the Royal Oak Foundation, whose Campaign for Country House Libraries ran between 1995 and 1999, raising the funds to endow the work of the Trust's Libraries Curator, and to pay for much-needed cataloguing and conservation of the Trust's collections. Readers should note that throughout the book 'Library' refers to a room, while 'library' is a collection of books.

Mark Purcell
2010

Prologue

The Big House Library

In 1850 there were perhaps 2000 country houses in Ireland.[1] Standing at the heart of its demesne, each Big House dominated its locality, though for many humbler folk the demesne wall would have been all that they ever saw. The inhabitants of the surrounding countryside worked for it and paid their rents to its owner, who not only owned the land, but very likely administered justice as the local magistrate. Whether an elegant Palladian box or a vast Gothic Revival castle, the Big House was far larger than any of its neighbours, built to inspire awe and deference, conceivably to intimidate, and certainly to serve as a political power-base, a place for hunting and shooting, for politics, and for the polite rituals of grand balls and parties. Its owner might indeed have spent long stretches in Dublin (where the 'season' ran from November to March each year, and before 1801 Parliament usually sat every second winter, and might indeed have been an absentee), but for many the Big House remained at the centre of life.[2] Perhaps surrounded by elaborate and well-tended gardens, or filled with works of art, it was at the same time both separate and different. The very term 'Big House', more likely to be used by the tenants than the owners, carried with it a certain undertow of resentment, because of course so many Big Houses belonged to the descendants of Protestant families who had settled in Ireland in the seventeenth and eighteenth centuries, and whose houses were built on land confiscated from its original Catholic owners in Penal Times. When Lord Ardilaun – born Edward Arthur Guinness (1840–1915) – built Ashford Castle in County Mayo in the 1870s, he explained to a friend that the cannons, battlements and moat were because he had 'a taste for the picturesque'. Nonetheless, they had the practical advantage that he would 'be able to defend myself in case of invasion, and as the drawbridge will be raised nightly it will be difficult for the dynamiters to get at me'.[3] Writing in the 1930s, the socialite Daisy, Countess of Fingall (1866–1944), the Nationalist wife of Ireland's senior Catholic peer, and the mistress of Killeen Castle in County Meath, articulated what had by then become something of a commonplace. The Big Houses of the Ascendancy were like artificial islands, she observed, shut off from the rest of Ireland behind high walls, 'raised by the incredibly cheap labour of the natives whom their ancestors had tried to exterminate'. They were separated from their neighbours not just by walls, but by wealth, cultural standing, political power (and of course in most parts of Ireland apart from north-east Ulster, by religion as well), 'making a world of their own, with Ireland outside the gates'.[4]

By the end of the twentieth century, only a few hundred Big Houses still survived intact. No more than a handful remained in the possession of their original owners, or survived in other hands but with a significant number of their original contents – including their libraries. But since books were – as another house-owner, the novelist Elizabeth Bowen, of Bowen's Court, County Cork, put it – among 'the proper fittings of a gentleman's house', almost every Big House would once have contained a library.[5] In some cases, this might well have been the only library in the district, though whether it was a carefully assembled collection or a haphazard accumulation of ancestral books would naturally have varied from place to place.

Writing in an essay republished in Dublin in 1736, the English schoolmaster John Clarke (1687–1743) had observed that four categories of person should properly devote themselves to study, for which purpose it was desirable that they should own a library. 'Gentlemen and such as live upon their estates' had been put into the world by God to serve their country – in the making of law, the encouragement of virtue, and the support of the poor – and so it was necessary that they should have a command of such subjects as logic, ethics and history. They ought not to believe that it was permissible for them to dissipate their time in frivolities, he admonished, because 'Heaven has relieved them from a life of Drudgery'.[6] 'Persons of Genteel Professions or Trade … as Lawyers, Physicians, Merchants, &c.', too, should read in so far as they could find time to do so, and it was appropriate that lawyers in particular should follow a similar programme to that prescribed for the gentry. Merchants, with still less time, were directed towards history, as well as volumes of essays like the *Tatler* and *Spectator*, while clergy, the third category, should be properly informed 'to explain and defend the true religion'. Taking a slightly starchy view of plays and romances – of which he disclaimed much knowledge other than that 'they are generally very indiscreetly and foolishly writ' – Clarke felt that his fourth group, ladies 'of Fortune', should stick to their own language. A little Latin was permissible, but French was imprudent, and it was more appropriate that they should explore history and geography, if only at a basic level. Of course these neat categorisations were apt, in England and Ireland alike, to break down, as Clarke would have known perfectly well. A family of country squires might creep up the social scale over several generations and join the ranks of the peerage, merchant cousins might inherit a country estate, younger sons be sent into trade or the law, or daughters marry country clergymen who might in time find their way onto the episcopal bench. Given the vagaries of inheritance and descent, ancestral shelves might become congested with books which had originally belonged to those in all four of John Clarke's categories, and certainly this is the case in those few Big House libraries which still exist in Ireland.

In the modern Republic no more than a handful of Big Houses still have their historic libraries, though the grandest house of all – Castletown, County Kildare, built for Speaker William Conolly in the 1720s – remained fully furnished long enough to have its Library photographed by *Country Life* in 1936, and still had its books as recently as the 1960s.[7] Today there are books at Castletown again, including some magnificent Irish bindings, but only ten are original to the house. Among other houses now in the care of the Irish state, the 700-odd volumes at Derrynane, the County Cork house of Daniel O'Connell (1775–1847), are O'Connell family books, but the Liberator's own library was sold in Dublin in 1849.[8] In Kilkenny, some 60 books from the original library of the Dukes of Ormonde (a collection was first mentioned there before 1539, and a catalogue created in 1685) have been returned to the castle, but most of those seen by visitors have been introduced from outside. Ilnacullin, on an island in Bantry Bay, has the mostly twentieth-century library of the Bryce family. The library at Farmleigh House, the Guinness house on the edge of the Phoenix Park in Dublin, is on an altogether grander scale, and was donated to Archbishop Marsh's Library in 2009, but the magnificent collection of books is, like the house, in the guardianship of the Office of Public Works.[9] In private hands, surviving libraries could probably now be counted on the fingers of one hand. Probably the most remarkable are at Tullynally Castle, County Westmeath

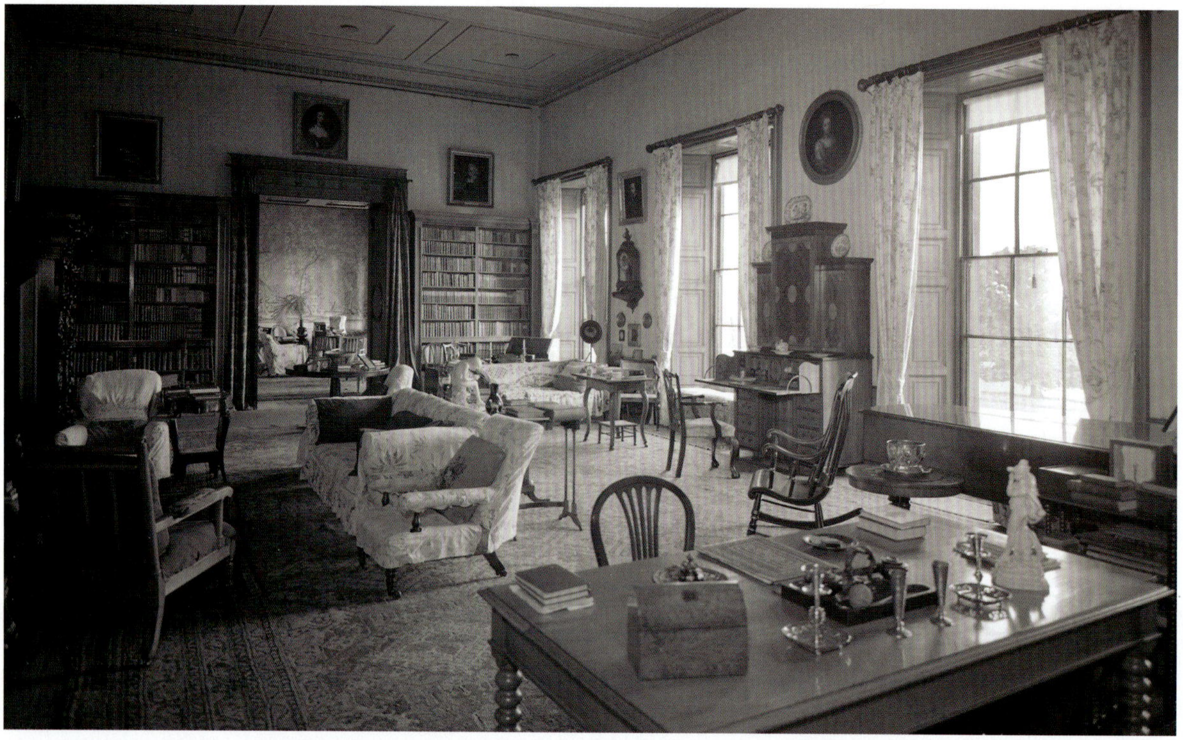

Above
The Library at Townley Hall, County Louth, in 1948 (Irish Architecture Archive)

(formerly known as Pakenham Hall) and at Clonalis, County Roscommon.[10] Both are either mentioned or illustrated in the standard guides to Irish houses. Clonalis, in particular, is fascinating as the library of an aristocratic Catholic family which can trace its pedigree back for well-on fifteen hundred years, and it includes the books of the Catholic antiquarian Charles O'Conor of Bellanagare (1710–91), many of them inscribed in Irish on their title-pages.[11] Other extant collections are much more modest, with the remnant of a library much depleted in the 1950s on show to visitors at Westport House, County Mayo, and a much smaller rump at Strokestown, the former home of the Mahons, in County Roscommon. No doubt a few more survive unseen in grand houses which are rarely, if ever, accessible to strangers, but several great Irish houses which otherwise retain many of their original contents have lost their libraries. At Glin Castle, County Galway, the Knight of Glin has bookcases and an eighteenth-century bookplate, but none of the original books; while Birr Castle, County Offaly, retains its historic archive, but the library was lost in an accidental fire in the 1920s. At least one Big House library, from Townley Hall, County Louth – originally housed in a magnificent room designed in 1796 for Blayney Townley Balfour (son-in-law of the Earl of Enniskillen of Florence Court) by the architect of the house, Francis Johnston – survives largely intact in an institutional collection, with some 3000 titles at Trinity College in Dublin.[12] Several hundred more books were purchased in the 1920s by the National Library of Ireland from the rather unusual library of Irish history and antiquities assembled by E. P. Shirley at Lough Fea, County Monaghan, between the 1850s and 1870s.[13] Hundreds of other libraries are now remembered only through ownership inscriptions and bookplates in individual books in collections in America, Ireland, and Great Britain.[14]

Unsurprisingly, the English nostalgia for the country house was not generally repeated in Ireland. In the Free State (and from 1948 the Republic) there was no equivalent of the National Trust to act as a safety net when owners fell on hard times, and though it would not do to forget the activities of the Irish Georgian Society, no-one could claim that it succeeded in capturing the imagination of the Irish public in the way that the equivalent polemicists – James Lees-Milne or Vita Sackville-West – did in England. The response of many Irish people to an often-unlamented past was much more ambivalent, and country-house visiting has never been the popular pastime it has become on the other side of the water; in both the Republic and Northern Ireland, very few privately-owned houses are open to the public on a regular basis, and some of those that are accessible receive very small numbers of visitors. Even without the economic realities underlying Irish life through much of the twentieth century, for some in the new Ireland the Big House still carried with it the stigma of association with the old ruling class. When Hazelwood, County Sligo, was acquired for demolition by the Land Commission in 1946 (it still stands, though seriously dilapidated), the editor of the *Sligo Champion* grumbled that in England such houses were preserved by the National Trust, and that it was deplorable that an Irish public body should value them only in 'the contents of the lead on the roof', but this was a rare view.[15] Of course English houses could also be sold for salvage, and hundreds were, but in England there was a perhaps surprising degree of agreement that country houses somehow encapsulated the soul of the nation, and were a cultural inheritance in which everyone could take pride.[16] This consensus has certainly not been present in Ireland. To some extent it still is not, as the sale of Lissadell, also in County Sligo, in 2003 showed, when even the combination of a magnificent and fully-furnished Georgian house with the impeccable Republican credentials of Countess Markiewicz did not provoke the public intervention that many had hoped for and expected. In the rather different climate of Northern Ireland, it is true, a handful of historic libraries do survive in private houses, but many others have been partially or entirely dispersed.[17] Caledon in County Tyrone is fairly typical. Nash's great Library room is still furnished with books, but the magnificent collection of Thomas Percy (1729–1811), the English-born Bishop of Dromore, and author of the best-selling *Reliques of Ancient English Poetry* (installed in the house by the 2nd Earl of Caledon in 1812) was largely sold to Queen's University, Belfast in 1969. By then it had already been raided by the great American dealer A.S.W. Rosenbach (with a little help from Shane Leslie of nearby Glaslough) in breach of the family entail. When the Caledon trustees later wrote to Philadelphia to demand their return, the canny dealer, confident that the law of entail had no power in America, simply ignored the letter.[18]

Set in this context, libraries in National Trust houses in the North start to assume a special interest, as remarkable and now extremely rare examples of a sort of domestic library which would once have been found in Big Houses all over Ireland. Private collections of books, have, of course, survived within a large number of institutional and particularly ecclesiastical libraries, with obvious examples including the library of the Antrim-born Archbishop William King (1650–1729) partly in the Bolton Library in Cashel, County Tipperary, or the books bequeathed by the Dublin physician Edward Worth (1688–1733) to Dr Steevens' Hospital in the Irish capital.[19] These libraries, and others less well-known, still lurking in the sometimes beleaguered libraries of the former established Church of Ireland, have much in common with those in the great Northern houses, but as essentially dynastic collections – as opposed to the libraries of successful professional men – there are also a good many differences as

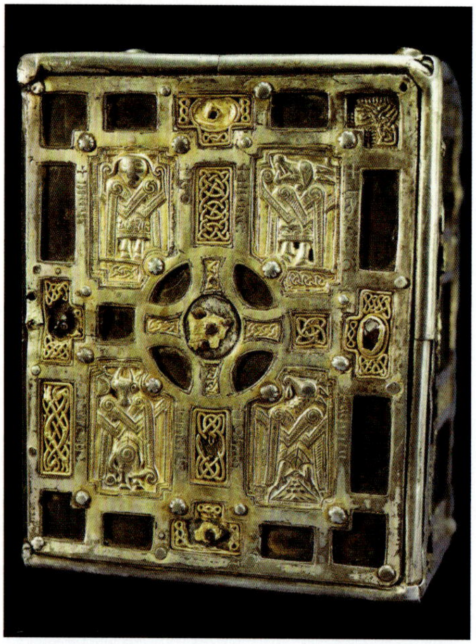

Right
The *Soiscel Molaise,* the book shrine of St Molaise, from Devenish Island, County Fermanagh, eleventh century (National Museum of Ireland)

well.[20] Another key distinction, of course, is that figures like King or Worth were in every sense collectors, clearly aware of the rarity, condition and value of their books, and conscious of them as valuable artefacts which themselves existed in an historical continuum. Only rarely would this have been so with the books in a Big House in the country, though whether owners were in agreement with John Clarke's view that 'the high value set upon these Old Editions is in a great measure whimsical' or had simply never paused to consider the question is perhaps another matter.[21] For all these reasons, what follows is a mixture of detailed description of libraries and their contents, as well as an attempt to examine them in a rather broader historical context.

In the last 30 years Irish historical studies have been dominated by the phenomenon of 'revisionism', with a new generation of scholars challenging many aspects of the received version of Irish history, and above all demanding due recognition of the range of 'varieties of Irishness', rather than traditional – if historically entirely explicable – Nationalist narratives.[22] But even the most enthusiastic controversialist would have to concede that the books on the shelves of a great Irish house did not and do not in any sense reflect the interests, opportunities and outlook of the vast majority of the Irish population, and certainly not of the Catholic majority. Nor, of course, do they represent the first chapter of the history of the book in Ireland.

Gaelic Ireland had its own very sophisticated literary and oral culture, and in 1518 the Anglo-Norman 9th Earl of Kildare had some 59 books at his castle in Maynooth – presumably both printed and manuscript – including works of piety, chronicles, and chivalric romances – of which 21 were in Latin, eleven in French, seven in English, and ten in Irish.[23] Cuchonnact Maguire (Cú Chonnact Mág Uidhir), Lord of Fermanagh, died in 1589, and 40 years later the *Annals of the Four Masters* memorialised him as 'a learned and studious adept in Latin and Irish'; and a Irish poembook that belonged to him is today in the Royal Library in Copenhagen.[24] Popular literacy may have been quite widespread, with 40% of the Catholic tenants on the Earl of Antrim's estates able to sign their names in the 1630s, and 85% on the Ulster estates of the Hill family in the later seventeenth century.[25] And it is an intriguing thought that the eleventh-century *Soiscel Molaise*, the gold book shrine of St Molaise, long associated with the ancient monastic settlement on Devenish Island in Lough Erne, was already 800 years old (and still in the hands of its hereditary keepers, the O'Meehans) at the time that the Victorian Earls of Enniskillen were buying books for nearby Florence Court.[26] Similarly, the manuscripts of Peregrine O'Clery (Cú Choigeríche Ó Cléirigh) – hereditary historian to one of the leading families of north-west Ireland, the O'Donnells of Tirconnell – were taken by him to County Mayo when he was dispossessed and expelled from his lands in 1632. They seem to have remained in the possession of his descendants but were brought to Dublin in about 1810, when they came into the possession of the Irish lexicographer Edward O'Reilly, before being purchased by George Petrie for the Royal Irish Academy at O'Reilly's sale on 30 November 1830.[27]

It is equally true that the owners of grand houses – the landed élite – were not even remotely typical of the 25% of the population who comprised the Protestant subjects of the early modern Kingdom of Ireland. But in certain respects their libraries are perhaps surprisingly uncontroversial. On the one hand, very few Catholic books were printed in Dublin until the arrival of the printer Ignatius Kelly in the city in 1740, and surviving libraries between them contain very few books of Catholic interest.[28] On the other hand, any collection of old books can be looked at fundamentally in two ways: from the perspective of the consumer or producer; and as a conflation of products once hawked on the market and as part of the surviving detritus of everyday life. The Big House may have belonged to the landowning élite, but the printers, booksellers, binders, chapmen, engravers of the bookplates, waggoners and boatmen who moved books to and from Dublin, agents who dealt with the financial paperwork, servants who cleaned the shelves – and even those who read now-vanished copies of books which today exist only on the shelves of an aristocratic library – may well have come from more varied strata of Irish society, Catholic and Protestant. And while landlords and their families may have comprised no more than a tiny fraction of the total population in a predominantly agricultural economy, the great majority of Irish men and women lived in landed estate communities.[29] In many parts of Ireland the fundamental patterns of the landscape are themselves the direct result of a process of estate formation in the seventeenth and eighteenth centuries, with a rural hinterland grouped around planned towns and villages still named – if not re-christened in the twentieth century – after their early modern owners.[30] To this extent the books on the shelves of those who once dominated those communities are of interest for that reason alone. What is more, aristocratic libraries do not just contain books produced for aristocratic consumers, but books which were read in less rarefied circles as well. The chances of the years being what they are, a copy of an eighteenth-century schoolbook used by an earl's son is far more likely to have survived than a copy of the same book which belonged to a tradesman's son – and the task of reporting the National Trust's books to the online *English Short Title Catalogue* (ESTC) has indeed revealed that its libraries in Northern Ireland between them contain considerable numbers of apparently quite ordinary British and Irish books which are in fact extremely rare survivals.

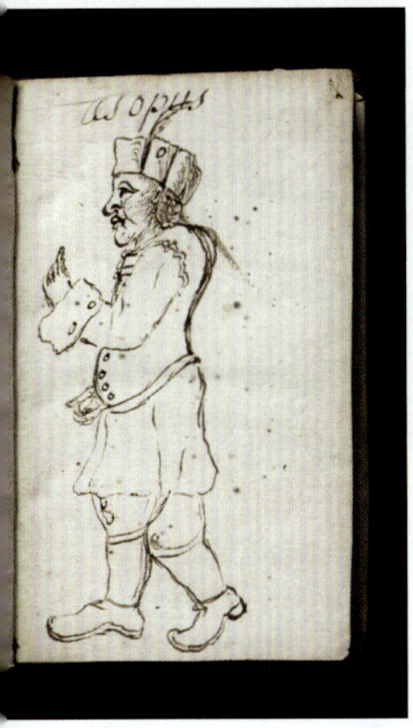

Above
Drawing of a schoolmaster on flyleaf of *Mythologia Aesopica* (London, 1682) (Springhill)

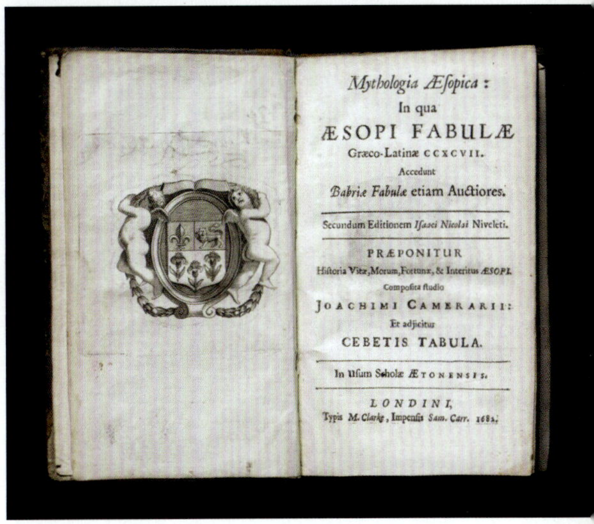

Mythologia Æsopica:
In qua
ÆSOPI FABULÆ
Græco-Latinæ CCXCVII.
Accedunt
Babriæ Fabulæ etiam Auctiores.

Secundum Editionem *Isaaci Nicolai* Niveleti.

PRÆPONITUR
Historia Vitæ, Morum, Fortunæ, & Interitus *ÆSOPI*.
Composita studio
JOACHIMI CAMERARII:
Et adjicitur
CEBETIS TABULA.

In Usum Scholæ ÆTONENSIS.

LONDINI,
Typis *M. Clarke*, Impensis *Sam. Carr.* 1682.

Above right
A seventeenth-century schoolbook: *Mythologia Aesopica* (London, 1682), Wing A730 (Springhill)

Unlike great research libraries in big cities, these collections have never been subject to atmospheric pollution or the attentions of reforming librarians, and they have not been heavily used in modern times. Many of the books still contain bookplates, ownership inscriptions, instructions to binders, binders' and booksellers' tickets, marginal notes, prices and price codes, and the overwhelming majority are still in unaltered contemporary bindings. Together, all of these features can tell us a good deal about the tastes and interests of the people who owned the books, and about the use, abuse and circulation of print across the whole of Ireland over a period of more than 300 years. Even if it is not always possible to be certain who owned and read what (and indeed who left what unread on the shelves), cumulatively the books themselves are very much more informative than subscription lists or the surviving catalogues of long-vanished libraries. They are more remarkable still in remaining in an intelligible historical context, and consequently susceptible to being investigated as more than mere passive curiosities or even as desirable collectables. The scrawled signatures of friends and relations become traceable because they are found in books whose history is already known in outline. The role of books in everyday life is easier to reconstruct when they are still shelved together in the Library designed to house them, rather than in alphabetical order in an underground strong room. The fittings and furnishings of a Library room themselves help to clarify the twin functions of books both as sources of information and entertainment, and as possessions which were themselves an important part of politeness and gentility.[31] The bookplate of a long-dead owner carries a special resonance when the ruffed face of a Jacobean ancestor, or a comfortable Georgian grandee in his expensive wig, peers down from a nearby wall. A woman's books are more interesting when her personal possessions – a miniature of a child perhaps, a teapot, or a walking stick – are still close by. An obscure tract on gardening or agricultural improvement carries greater weight when a park and garden are just outside the front door. And when all of this is set against the archival material mostly in the Public Record Office of Northern Ireland (PRONI) – inventories, commonplace books, wills, bills and correspondence so voluminous that the subject must inevitably await fuller treatment – it is not difficult to appreciate that these libraries together constitute a very significant source for the history of private book ownership in Ireland. For a whole variety of reasons, some purely accidental and others rather more predictable, they are a source which has remained almost entirely unknown and unstudied.

The National Trust's interest in Ireland pre-dated Partition by over twenty years, and its first property there was Kanturk Castle in County Cork, given by Lucy, Countess of Egmont in 1900. A roofless prodigy house built by MacDonagh MacCarthy in about 1609 and apparently abandoned when suspicious English neighbours reported him to the Privy Council for building a fortress, it was handed over to An Taisce (the National Trust's nearest equivalent in the Republic of Ireland) on a 1000-year lease in 1951, and formally transferred to the Irish state as recently as July 2000.[32] But the National Trust's story in Northern Ireland really began only in 1936, when (after receiving confirmation from the lawyers that the 1895 National Trust Act did indeed 'run' in the Province) a Northern Ireland Committee met for the first time.[33]

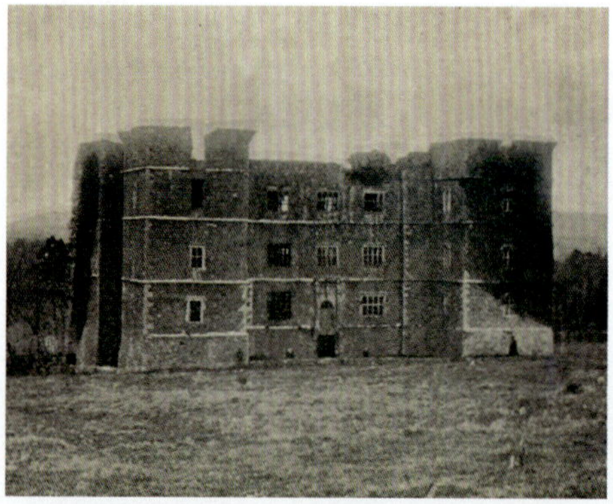

Right
Kanturk Castle, County Cork

Properties of all kinds soon followed, but the first with a library was Castle

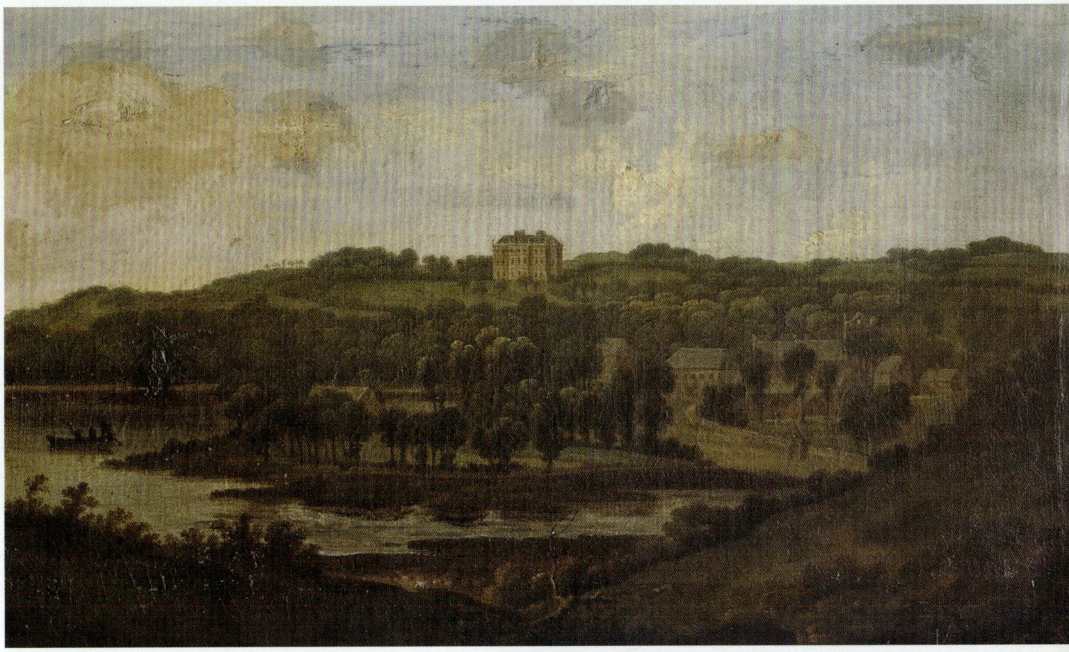

Right
The demesne of Castle Ward, County Down, as depicted by Jonathan Fisher in the eighteenth century

Coole, James Wyatt's neo-classical mansion just outside Enniskillen, which was purchased by the Ulster Land Fund in 1951. Today there are seven National Trust houses in Northern Ireland with books: Castle Coole and Florence Court, both in County Fermanagh; Castle Ward and Mount Stewart, both in County Down; Springhill, in County Londonderry; and Ardress and The Argory, both in County Armagh. Ardress can effectively be discounted from the story. A seventeenth-century Plantation house with elegant Georgian additions, it must once have had a library of some sort. Today there are only eighteen books, mostly imported to fill empty shelves. At Castle Coole the library remains with the family of the original donor, and this is also partly true of the books at Mount Stewart, in County Down.[34] The two greatest collections are those at Springhill, a mid-Ulster Plantation house built some years before the Battle of the Boyne, and Castle Ward, a splendidly unconventional house, which displays a sober Palladian façade to visitors arriving from Downpatrick, but sports an exotically Gothick rear to those approaching by water via the quays of Strangford Lough. Springhill has the larger library, but both collections are remarkable for the quality and interest of their books, and for their antiquity. In both houses the core of the library was assembled before the Williamite Wars of the 1690s. The story at Florence Court, one of the grandest surviving Irish Palladian houses, situated (as an eighteenth-century traveller put it) 'on an eminence under a great ridge of mountains' near the border between County Fermanagh and County Cavan, is more complex.[35] The house – but not the contents – passed to the National Trust in the 1950s, but the title was unexpectedly

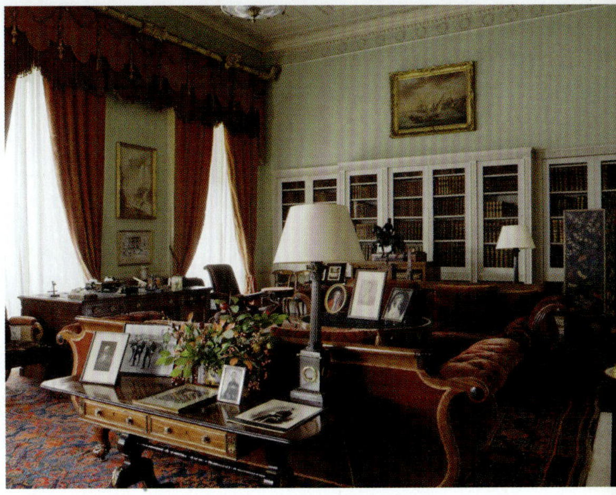

Right
The Wyatt Library at Castle Coole, County Fermanagh

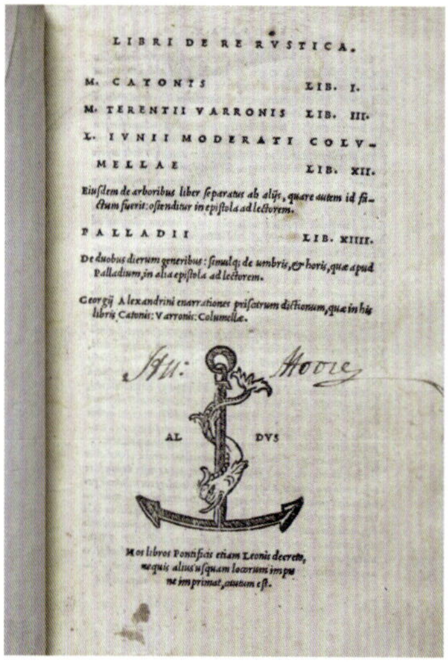
LIBRI DE RE RVSTICA.

M. CATONIS LIB. I.

M. TERENTII VARRONIS LIB. III.

L. IVNII MODERATI COLVMELLAE LIB. XII.

Eiusdem de arboribus liber separatus ab aliis, quare autem id factum fuerit: ostenditur in epistola ad lectorem.

PALLADII LIB. XIIII.

De duobus dierum generibus: simulq; de umbris, & horis, quae apud Palladium, in alia epistola ad lectorem.

Georgij Alexandrini enarrationes priscarum dictionum, quae in his libris Catonis: Varronis: Columellae.

AL DVS

Nos libros Pontificis etiam Leonis decreto, nequis alius usquam locorum impune imprimat, cautum est.

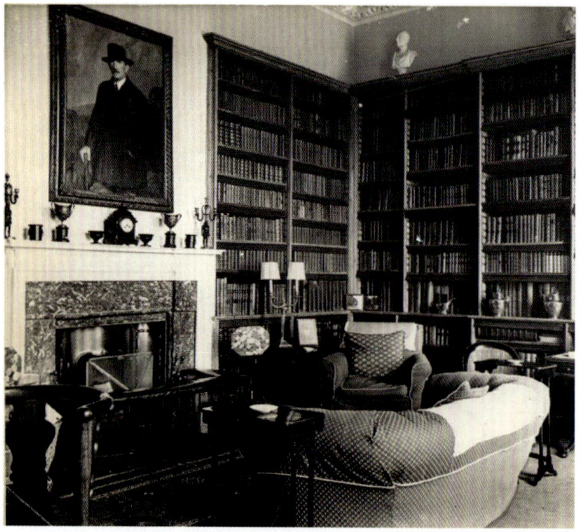

Right
The Aldine *Libri de Re Rustica* (Venice, 1514), from the library at Rowallane (now at Florence Court)

Far right
The Library at Florence Court, as it was when photographed by the *Irish Times* in 1963

inherited by a cousin. The Trust and the 6th Earl of Enniskillen (1918–89) quarrelled in the early 1970s, and he and his American second wife moved to Scotland, taking all of the historic chattels from the house with them, including a large and interesting library. Somewhat more friendly relations were eventually restored almost 30 years later, and Lady Enniskillen presented the family portraits to the National Trust shortly before her death. The Trust has purchased many more of the original contents since, but by then some of the books had unfortunately already been dispersed. The rest were bequeathed to Cambridge University Library, which has retained 591 of them, and has kept them together as a collection.[36] But about half of the original books returned to County Fermanagh in 2002, where they now fill one side of the Library; the other half of the room houses 'furniture' books brought in by the National Trust, as well as the homeless remnant of the library of Rowallane House, County Down. This then leaves only The Argory, a remarkable Greek Revival house near Portadown, where for very good historical reasons most of the books date from the late nineteenth and twentieth centuries, though others were transferred from nearby Drumsill House in the Edwardian period.

This modest roll-call masks the fact that the National Trust's holdings of books in Northern Ireland are considerably more wide-ranging than first impressions might suggest. In the first place it would not do to forget Gray's Printing Press, a remarkable early nineteenth-century print shop in Strabane, in the west of County Tyrone, one of the best preserved of its kind in Great Britain or Ireland. Then there are two properties – Downhill Palace on the north coast, and Derrymore, a delightful eighteenth-century *cottage orné* in Bessbrook, County Armagh – which once had libraries, but where no books are visible today, though a single book from the collection of Isaac Corry (1755–1813), the builder of Derrymore and last Chancellor of the Exchequer in the Dublin Parliament, has washed up at Florence Court.[37] Downhill, on the other hand, burned down in the nineteenth century, was rebuilt, and fell into ruin again after the Second World War.[38] No books survive today, though the estate records do, as does something rather stranger: the Mussenden Temple ('a beautiful and singular erection' thought the topographer G. Vaughan Sampson in 1802), a domed rotunda originally built as a summer library by the eccentric Frederick Hervey (1730–1803), 4th Earl of Bristol and Bishop of Derry.[39]

But more important than these ghostly libraries, and far less visible,

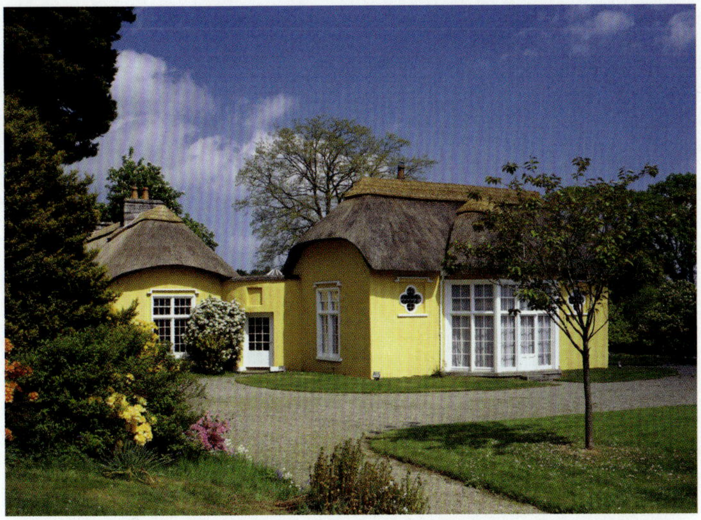

Above
Derrymore, County Armagh

are the libraries within libraries; whole collections or sometimes just single books transplanted from one house to another, sitting quietly unobserved on the shelves as mute witnesses to long-dispersed collections. It is a pattern which goes back many centuries, and as long ago as 1781 a correspondent of the Earl of Abercorn was urging that his employer might consider purchasing books from a neighbouring house, Creghan, and recommending that 'Your Lordship might think it convenient to procure part of the library furniture for your library at Barons Court'.[40] In the far west of County Tyrone, the sheer practical convenience of acquiring books and furniture from close by must have been very appealing, and the pattern was often repeated elsewhere. Castle Ward, to all outward appearances a mid-Georgian house, has not only the books bought by the Wards in the early eighteenth century, but part of the seventeenth-century library of the Hamiltons of Bangor, a cadet branch of one of the most powerful Plantation families, and itself containing books which had probably been in Ireland since the 1590s. Castle Ward also has books from several southern houses, including Ballylin, County Offaly, and at least one – a copy of Henry Milman's poem *The Martyr of Antioch* (London, 1822) – which was in the library at Stradbally Hall, County Laois in 1823. At Springhill there are substantial numbers of books from at least five other Ascendancy houses. Two are local: Lissan House and John Nash's Killymoon Castle (placed on the market following an order from the Court for the Sale of Encumbered Estates in 1850), both in nearby County Tyrone.[41] Others came from Drenagh and from Bellarena, both near Limavady in County Londonderry. The fifth, and much the most important, was Blessington House in County Wicklow, destroyed in the 1798 Rising, though by then the books were already in Ulster. Florence Court has even more strays, though these have been installed by the National Trust as set-dressing in the last 30 years. Part of the homeless library from Rowallane House, County Down (the gardens are open to the public, but since 1976 the house has been used as the National Trust's office in Northern Ireland), has been stored there for a number of years. Equally, many of the imported books at Florence Court originated in various historic Irish collections. They include more than 50 with the elegant armorial bookplate of Michael Kearney (1733–1814), Professor of History at Trinity College, Dublin from 1769 to 1778, and from 1798 Archdeacon of Raphoe in County Donegal; there are books from the library of the Divinity Hostel in Dublin (the present Church of Ireland Theological Institute), and smaller numbers of books which appear to have come from various defunct houses north and south of the border. The precise

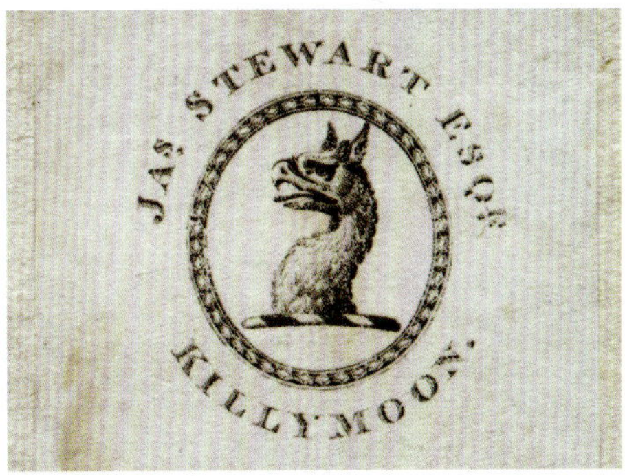

Right
Bookplate of James Stewart of Killymoon Castle, Franks 28156 (Springhill)

history of most of these can no longer be reconstructed, since the National Trust's curatorial records in Northern Ireland were destroyed when the IRA bombed Malone House in Belfast in 1976.[42] Many appear to have been purchased by the National Trust, apparently as set-dressing for Derrymore in the 1950s and 60s, and were moved to Florence Court in 1979.[43]

Consequently the Trust's libraries in Northern Ireland contain a surprisingly broad cross-section of the books which could be found in the Irish Big House during the *ançien régime* of the Protestant Ascendancy (from the Restoration in 1660 down to Catholic Emancipation in 1829) and during its long decline. These libraries, like their counterparts in England, Scotland and Wales, are fascinating social documents and packed with interesting books, but viewed in a more specifically Irish context, their survival is all the more remarkable. Across the water, libraries in British country houses have been the victim of endless sales ever since the Settled Lands Acts of the 1880s first allowed the sale of previously entailed chattels. The survivors remain vulnerable to dispersal – a natural and inevitable process, perhaps, but one where the satisfaction of the modern-day collector is necessarily bought at a price – the dispersal of historic libraries which, intact, usually mean much more than the sum of their parts. But things have evolved quite differently in Ireland, where far fewer houses and even fewer libraries have survived. The relationship between the Irish Big House and the estate which supported it was of course quite different from the English model. In Ireland the term 'demesne' was traditionally used to refer to a great house, its gardens, parkland and woods, deer-park and farm buildings, the whole surrounded by a demesne wall and kept for the landowner's private use. The demesne was quite distinct from the wider estate, a term used to refer to all the landowner's holdings, including land that might be dispersed across several counties and cultivated by many tenant farmers. The social and legal position of landowners was also very different from England. Despite the parade of legislative independence in the Dublin Parliament, seventeenth- and eighteenth-century Ireland functioned in many respects like a colony. Grandees like the Dukes of Ormonde belonged to families which had been resident in Ireland for many hundreds of years, but many other Protestant landowners were *nouveaux riches* settlers, and very likely regarded by their tenants as aliens and interlopers, even if they gradually came to think of themselves as Irish patriots. And if civil commotion certainly saw to some libraries – those destroyed in the 1641 rising, the Williamite Wars and the 1798 rebellion, those burned out in the Irish Civil War in the 1920s, and at least one (Tynan Abbey, County Armagh) burned by the Provisional IRA in 1981 after the shooting of its owners, the Stronges – the crucial element in the destruction of the Big House library was earth rather than fire. Certainly, houses were destroyed in some numbers, along with their contents, including their books: 76 in the 26 southern counties during the War of Independence between January 1920 and July 1921, and a further 199 in the ensuing Civil War in the Free State between January 1922 and April 1923.[44] At Mitchelstown Castle, County Cork – a county which saw a disproportionate number of burnings – Edith Somerville in July 1922 noted that 'all the books in the library are being used as barricades for the windows, & as there are not enough, valuable old furniture is being used as well'. The castle, vast home of the Earls of Kingston, was torched by Republican forces a month or so later.[45] In County Wexford the former Nationalist MP Sir Thomas Esmonde (1862–1935) was so dismayed by the destruction of his house, Ballynastragh, in 1923, and especially by the loss of his library, that he lost all interest in books, and refused to accept them as gifts from friends on the grounds that he had nowhere to put them.[46]

But to focus too much on these dramatic events overlooks that all the great Ascendancy houses were founded on and funded by the income-generating estates of their owners, and that for every one which was burned out many others gradually went under for less dramatic reasons. With the advent of the Land War, the campaign of agrarian agitation which began in Connacht in 1879, it must have become increasingly apparent that the writing might be on the wall for the great Irish landlords, many of whom were already heavily in debt in the aftermath of the Famine. The Land League's campaign in the north of Ireland was launched by the Nationalist leader Charles Stewart Parnell at Belleek in the far west of Fermanagh in November 1880; over the next two years there were rallies and demonstrations all over Ulster.[47] Faced with disorder on this scale, the landlords and the authorities alike began to look for a way out. As early as May 1889, the owners of Springhill had equipped themselves with a copy of Sir George Fotterell's newly-published *Practical Guide to the Land Purchase Acts (Ireland)* (Dublin, 1889). By 1903, the year of the Wyndham Land Act, named after George Wyndham (1863–1913), the Conservative Chief Secretary – the principal working minister, as opposed to the by then more ceremonial functions of the Lord Lieutenant – in the Dublin Castle administration from 1900 to 1905, the process was becoming irreversible. By 1914, three-quarters of Irish tenant-farmers had bought out their landlords, and Ireland had witnessed a redistribution of land scarcely paralleled in any other western European country.[48] Between 1903 and 1921, Irish landowners received some £86 million in payments under the 1903 and ensuing 1909 Land Acts, having already received a further £25 million under previous Acts passed between 1870 and 1896.[49] The process was of such labyrinthine complexity that the novelist's father Henry Cole Bowen spent sixteen years writing his *magnum opus* on the subject, an ultimately fruitless activity as subsequent developments rendered much of his work obsolete before it was even published.[50] But the effects could be dramatic, and the estates of the Coles of Florence Court, for example, shrank from 12,140 hectares to less than 2,833.[51] The Earls Erne, of Crom Castle in County Fermanagh, had been the owners of one of the largest estates in the north-west of Ireland, including substantial lands in County Mayo. The Mayo agent Charles Boycott, an employee of the 3rd Earl (1802–85), gave a new word, boycott, to the English language when, at Parnell's suggestion, he was ostracised by his neighbours for evicting tenants, but between 1904 and 1909 the 4th Earl (1839–1914) sold land to the value of £240,440 to the Land Commission, retaining only £12,770's worth on his own account.[52]

Below
Mitchelstown Castle, County Cork, burned in 1922

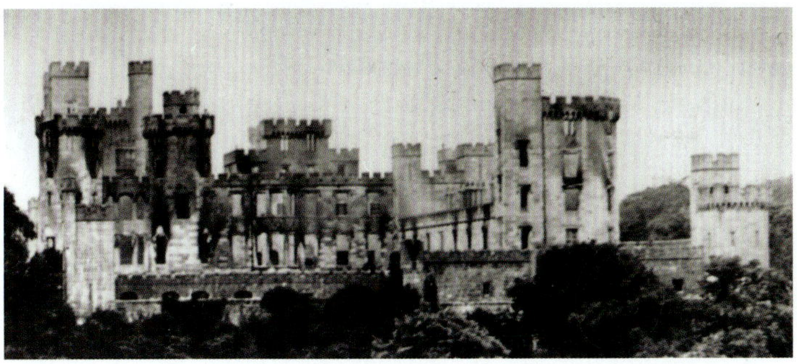

Without the landholdings which had supported them, it was only a matter of time before many Big Houses started to fall into decay, and their contents – including their libraries – to be dispersed. As early as 1882, the historian J. P. Mahaffy (1839–1919) had lamented in the columns of *The Contemporary Review* that 'the splendid libraries so common before the famine times are scattered and it is now an exception to find a good library in any country house'.[53] But though a good number of Irish libraries survived

Right

Second Report from the Select Committee of the House of Lords on Land Law (Ireland) (London, 1882), extract from land returns for County Fermanagh (Florence Court). The left-hand column gives the annual rental in £. s. d, and that on the right the total acreage of the estate

.	Trillick, . . .	95	2	20	18	5
.	Dromard, . . .	326	3	8	231	5
.	Mullaghsilogagh, .	161	2	20	109	15
.	Drumswords, . .	253	0	19	136	0
.	Salry, . . .	12	3	30	9	15
.	Pettigo, . . .	12	1	0	9	10
.	Florence Court, .	68	3	20	42	0
.	Ely Lodge, Enniskillen,	34,879	2	0	13,983	0
.	Florence Court, Enniskillen.	29,635	0	31	18,795	7
.	Dublin, . . .	1,043	0	0	768	12
.	Crom Castle, . .	31,389	1	30	17,039	0

for several decades longer, many were living on borrowed time. The Wyndham Land Act – 'that big bribe', thought Lady Fingall – had compensated landowners with a cash 'Bonus' of 12%. Funded by a Land Purchase Fund underwritten by the United Kingdom's National Debt, it was designed to bridge the gap between the prices that owners would accept and those which their tenants could afford to pay.[54] If well-invested, the Bonus plus the purchase price should have been more than enough to keep owners afloat, and some indeed were able to renovate their houses, or even build new ones, and certainly to keep up a traditionally grand and leisured lifestyle for several decades more. But inflation and fluctuations in the markets eroded the value of invested capital in the years after the Great War.

Many of the landowners (and former landowners) who stayed on in the Free State after 1922 found it ever more difficult to make ends meet. Further Land Acts were introduced there in 1923 and 1933 on terms markedly less generous – some would have said confiscatory – than those offered by the Wyndham Act, while Northern Ireland, introduced its own Compulsory Land Purchase Act in 1925.[55] A large house which had once been financed by the proceeds of a great estate simply could not be maintained on the back of a few hundred acres of parkland, and those who continued to farm a remnant of their lands were badly hit by the agricultural depression of the 1920s. Unsurprisingly, the Free State authorities were far more concerned with the ever-present problem of emigration – and with the appalling levels of rural poverty which so shocked interwar visitors to the west of Ireland – than with the tribulations of the former ruling class.[56] Northern landowners found themselves subject to similar pressures as well, and at Springhill, the estate was sold off under the terms of the Wyndham Land Act shortly before the death of Sir William Lenox-Conyngham in 1906, and (as his daughter-in-law subsequently recalled) 'a good deal of income was lost through insecure investments.'[57] In the Free State, the 1930s saw economic war with the United Kingdom, with punitive duties levied on Irish goods in retaliation for the Fianna Fáil government's refusal to transfer payments made by former tenant farmers to the Land Commission under the terms of pre-1922 Land Acts, as had been agreed in the 1921 Anglo-Irish Treaty, a treaty which De Valera and his supporters had of course rejected.[58] As time passed, the money ran out and the last retainers died off, dozens of Irish big houses were abandoned or sold for salvage by owners hit by death duties, or unable to pay for their upkeep and their often enormous rates bill. Those which survived, did so by good luck, tenacious good management, or as often as not because their owners – families like the Guinnesses in the South or the Londonderrys in the North – had substantial sources of income originating outside Ireland. When houses disappeared, their libraries vanished with them, if they had not already been sold – along with other chattels – to pay death duties. Libraries had, as in England, been sold right through the eighteenth and nineteenth centuries, at least when the family entail allowed, and the sale of the Earl of Gosford's books from Gosford Castle, a massive neo-Norman mansion in County Armagh, had taken eleven days in 1884, raising over £11,000; if most of the books were at that time considered quite ordinary, the pickings included a

Gutenberg Bible and a Shakespeare First Folio.[59] But by the period after the First World War the seepage of books grew to a great flood, and a few examples illustrate the point. The library at Braganstown, County Louth, was sold in 1918 to pay debts; Hillsborough Castle in County Down in 1924; books were sold from the ducal residence of Carton, County Kildare, in 1927, the library at Kilkenny Castle in 1935, and 5000 books from Lady Edith Windham's house at Dartrey, County Monaghan, in 1937, with special buses laid on from Dublin for the sale.[60] The trend continued after the Second World War ('The Emergency' in the South), with books from the library of the Marquess of Sligo at Westport sold in London in 1955, the 'fine Country House Library' from Gloster House, Brosna, County Offaly sold at Naas, County Kildare in 1956, Castlewellan Castle, County Down in the 1960s, Malahide Castle in County Dublin in 1976, and the great library of the Earls of Granard, from Castle Forbes, County Longford sold in London by Sotheby's in 1993. In the same year books were sold from Woodstock, Newtownmountkennedy, County Wicklow, and from Slane Castle, County Meath, rich in nineteenth-century novels which made 'enormous prices'.[61] In Northern Ireland, too, the library of Mourne Park, Kilkeel, County Down, was sold in April 2003, part of the fall-out from a family feud which had landed its chatelaine with a week in Maghaberry Gaol for contempt of court. Generally speaking, the only thing that unites any of these various sales is that the books clearly found willing purchasers, and none of these collections had been subjected to serious study, and now no longer can be, since they no longer exist.

Below
Thomas Hopper's neo-Norman Library at Gosford Castle, County Armagh, as it was in 1963; the books had been sold in 1884

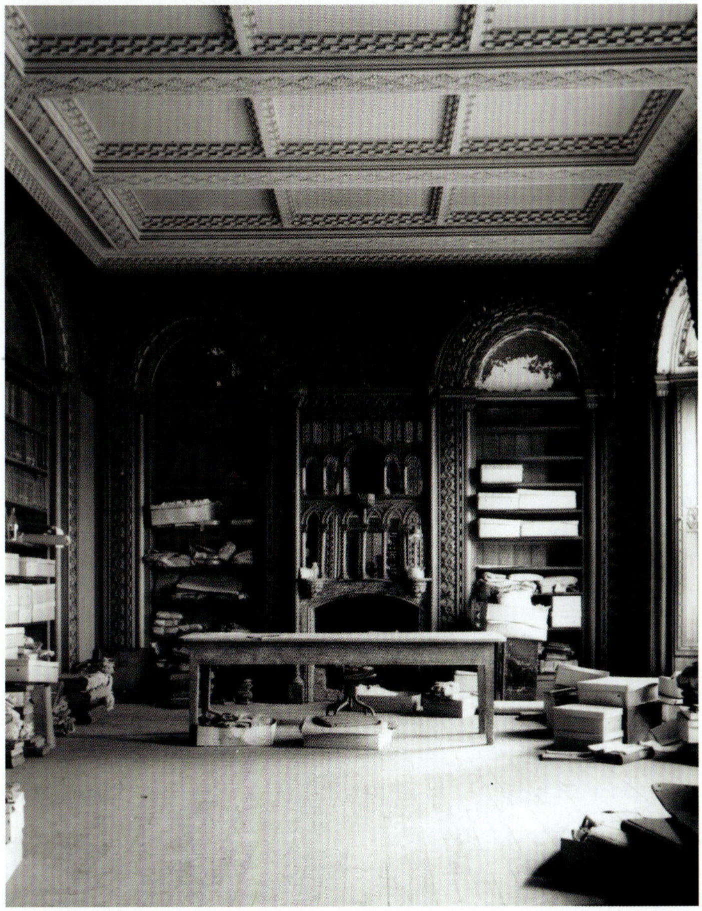

The sceptical have been able to convince themselves that the loss of Big House libraries has been of no great significance, with one commentator in the early 1990s airily observing that 'the descendents of Cromwell's adventurers were non-literary by nature' – a bold assertion indeed, made without any accompanying evidence, and further undermined by the same author's curious belief that books were few in Irish Big Houses 'because of the difficulties of reading by candlelight', as if Irish candles were somehow more intractable than those found in Britain and Continental Europe.[62] In Great Britain, indeed, hundreds of thousands of books have been sold from country houses over the last century and a half, but thousands more still remain. In Ireland the process of attrition has now advanced much further. With a handful of exceptions, the history of the Big House library is not only a story which has run its course, but one which has come to an end without having been studied, and with the permanent and irreversible loss of much of the evidence. Ultimately, this is what gives the National Trust's collections in Northern Ireland their special interest.

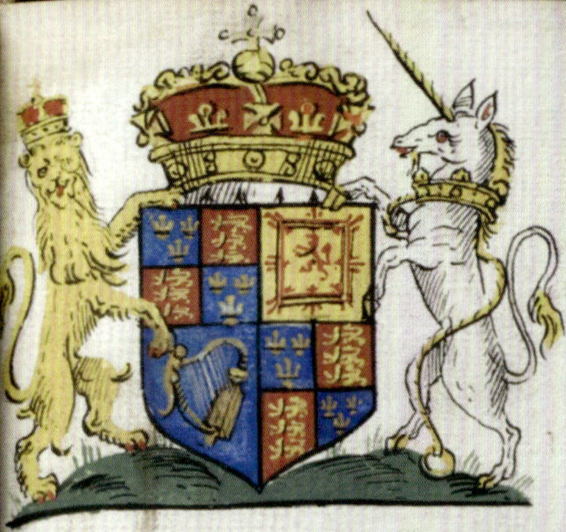

Robert Cicell Baron of Essington

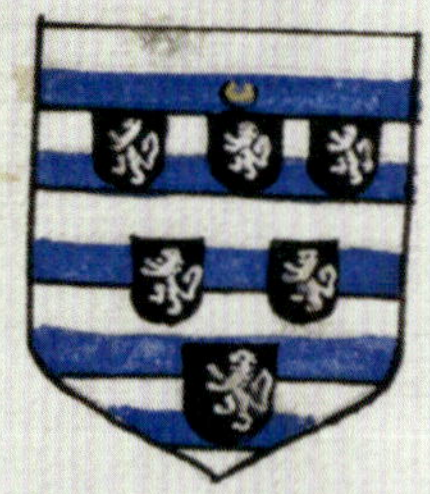

Robert Sydney Baron of Penshurst.

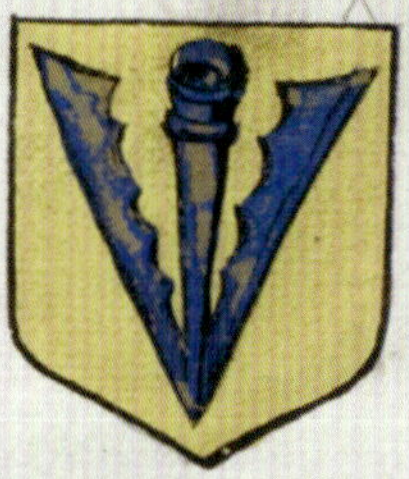

William Knoles Baron of Grais.

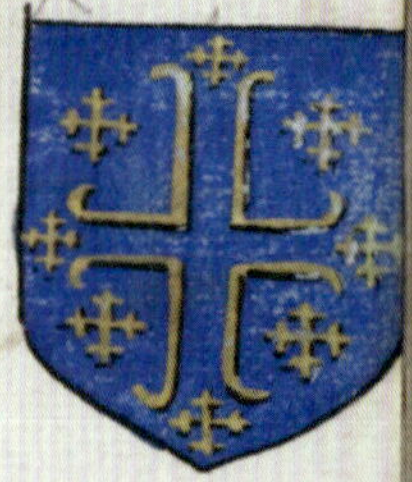

Edward Baron Wotton.

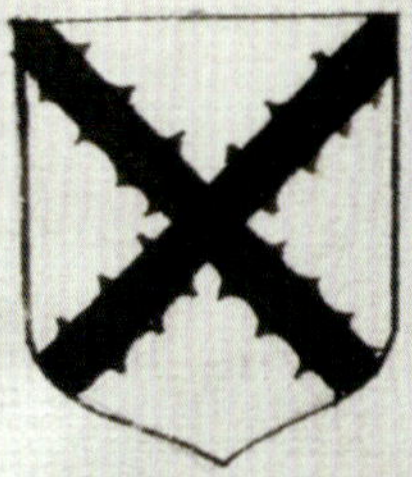

Thomas Sackuill Baron of Buckhurst created Earle of Dorsett

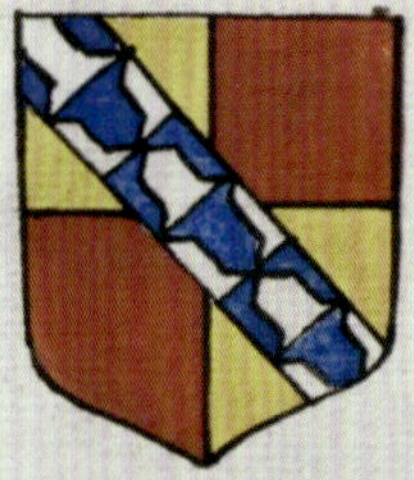

Robert Cicell Baron of Essington Viscount Cranborne.

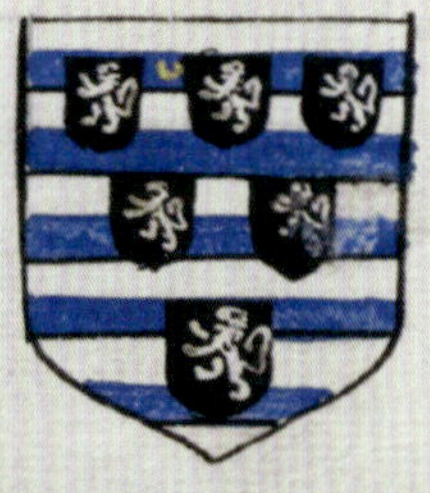

Henry Wriothesley restored Baron of Tichfeild and Earle of Southampton.

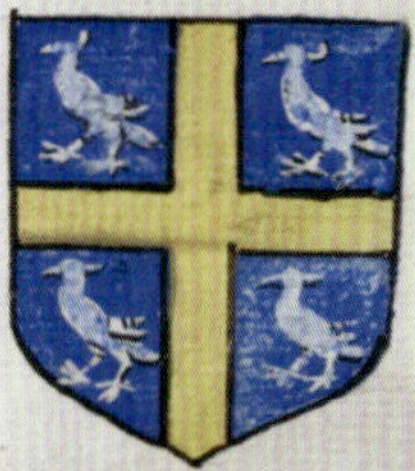

Thomas Howard Lord Walden created Earle of Suffolke.

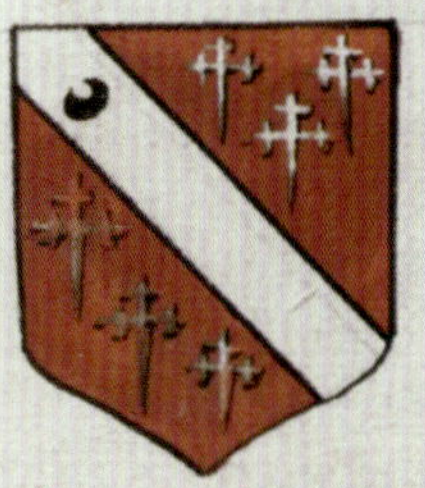

Charles Blount Lo: Mountioy & Earle of Devonshire.

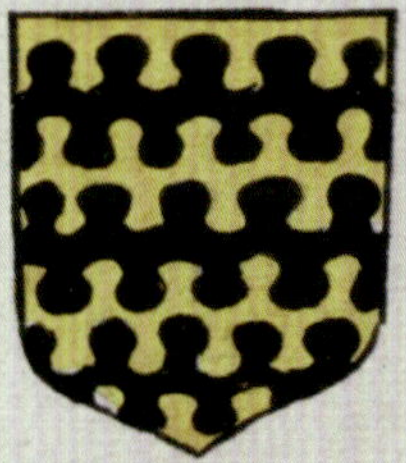

Henry Baron Gray of Groby.

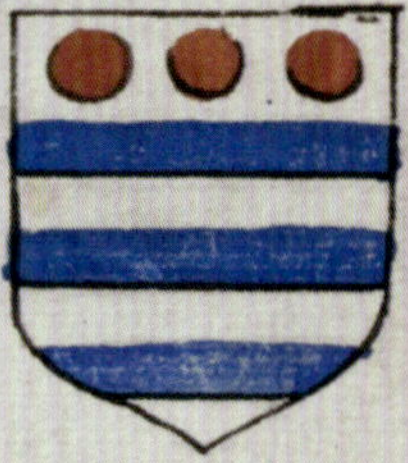

John Baron Peter of Writle.

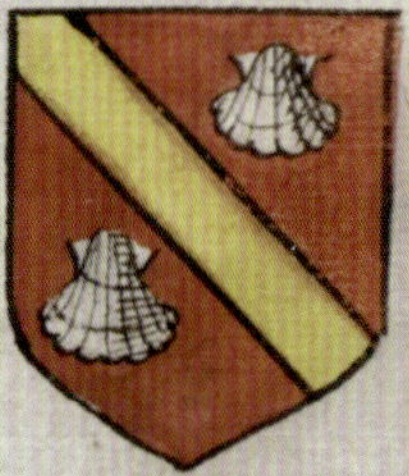

John Baron Harington of Exton.

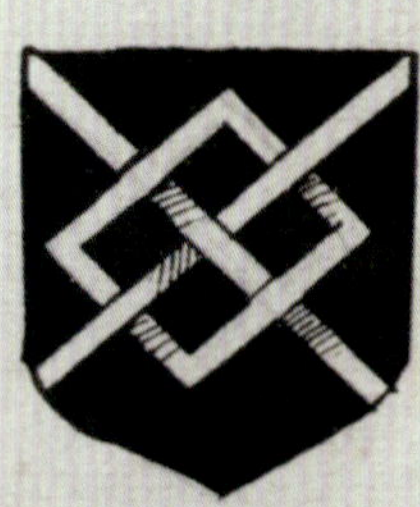

Henry Baron Danvers of Dauntesey.

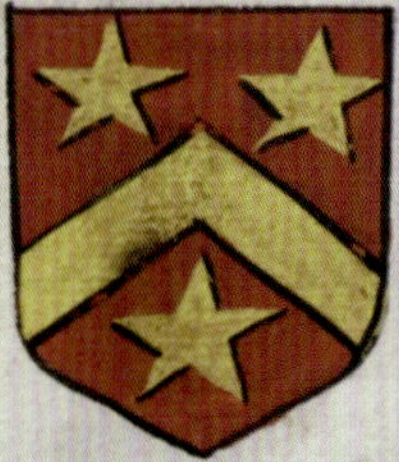

Thomas Baron Gerrard of Gerrards Bromley.

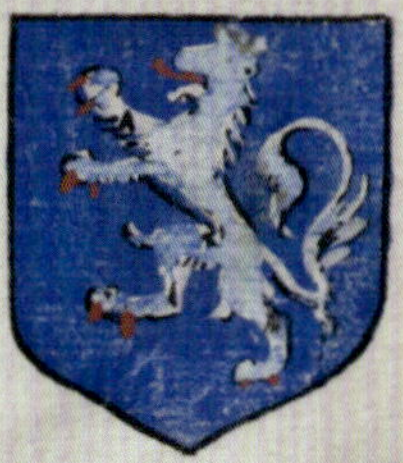

Robert Baron Spencer of Wormleighton.

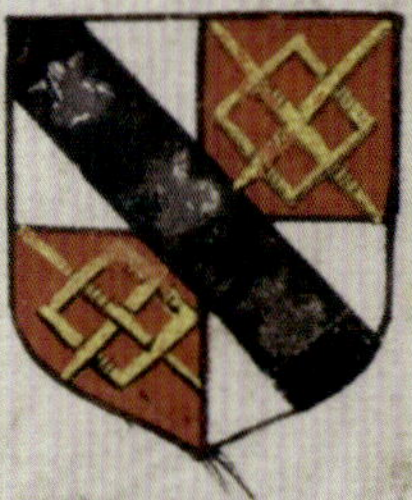

1 Plantation

Castle Ward, County Down, 1584–1690

Left
Heraldic manuscript, after 1580, probably owned by James Hamilton, 1st Viscount Claneboye (Castle Ward)

In 1978 Edward Miller (1914–80), the National Trust's then Libraries Adviser, visited Castle Ward to see the library, which he described as 'a good typical country house library, with particular reference to classics, law and topographical works'.[1] At first sight this is exactly what it appears to be. The standard nineteenth-century bookplates, and the heavy grille-fronted Library bookcases installed by the 3rd Viscount Bangor in 1835 all conspire in this illusion of uniformity, an illusion which is dispelled by a more detailed examination of the shelves. Only then does it become apparent that far from being a collection of grand but unexceptional Georgian and early Victorian books, the library is rich in English and Irish imprints from the period 1660 to 1740, and contains significant numbers of learned books from the great Continental presses of the sixteenth and early seventeenth centuries. And while there are certainly the sort of books which are often associated with country houses – William Alexander's *Costume of China,* his *Costume of Turkey*, and his *Costume of the Russian Empire*, all of 1804 and handsomely bound in blue morocco; a finely-bound *Votes and Proceedings* of the Irish House of Commons; and a grand copy of Colen Campbell's *Vitruvius Britannicus* (1722) – there are many more which had clearly found their way to this corner of Ireland something between 50 and 150 years before the construction of the present house in the 1760s. The Castle Ward library is full of surprises, and the reasons for this are tangled up with the complex history of the Ward family and the seventeenth-century plantation of County Down.

The Wards originated in Cheshire, and the first to own land in Down seems to have been Bernard Ward (d. 1584), who bought land at Carrick na Sheannagh ('Rock of the Foxes') from about 1570, and renamed the demesne in honour of his own family.[2] The first Castle Ward was (and still is) a tower house, surrounded by a fortified farmyard or bawn, and apparently built by Nicholas Ward in about 1610. Its successor was an elegant Queen Anne house, replaced in its turn by the present house, which is the third Castle Ward. All this might be taken to suggest a distinguished lineage for the future Viscounts Bangor, but the truth seems to have been that the Wards were comparatively small fry in the seventeenth century, and the real founder of the family fortunes was Michael Ward (1683–1759), a Justice of the King's Bench in Dublin for 31 years from 1727. 'The most important man in the county in the first half of the eighteenth century', Judge Ward was a prolific correspondent, a great fixer and – eventually – a very rich man.[3] He married well, in 1709, to Anne Hamilton, daughter and co-heiress of James Hamilton of Bangor (d. 1707), who was himself the owner of a significant portion of the vast inheritance in County Down originally granted by James VI and I to his namesake James Hamilton, 1st Viscount Claneboye (1559–1643). The marriage brought £4000 in cash to Castle Ward, and Anne Hamilton evidently brought a considerable number of family chattels with her. They included many of the family portraits, as well as a considerable number of Hamilton books.

So Michael Ward's marriage in 1709 was in effect the crucial event in the history of the Castle Ward library, explaining as it does why the collection has three distinct layers

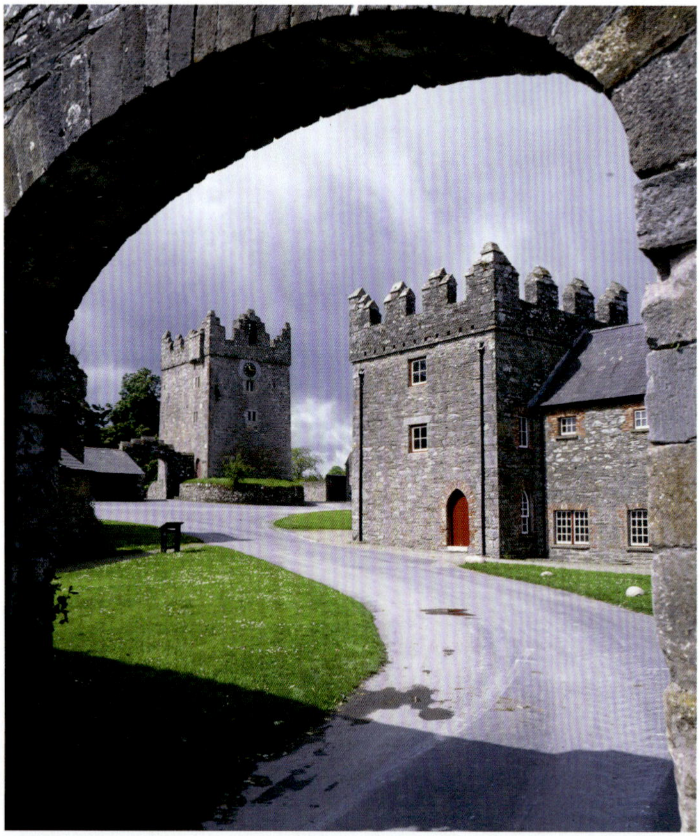

Above
Old Castle Ward

within it: Michael Ward's own books, the books added by his descendents later in the eighteenth and nineteenth centuries, and the seventeenth-century library inherited from his father-in-law, James Hamilton of Bangor. Each one of these layers is fascinating in its own right, but the Hamilton books are very remarkable indeed.

James Hamilton of Bangor was obviously interested in books, and his signature can be found in about 60 on the shelves at Castle Ward. Yet he never lived there, and his mansion house in Bangor, by then seriously outmoded, was described in 1744 as 'a low moderate structure'. In his lifetime Hamilton was patron of the church at Bangor, a building 'afterwards beautified' by his widow Sophia Mordaunt, and by his eldest daughter Anne, who set up a handsome monument there by Peter Scheemakers in her parents' memory.[4] But James Hamilton was much more than a north Down squire, and a simple outline of his family connections starts to makes sense of his library.[5] His wife Sophia was the daughter of the Cavalier conspirator John Mordaunt (1627–75), younger brother of Henry Mordaunt, 2nd Earl of Peterborough, and created Viscount Mordaunt for services to Charles II in 1659. Hamilton's mother-in-law was Elizabeth Carey (d. 1679), in her youth described by Clarendon as 'a young, beautiful lady, of a very loyal spirit and notable vivacity of wit and humour', and in old age by John Evelyn as 'the most virtuous lady in the world'.[6] The Mordaunts were a court family, with friends in the highest echelons of the state. But James Hamilton was himself the scion of a still grander Scottish family, and one which had benefited greatly from the Jacobean Plantation of Ulster. The County Down Hamiltons were descended from the six sons of the Revd. Hans Hamilton (1535/6–1608), minister of Dunlop in Ayrshire: in due order James (1559–1643), Archibald, Gavin, John (d. 1639), William and Patrick. The oldest, James, moved to Dublin in 1587, ostensibly 'to keep a public Latin school', but in fact to act as James VI's confidential agent in the city in the anxious years before the death of Queen Elizabeth. Hamilton was educated at St Andrews University, and his scholarship seems to have been real enough, for his pupils included the future Archbishop Ussher (1581–1656), and he was one of the first Fellows of Trinity College, Dublin, when it opened in 1592. With James VI's successful translation to Whitehall in 1603, his Ayrshire *protégé* followed him, was knighted, and eventually (1622) created Viscount Claneboye. By this stage he was back in Ireland, in County Down, where the king had granted him substantial estates in 1606. A formidable operator, Claneboye 'made a great use of the services of his brethren and nephews', and all of his brothers ended up in Ireland. The lawyer Archibald

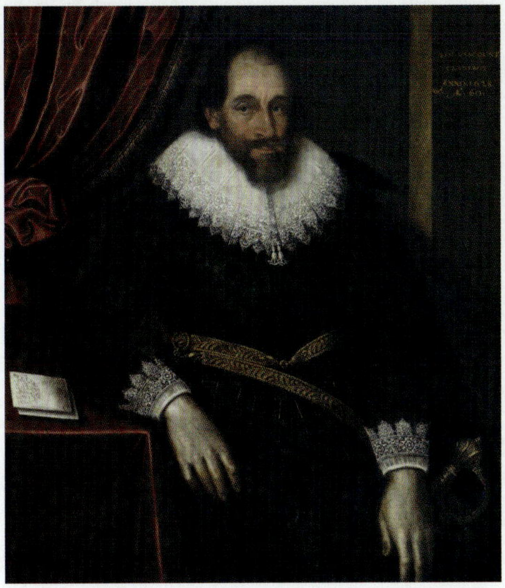

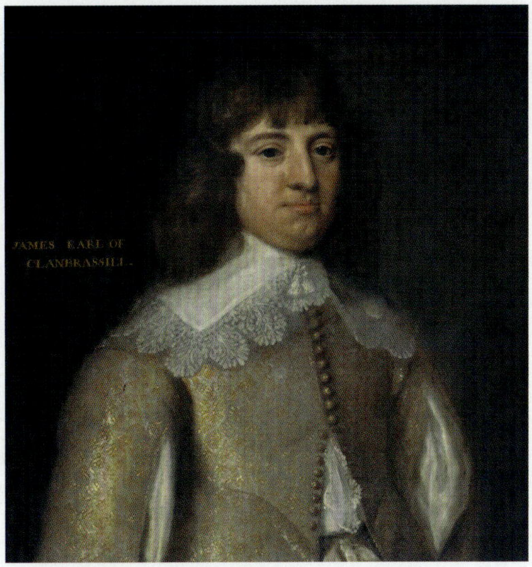

Right
James Hamilton, 1st Viscount Claneboye (1559–1643), artist unknown (Castle Ward)

Far right
James Hamilton, 2nd Viscount Claneboye, later 1st Earl of Clanbrassil (d.1659), in the manner of William Dobson (Castle Ward)

Hamilton, 'educated in learning in Edinburgh', and then 'bred a Writer to the Signet', purchased large estates in County Limerick, while Gavin, a Glasgow merchant, was involved in his brother's business activities in Ireland, and drowned in the river Bann, to which Claneboye had secured the fishing rights in 1606, in the teeth of local opposition. The middle brother, William, was brought to County Down. He acted as agent to his brother Claneboye, but also managed to build up substantial estates of his own, property which passed first to his son James (killed at the Battle of Benburb in 1646), and ultimately to his grandson James Hamilton of Bangor – Michael Ward's father-in-law. But the great Lord Claneboye died in 1643, and his successors clearly lacked his skill and ambition. His son James Hamilton, 2nd Viscount Claneboye (d. 1659) was sent on a Grand Tour by his father in 1633, and created Earl of Clanbrassil by Charles I in 1647, but the senior branch of the family did not prosper, and when Henry, 3rd Earl of Clanbrassil died in 1675, many of the family estates ended up in the hands of a cousin, James Hamilton of Bangor, who thereby came to control not only the estates he had inherited from his grandfather William Hamilton, but a substantial proportion of James I's original grant to his great-uncle, the 1st Lord Claneboye. It was part of this great inheritance on both sides of Strangford Lough which ultimately passed into the hands of Michael Ward, and made the Wards the rich and powerful figures that they became.

The Hamilton books are remarkably varied and interesting, and the great majority of the 325 sixteenth- and seventeenth-century books at Castle Ward today have a Hamilton provenance. The largest group of these, unsurprisingly, belonged to James Hamilton of Bangor. So far as one can judge, he was not an especially learned man, but appears to have taken an intelligent interest in the world around him. He certainly owned an attractive collection of late seventeenth-century books on travel and historical geography – books like William Drummond's *The History of Scotland* (London, 1681), Jacob Spon's *History of the City and State of Geneva* (London, 1687), and Paul Rycaut's *History of the Turkish Empire* (London, 1680). Then – and perhaps rather more predictably – there is Rycaut's translation of Platina's *Lives of the Popes* (London, 1685), and of course a good deal of religious polemic: Michael Geddes's *The Council of Trent no Free Assembly* (London, 1697) is a typical example. But in general Hamilton does

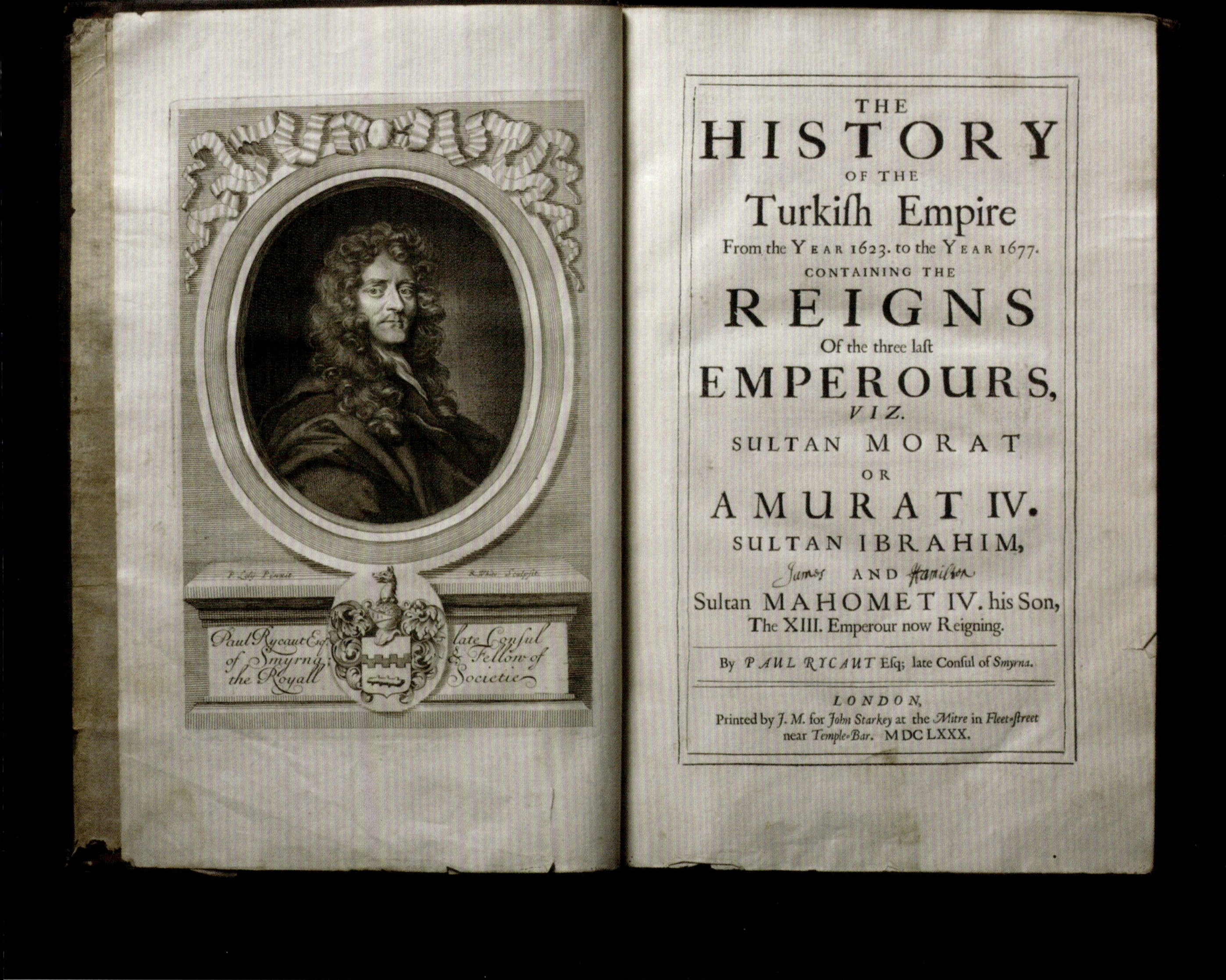

Above
Paul Rycaut, *The History of the Turkish Empire* (London, 1680), Wing 2406 (Castle Ward)

not seem from his books to have been much of an intellectual, notwithstanding his ownership of more substantial fare like Francis Willughby's *Ornithology* (London, 1678) and the 1676 edition of Bacon's *Sylva Sylvarum*. Nor does he seem to have been much of a linguist. There is the odd Latin book, and some of the many late seventeenth-century Dutch books in the French language may perhaps have been his, but it is striking how many of the foreign texts in James Hamilton's library are present only in English translations. Of course, these conclusions must of necessity be somewhat tentative, based as they are on books which Hamilton bothered to sign; there are books of similar type and date, in similar bindings with no ownership marks. These probably belonged to him as well, but unless some sort of inventory turns up, this is something which can only be inferred. Nor can we draw many conclusions about Hamilton's reading habits, since he does not seem to have been much of an annotator, though a list of 'Books of My Lady Dowager of Peterboros' written into a copy of Ussher's *Annals of the World* (London, 1658) provides an intriguing glimpse into the library closet of his Mordaunt in-laws:

1. A Tretis against Athisme by Will: Towres
2. Bishop Ushers Observations upon the Old Testament
3. Bishop Coopers Works
4. The desatefulness of plan Hart by Danyell Dick
5. Selecte Thoughts by Bishop Hall
6. The Consecration of Bishops by Francis Mason
7. Eusebius, Ecclesiastical History
8. A paraphrase upon the Salmes
9. A sperituall and pretious pearle
10. Doctor Hamon against the papistrie of Jesuisme
11. Fishers defence of the Common Prayer
12. Bonde upon the Sabbath
13. In defence of the King's boock
14. Doctor Usher Bishop: the Prinsis pour
15. The King's boock
16. Doctor Bramons Vindication of the Church of England
17. Boultons Cardinall Professor
18. The daily prais of pyety
19. Prayers
20. 3 books of notes of my Ladys
21. My Lord Primats Catecis. Refor
22. St Ostin
23. Mr Gals practick theoris unbound
24. The Holy Warr by Fuller

Finally, Hamilton is a disappointing book-owner because he rarely made any note of where and when he bought his books. His copy of the fourth edition of John Guillim's *A Display of Heraldrie* (London, 1660) – a favourite work of many a Restoration squire – is a rare exception. Though we do not know where it came from (presumably bought in London or Dublin, or conceivably even in Scotland), we do at least know when, since it is carefully signed 'James Hamilton 1663 August: 31'. But if James Hamilton's books are interesting, the antecedents of his library are yet more intriguing. Apart from a few hastily-scrawled ownership inscriptions, there is very little definite evidence as to where the many sixteenth-century books now at Castle Ward came from, but it seems all but certain that the Hamiltons of Bangor took them on from the senior branch of the family, and some have consequently been in Ireland for the best part of 400 years.[7] In the first place, they simply look different, with distinctive bindings very different from the plain trade bindings which clothe James Hamilton's books. Then there is their subject matter, and their places of production: not plain and simple books printed in England or Ireland, but learned texts in Latin, Greek, and even Hebrew, the products of presses like the Wechels in Frankfurt, Christophe Plantin in Antwerp, and the Lyon printer Jean de Tournes (1539–1615). What, for example, is one to make of a Hebrew grammar by the humanist scholar Sante Pagnini (1470-1536), printed in Lyon by Antoine Gryphius in 1577, in a probably sixteenth-century gold-tooled Oxford binding, with scraps of a medieval manuscript embedded in it? Or of books like Junius's *Grammatica Hebraeae Linguae* (Geneva, 1590), or for that matter of a massive made-up set of Cardinal Baronius's *Annales Ecclesiastici* (the official Counter-Reformation history of the Church), in part from the Plantin presses in Antwerp? It seems obvious that these and others like them belonged to a seventeeth-century scholar, and a wealthy one at that, because many of them would have been far beyond the pocket of an ordinary student. It seems clear that they belonged to the 1st Lord Claneboye, *quondam* Dublin schoolmaster, Fellow of Trinity, a graduate of St Andrews in his native Scotland, and described (admittedly by his nephew) as 'very learned, wise, laborious, noble (especially to strangers and scholars)'.[8] If so, these books constitute a remnant of one of the earliest surviving private libraries in Ireland, presumably brought to Ireland at a time – roughly 1590 to 1612 – when English port books show a five-fold

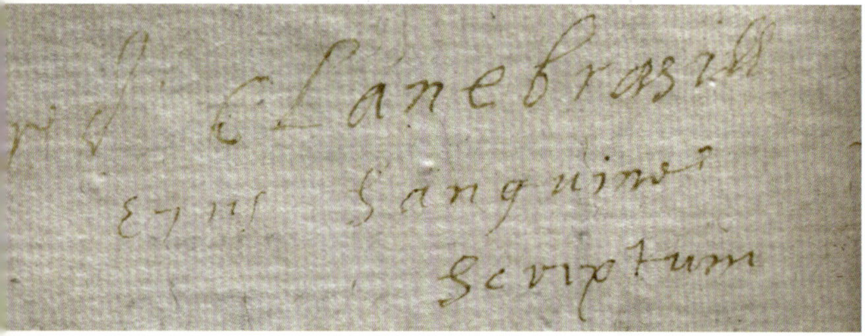

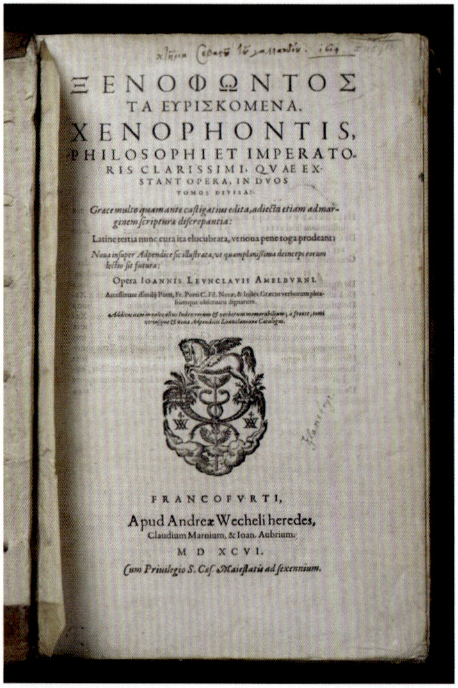

ΞΕΝΟΦΩΝΤΟΣ
ΤΑ ΕΥΡΙΣΚΟΜΕΝΑ.
XENOPHONTIS,
PHILOSOPHI ET IMPERATORIS CLARISSIMI, QVAE EXSTANT OPERA, IN DVOS TOMOS DIVISA:

Græce multo quam ante castigatius edita, adiecta etiam ad marginem scripturæ discrepantia:

Latine tertia nunc cura ita elucubrata, vt noua pene toga prodeant;

Noua insuper Adpendice sic illustrata, vt quamplenissima deinceps eorum lectio sit futura:

Opera IOANNIS LEVNCLAVII AMELBVRNI.

FRANCOFVRTI,
Apud Andreæ Wecheli heredes,
Claudium Marnium, & Ioan. Aubrium.
M D XCVI.
Cum Priuilegio S. Cæs. Maiestatis ad sexennium.

Above
Endpaper of Cicero, *Opera Omnia quae Extant* ([Geneva], 1594) signed in blood by Henry, 3rd Earl of Clanbrassil (Castle Ward)

Right
Xenophon, *Quae Exstant Opera* (Frankfurt, 1596), Adams X16 (Castle Ward), with signature of the (1st?) Lord Claneboye

increase in the number of books being shipped into Dublin.[9] They would have been a tremendously valuable asset in Elizabethan and Jacobean Dublin, where there was no publicly accessible library until the foundation of Trinity College in 1592. Some may equally have been connected with the future Lord Clanbrassil's Grand Tour in 1633, though there is also a 1594 Cicero apparently inscribed by Clanbrassil's son and heir Henry, 3rd Earl of Clanbrassil (1647-75) in his own blood. It seems a fairly extraordinary thing to do, though it is difficult to say whether the choice of medium actually means anything very profound, or whether signing in blood was an act of youthful bravado or friendship. Perhaps young Clanbrassil had been reading in *De Amicitia (On Friendship)* that 'the good love the good and attach them to themselves as though they were united by blood and nature.'[10] Finally, it is worth considering the earliest Irish book at Castle Ward today: Ussher's *Britannicarum Ecclesiarum Antiquitates* (Dublin, 1639). Could it be the copy which belonged to the Archbishop's former teacher, Claneboye, or did it come from James Hamilton's mother-in-law Elizabeth Carey, who was the prelate's most intimate friend?[11] This is, of course, pure speculation, but we can be rather surer about where all these books were actually kept. The surviving Hamilton books include only one manuscript of any note, a brilliantly-coloured heraldic compilation, probably made in about 1580. It is an attractive but unsurprising possession for a man like Claneboye, detailing the pedigrees of a large number of English, Scottish and Continental families, but, more importantly, inscriptions in the book suggest that it was kept in his principal residence, Killyleagh Castle, about ten miles from Castle Ward on the western shore of Strangford Lough. Presumably in the 1590s the future Lord Claneboye's books were with him in Dublin, but the manuscript seems to imply that after 1606 Claneboye's books were kept at Killyleagh as well. If so, the Hamilton books have enjoyed a remarkably eventful history, some perhaps having migrated in just over a century from Scotland to Dublin, from Dublin to Killyleagh (where they still were in 1666 – we know this from the second of the two books inscribed by Clanbrassil)[12], from Killyleagh to Bangor Castle, in 1709 from Bangor Castle to Castle Ward, and in the 1760s to the present house there.

It says a good deal about the resilience of books that such apparently fragile objects have survived moves by sea and by waggon, the Parliamentarian capture of Killyleagh Castle in a waterborne assault in 1649, and the Williamite wars.

The Wards of Castle Ward

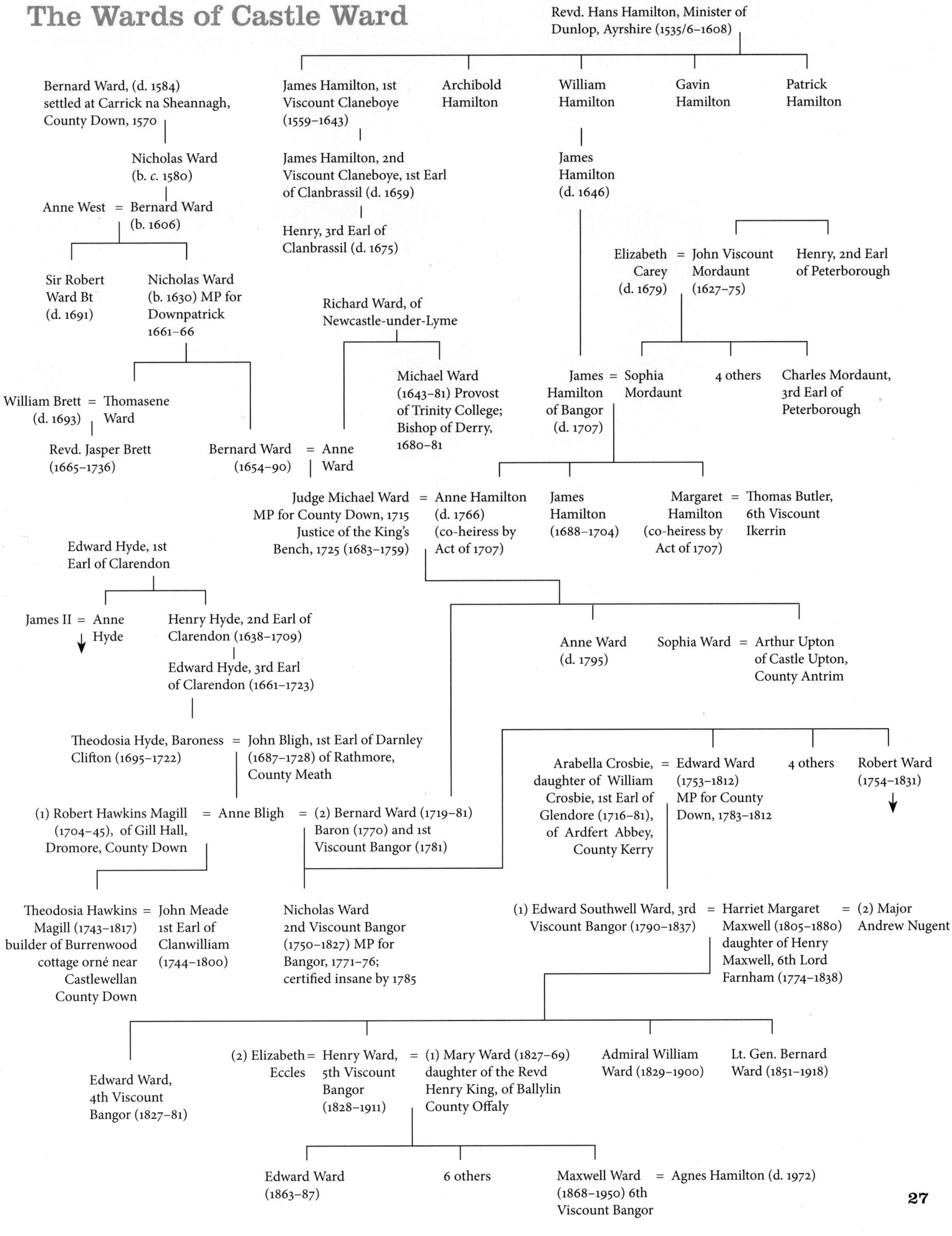

2 This Book is Mr Justice Ward's

Castle Ward, County Down, 1690–1950

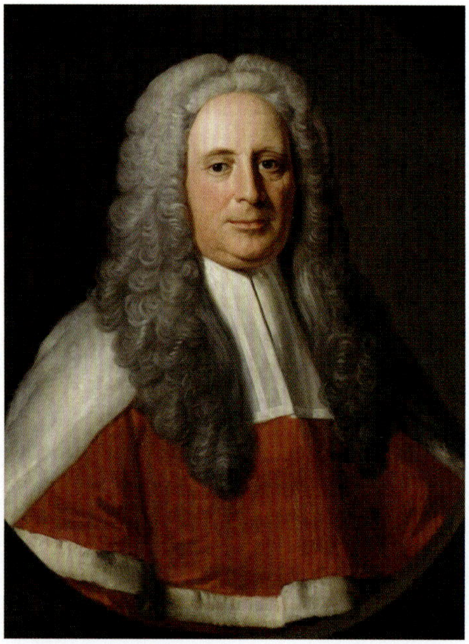

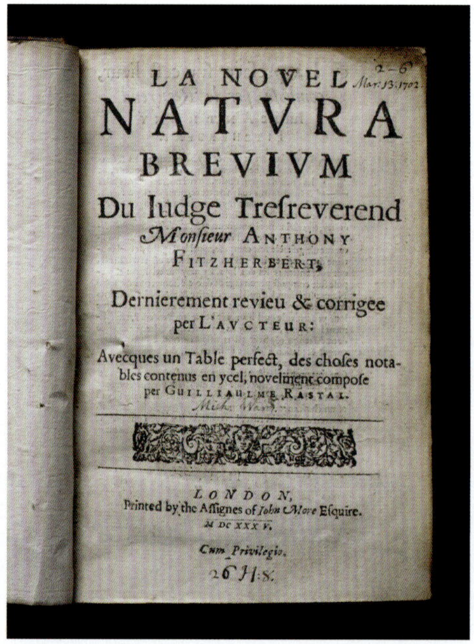

Right
Judge Michael Ward (1683–1759), portrait in the manner of Allan Ramsay (Castle Ward)

Far right
Sir Anthony Fitzherbert, *La Novel Natura Brevium* (London, 1635), STC 10967, signed by Michael Ward (Castle Ward)

In 1690 the seven-year-old Michael Ward of Castle Ward was orphaned when his father Bernard Ward (1654–90) was killed in a duel in Downpatrick. He was named after his maternal uncle Michael Ward, (1643–81), Bishop of Derry, and Provost of Trinity College, Dublin – no mean bookman himself, with a library of over 1200 titles in the early 1680s.[1] Educated in Dublin by his tutor Mr Jones, the bishop's nephew matriculated at Trinity College in 1699, and was a student there at a time when the Irish capital was, thought one resident, 'marvellously increased in wealth, trade, splendour and civility'.[2] After further studies at Gray's Inn in London, Michael Ward returned home to a city which was by then reckoned the fourth largest in Europe, and was called to the Irish Bar in 1705 – four years before his marriage to the heiress Anne Hamilton.[3] By then, it is clear, he had already been buying books – starting with a small legal reference collection – for some years, and Dublin, with its viceregal court, parliament, its lawyers, clergy and physicians, was a good place to do it. Many of the Castle Ward books have a small cipher scribbled onto their endpapers. Looking at isolated examples, this is rather puzzling, but working through the entire library, it becomes perfectly obvious that it is a highly stylised version of the initials 'MW': Michael Ward. A few books have both the cipher and a signature: for example *La Novel Natura Brevium du Iudge Tresreverend Anthony Fitzherbert* (London, 1635), inscribed 'Mich: Ward 2s 6d Mar. 13 1702' and 'MW', and presumably made up the nucleus of a small legal reference collection. And since the handful of inscribed books seems to have been purchased at the very beginning of the eighteenth century, the obvious inference is that Michael Ward habitually signed his books as a young man (he would have been nineteen in 1702), and that the cipher gradually took over as his sole method of indicating his ownership. An exception is his copy of Bishop Burnet's *History of His Own Time* (London, 1724), carefully marked 'Judge Ward': presumably not by the Judge himself, but by a bookseller, or a binder, or even by a zealous clerk. Looking through these books, recently catalogued for the National Trust, one gains the distinct impression that this was the library of an urbane man of the world: a suitable collection for a founder member of the Royal Dublin Society.[4] No doubt such books as M. de Vaumorière's *L'Art de Plaire dans la Conversation* (Paris, 1690) would have been useful to a young Dublin lawyer seeking to acquire a little Parisian polish, at a period which saw a great increase in court business in Ireland and the final exclusion of Irish Catholics from the legal professions.[5] But Judge Ward owned much more varied fare, ranging from law books to a large set of almanacks produced for the Dublin bookseller John Watson.[6] And then there are religious works, among them John Kettlewell's *An Help and Exhortation to Worthy Communicating* (Cambridge, 1701), signed in its owner's seventeenth year 'Mich: Ward prêt. 4s-0 Dec: 1701', or John Wilkins's *Of the Principles and Duties of Natural Religion* (London, 1715), marked (perhaps disapprovingly) 'foelix qui pius MW' ('happy is the pious man'). The several hundred late seventeenth- and early eighteenth-century sermons, printed in London and Dublin, may well have been Judge Ward's as well. In tune with the spirit of his age, he appears to have been a man who took his religious duties rather seriously. At any event he spent considerable sums refitting the nearby estate church at Ballyculter in 1736.[7] Equally, some of the devotional and religious books may have belonged to his wife Anne or to her family: a *Book of Common Prayer* (Dublin, 1700) certainly did, since Ward's mother-in-law Sophia Hamilton signed it in 1706/7, three years before her daughter's marriage. There are also books at Castle Ward with Sophia's initials tooled in gilt on their spines. This apparently trivial detail is at least evidence that she was fashionable enough to shelve them spine-outwards. We know little about how Judge Ward kept his books, but in 1685 the Duke of Ormonde had kept his books at Kilkenny Castle on shelves in a closet, and it seems likely that Michael Ward would have stored his in a similar fashion.[8] As his voluminous correspondence shows, Ward spent a large part of each year in Dublin, living in the 1720s on Ormonde Quay, so presumably at least some of his books were kept in his lodgings there.[9] Any books at Castle Ward would have initially have been kept in the first castle, a seventeenth-century tower house which still stands on the shores of Strangford Lough, where the Wards lived until about 1710. Later they would presumably have been installed in the now-vanished second Castle Ward, 'a large and handsome Improvement of Mr Justice Ward', thought a visitor in 1744; and certainly Michael Ward kept his plate trunk in his closet in this Queen Anne house in the early years of his marriage.[10]

Judge Ward's eldest son and successor, Bernard Ward (1719–81), was ennobled as 1st Baron Bangor in the Peerage of Ireland in 1768, a reward from the Lord Lieutenant, Lord Townshend, who recommended him to George III as a gentleman 'of very considerable property' of 'an ancient' Protestant family, who had consistently given the government's measures 'a

Right
Abraham Swan, *A Collection of Designs in Architecture* (London, 1757), ESTC T101999 (Castle Ward)

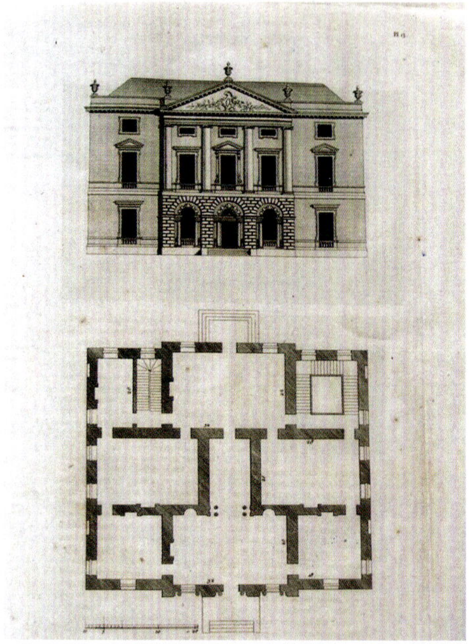

firm and honourable support'; in 1781 he was elevated to a viscountcy.[11] He found time both to build the present house and to quarrel with his wife Lady Anne Bligh, a sister of the 2nd Earl of Darnley, of Athboy in County Meath, and widow of the County Down MP and landowner Robert Hawkins Magill (1704–45). Family tradition has it that the marital breakdown was caused by arguments about architecture – Lord Bangor favoured a good solid Palladian house, while his wife inclined to the Gothick; Mrs Delany was critical of both, observing that 'he wants taste and Lady Anne is so whimsical that I doubt her judgement'.[12] With the recent publication of material which suggests that in her youth Anne had been engaged in a passionate emotional relationship with an older gentlewoman, Letitia Bushe (*c.*1705–57), which began probably in 1739, when Anne ('my own sweet jewel and petsy') was 21 and Letitia in her mid-thirties, it seems that architectural preferences may not have been the only cause of domestic disharmony. The precise nature of the relationship, which continued after Anne's marriage to Robert Hawkins Magill in September 1742, is difficult to determine, but it may be significant that Lady Anne saw it as something to be kept secret, and so presumably not entirely respectable. Disappointingly, none of Lady Anne's books is obviously at Castle Ward, and she may perhaps have taken them with her when she left her husband for Bath; certainly her friend Letitia moved in sophisticated circles, was both well-read and an accomplished letter-writer, able to quote from Seneca and Socrates in French translation, and delighting in the sociable reading of Shakespeare, biographies, and Fielding with her friends.[13] A friend of Mrs Delany's, whose letters she read with interest, Letitia Bushe had strong views on books, in 1740 dismissing collections of published correspondence as generally disappointing, and eager to tell her own correspondents what she herself was reading.[14] But there is at least one direct connection between books and building at Castle Ward since designs in Lord Bangor's copy of Abraham Swan's *Collection of Designs* (London, 1757) clearly inspired not only the Palladian north front but the details of the main staircase as well.[15] The 1st Lord Bangor's wide-ranging interest in the Antique evidently went some way beyond architecture – though he did own standard pattern books by Isaac Ware, as well as a set of Colen Campbell's best-selling *Vitruvius Britannicus*. His was probably the Castle Ward copy of Pierre-Jean Mariette's *Traité des Pierres Gravés* (Paris, 1750) – were there once engraved gems in the Ward collection? – and either he or his father might have owned the English translation of the standard text, Montfaucon's *Antiquity Explained* (London, 1721). He also took an interest in pictures, owning a copy of Robert Dossie's *The Handmaid to the Arts* (London, 1758), which half a century after the first sale of pictures in Dublin in 1707, claimed

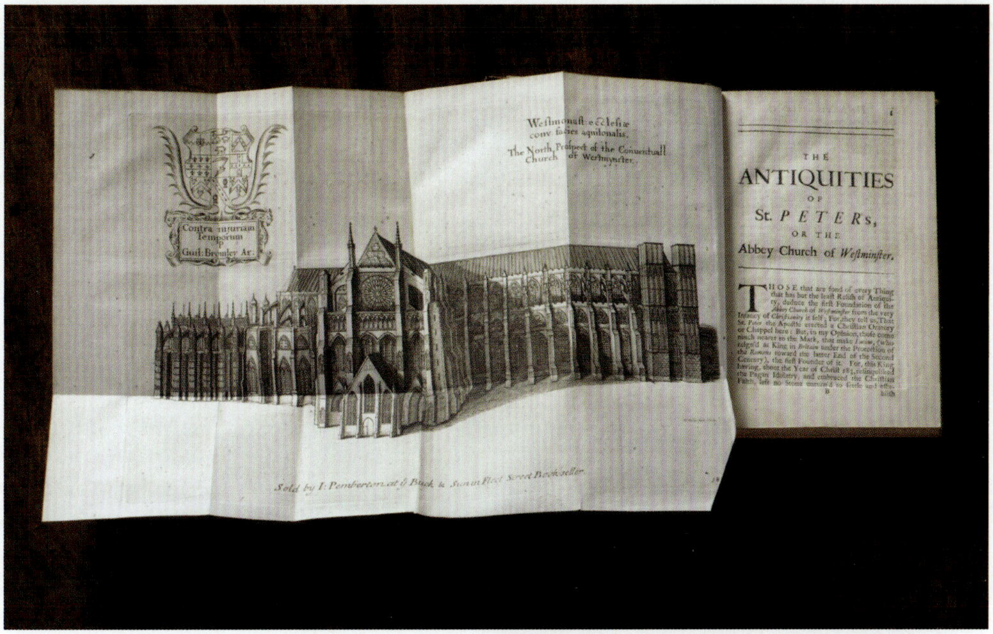

Right
Jodocus Crull, *Antiquities of St Peter's, or the Abbey Church of Westminster* (London, 1711), ESTC T72143 (Castle Ward)

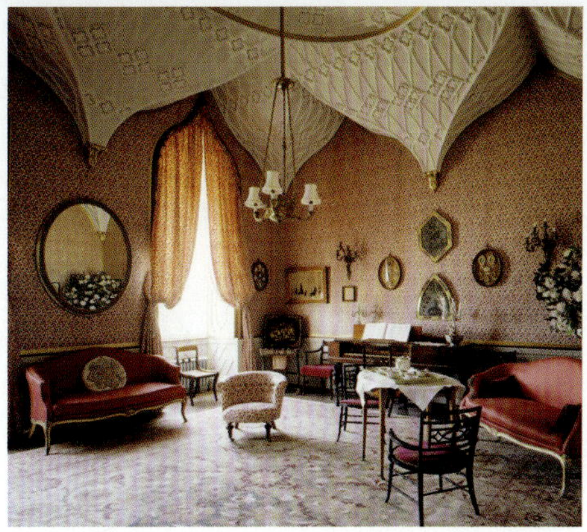

Right
The Gothic Boudoir at Castle Ward

to equip cultivated gentlemen not only with 'a perfect knowledge of the materia pictoria', but also advised on the various methods of gilding their frames.[16] The many books on British (though only rarely Irish) antiquities are also noteworthy, ranging as they do from Plot's *Natural History of Stafford-Shire* to Edward Lhuyd's *Archaeologia Britannica* (Oxford, 1707) and Jodocus Crull's *Antiquities of St Peter's, or the Abbey Church of Westminster*. The last was Michael Ward's, but surely significant in a house whose Gothick fan vaults were inspired (as Lord William Gordon noted in a letter to Bernard Ward in 1764) by the Henry VII Chapel at Westminster.[17] For them, as for the contemporary County Down amateur Samuel Waring of Waringstown (1660–1739), who copied by hand the plates in a borrowed *Vitruvius Britannicus* in the 1720s, books were the keys which unlocked the mysteries of refined architecture, allowing gentlemen to design their own houses in an appropriately up-to-date and fashionable style.[18]

In the days before the Union, the Wards and their clients did not sit in the Westminster Parliament, but in the Irish Parliament on College Green in Dublin. Bernard Ward was a member of the Commons from 1745 to 1760 and from 1761 to 1768, and sat in the Upper House after his ennoblement.[19] Presumably, he was the purchaser of Castle Ward's very handsomely-bound nineteen-volume set of the *Journals of the Irish House of Commons* – an obvious gesture at a time when many members of the Ascendancy were increasingly keen to articulate their own brand of Irish patriotism. But equally affairs in London evidently continued to influence the Wards – as witnessed by the four-year run

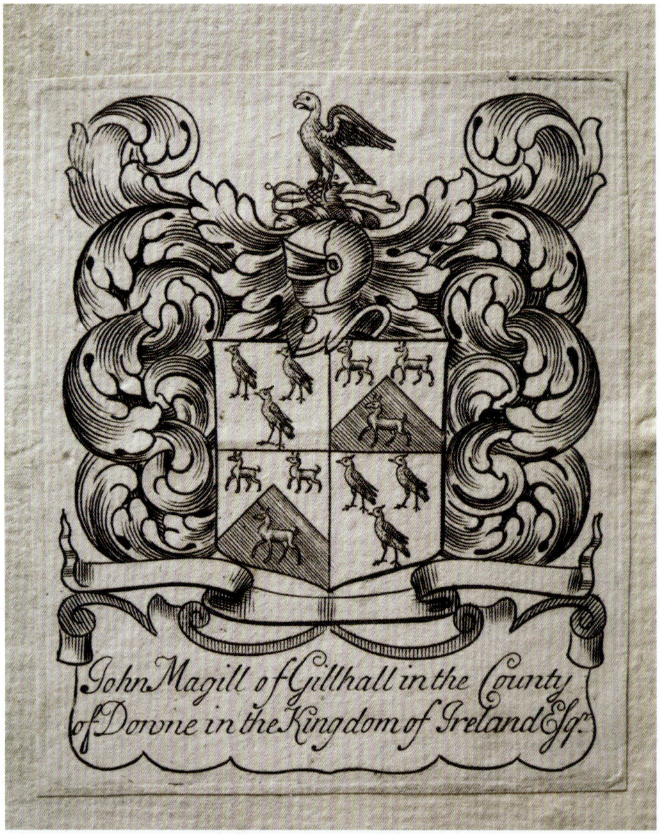

Above
Bookplate of John Magill of Gill Hall, Franks 19453 (Castle Ward)

of the *London Chronicle* (1758–62). And if the shelves at Castle Ward appear to groan under a great weight of eighteenth-century Irish books (126 titles today) – to seize on just a couple of examples, books like John Rutty's *An Essay towards a Natural, Experimental and Medicinal History of Mineral Waters of Ireland* (Dublin, 1757) and a 1749 Dublin edition of Robertson's best-selling *History of Scotland* – less than a quarter of the contemporary books are of local manufacture, and there are many more from Great Britain (582 in total, all but 12 printed in England). Some of these, no doubt, were acquired in Ireland, but the English connection was clearly important, and when Nicholas Ward, the future 2nd Lord Bangor (1750–1827), was sent to university, it was to Christ Church, Oxford, and not to Trinity College in Dublin. Nicholas's set of the University statutes, *Parecbolae sive Excerptae e Corpore Statutorum Universitatis Oxoniensis* (Oxford, 1766), neatly signed 'N. Ward Ecclesiae Xti Oxon', is still at Castle Ward, as are a considerable number of books which can only have been school or university textbooks. The most amusing of these is a copy of François Porney's *The Pantheon, Representing the Fabulous Histories of the Heathen Gods and the Most Illustrious Heroes* (Dublin, 1738) – a useful crib for a young man struggling to remember his classical mythology, and waggishly inscribed 'Nicholas Ward, for his Pantheon'. Alas, the 21-year-old Nicholas found it difficult (as his Swiss tutor M. Delafare complained) to shed his 'whimsical habits', and cursed with an 'untameable temper', was brought back from Geneva in disgrace in 1771, his ambitions to learn French unfulfilled.[20] The daughters of the family, too, have left their mark. It may well have been they who followed Letitia Bushe in reading (or at least buying) modish French language books in the second half of the eighteenth century. There are about 40 in all, including a 1750 edition of Rousseau's letters, all bought at precisely the time when a knowledge of French was becoming fashionable both among the Irish gentry and the middling sort.[21] The Castle Ward copy of Boyer's *Dictionnaire Royal* (London, 1764) belonged to the 1st Viscount's future daughter-in-law, the eventual wife of Edward Ward (1753–1812), who was the daughter of William Crosbie, 1st Earl of Glandore (1716–81), of Ardfert Abbey, County Kerry. Like several of her French books, she proudly inscribed it in her best French: 'Ce livre appartient à Mademoiselle Arabella Crosbie'.

The 1st Lord Bangor's tangled marital affairs were responsible for yet another layer within the Castle Ward library, in the form of books which had formerly belonged to his estranged wife's first

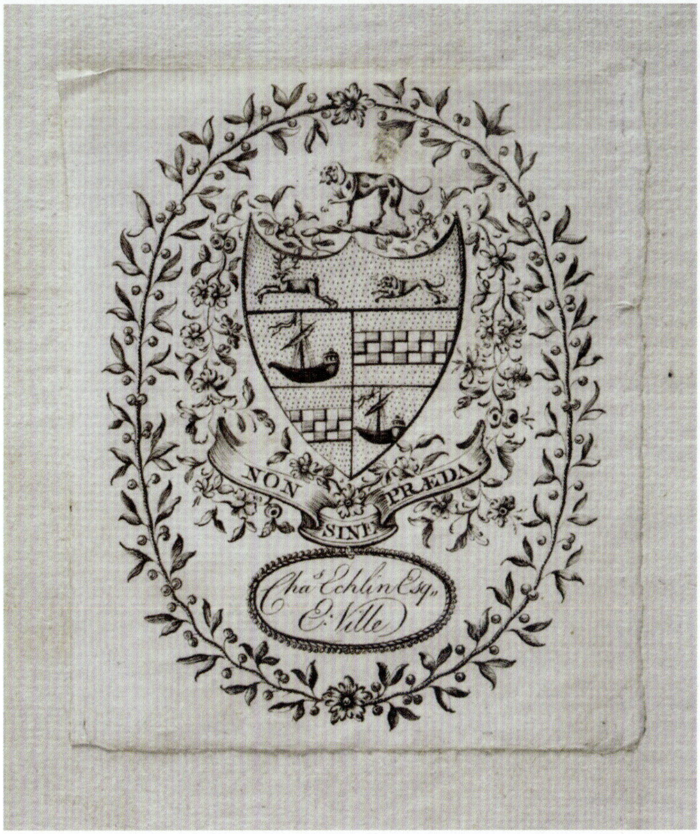
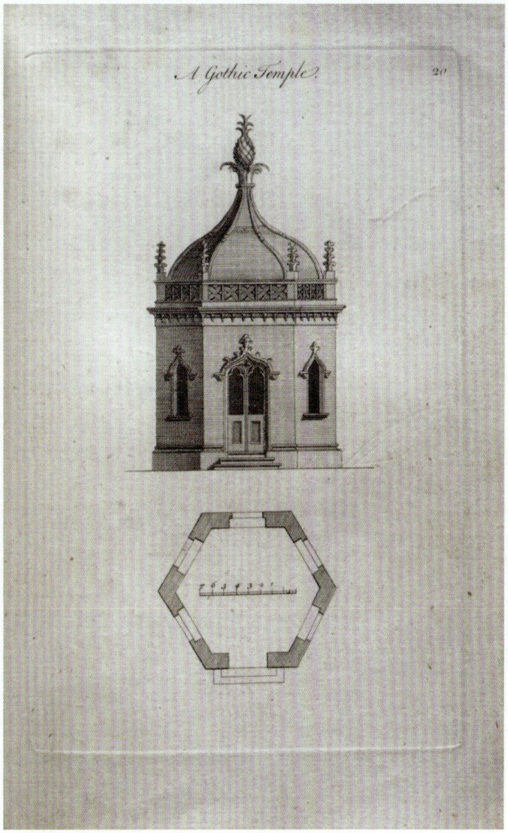

Above
Bookplate of Charles Echlin (Castle Ward)

Right
Plate from Charles Echlin's copy of Charles Over, *Ornamental Architecture in the Gothic, Chinese, and Modern Taste* (London, 1758), ESTC T132234

husband, Robert Hawkins Magill (1704–45), through his mother a descendant of the great Lord Clarendon and a distant cousin of Queen Anne. The family seat was Gill Hall, a mile and a half west of Dromore, and by hook or by crook his grieving widow seems to have retained at least some of the Gill Hall books. Unlike her own books, they at least remained at Castle Ward when she left, and there are several at Castle Ward today still with the very handsome eighteenth-century bookplate of 'John Magill of Gillhall in the County of Downe in the Kingdome of Ireland'. These include his copy of Fynes Moryson's classic *An History of Ireland, from the Year 1599, to 1603* (Dublin, 1735), and a translation of Mariana's *General History of Spain* (London, 1699). Another local bookplate is the extremely elegant *ex libris* of Charles Echlin of Echlinsville, County Down, a copy of which is pasted into an appropriately elegant little book, Charles Over's *Ornamental Architecture in the Gothic, Chinese and Modern Taste* (London, 1758). The Echlins were another local gentry family, originally from Fife in eastern Scotland, and the senior branch lived just across Strangford Lough from Castle Ward, at Ardquin, on the Ards peninsula near the little town of Portaferry.[22] In the seventeenth century Robert Echlin (d. 1635), the builder of the manor house at Ardquin, had been Bishop of Down and Connor and had harried Scots Presbyterians in his diocese in a vain attempt to compel them to conform to the rites and practices of the Church of Ireland.[23] A junior branch of the family lived not far away at Echlinsville, where a substantial single-storey Library was added to the house in the late eighteenth century, and two generations, father and son, both named Charles, were agents to the Wards in the eighteenth century. The older of the two seems to have managed the lands in and around the town of Bangor which Judge Ward had inherited from his wife's Hamilton ancestors, but the bookplate seems more likely to have belonged to the son.[24] We may never know how one of his books ended up in his patron's library, and perhaps it does not greatly matter. Ultimately, what is perhaps more telling is the tangible physical reminder that by the middle of the eighteenth century a library and its associated paraphernalia had become an essential component of a genteel life-style. Of libraries sold at auction in Dublin between 1741 and 1760, only 12.6% belonged to the nobility and gentry, but fully 67.6% to professional men like the two Charles Echlins, and if clergy were in the lead with just over a third of the libraries, together the lawyers, physicians and army officers were not so very far behind.[25] There are many pre-1800 books on the shelves at Castle Ward with the signatures of as yet unidentified owners who no doubt came from precisely these strata of society: books like Guy Miege's *The Great French Dictionary* (London, 1688), signed 'Dorithea Cressy' or Michael Geddes, *Several Tracts Against Popery* (London, 1715) ('E. Cairnes').

The present Castle Ward has probably included a Library room of some kind ever since it was built, quite possibly in the room to the right of the front hall which still houses the books today. In 1774 it seems usually to have been kept locked, as when the Dublin clergyman Edward Smyth was enticed north by Lord Bangor to become curate of nearby Ballyculter, he was promised that he should 'have a hunter always at my command, and a key to a large library, from whence I might select any book I pleased.'[26] And indeed by the standards of the libraries available to many local people, Castle Ward did have a large library, with the Mechanics Library in nearby Portaferry holding only 258 volumes in the third decade of the nineteenth century, and the subscription library founded in Bangor by the Wards with only a 'limited number of religious and moral works'.[27] But all of these libraries – including Castle Ward's – were dwarfed by the Earl of Moira's library at Montalto, near Ballynahinch, described in fulsome terms by John Moore Johnston, his Lordship's Receiver of Rents between 1780 and 1796:

> His Lordship had one of the largest and best collection [*sic*] of books (about Thirty Thousand volumes) of any private library perhaps in this Kingdom, he readily lent books to any Lady or Gentleman who asked them; he always permitted me to read any book I chose, provided I returned it without damage, which order I strictly adhered to. When in dublin [*sic*] he left the key of the library with me, (and an injunction not to suffer a book to leave the library, unless to … a few … and in that case to take a memorandum of the book and day of the month got)…. He was a great friend and benefactor to booksellers in general buying every new publication…. I had the use of the … library … – Books in all languages, history, antiquities, arts and sciences, for sixteen years, which equaled [*sic*] College education.[28]

By comparison only occasionally is it possible to see where successive generations of Wards purchased their books. Some might have been ordered by mail, and many, surely, were bought in bookshops in Dublin, and others perhaps in England. In 1735, for example, Michael Ward's friend, the MP Arthur Dobbs (1689–1765), wrote from London to the Judge (then in Dublin) to report that he had dispatched books 'by long sea to Belfast', presumably meaning that they had been sent direct to the north, rather than via the Irish capital. Trips to take the waters in Scarborough (1746) and Bath (1757) perhaps provided further opportunities for shopping in England.[30] Other books may have been purchased in Belfast, and others, quite conceivably, in smaller provincial towns like Downpatrick, Newry and Dundalk, all on the way to Dublin. Judge Ward, of course, routinely travelled round Ireland in pursuit of his official duties: in 1740, for example, he was much criticised for rebuking a prosecuting counsel in Monaghan for opposing the provision of an Irish-speaking interpreter.[31] For the most part we can only speculate, though the Wards habitually kept a house in the capital, and Judge Ward spent much of his time there, laying out £50 on books and physicians in the city in 1729, though, frustratingly, we do not know the precise breakdown of the expenditure.[32] Some of his books would undoubtedly have been kept in the Dublin house, but it would have been easy enough to shift books or any other goods up and down the coast. A hogshead of wine was dispatched from Dublin direct to Castle Ward via the little port of Strangford in 1733.[33] Moving books by sea would have presented few difficulties by comparison, while the introduction of a scheduled coach service from the city to Belfast in 1740/1 would have facilitated the passage of books and ideas, even for those who did not have their own coach and horses.[34] Certainly Michael Ward's near-contemporary Francis Hutchinson, Bishop of Down and Connor from 1721 to 1739, was routinely moving books back and forth from Dublin to his residence at Portglenone Castle, County Antrim, in the 1730s.[35] Of course some of the Hamilton books may even have come to Down directly from Scotland in the Plantation period – indeed the circumstantial evidence of Claneboye's choice of editions and the occasional rather cryptic inscriptions perhaps suggests that they did.[36]

The most detailed evidence on the workings of the Irish booktrade at Castle Ward is provided by a clergyman called Jasper Brett (1665–1736), whose books, or at least some of them, seem to have come into Judge Ward's possession. Brett came from Ballynewport, and was Vicar of Rathmullan, Bright and Tyrella from 1709 to 1736. He was also Michael Ward's cousin, his father having married the Judge's aunt, Thomasene Ward.[37] Brett was also one of those collectors who liked to note on the flyleaf where he had bought his books. Of the quite small number which can be positively identified as his, most are inscribed in this way. His copy of John Scott's *The Christian Life* (London, 1695), for example, is carefully inscribed: 'bought from Jacob Milner in Essex Street Dublin Sepr 1697'. Milner (d. 1701) was a leading member of the Dublin

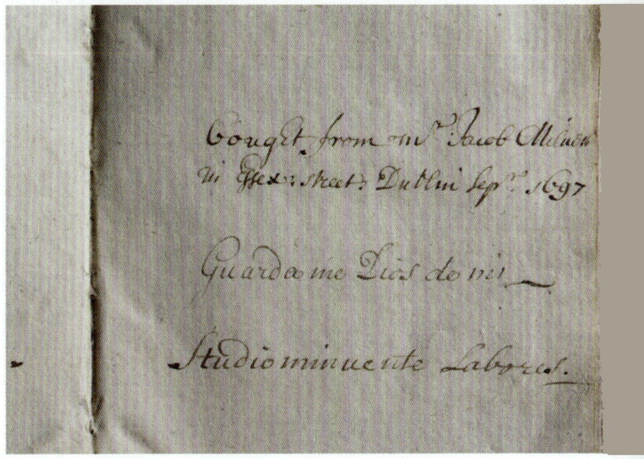

Right
A characteristic inscription in a book owned by the Revd. Jasper Brett (1665–1736), in his copy of John Scott's *The Christian Life* (London, 1695), Wing S2052 (Castle Ward)

trade.[38] Then there is Brett's copy of a work of the bookish bishop William Nicolson, inscribed 'bought from Mr North in Skinner's Row Sepr 1697'. Perhaps the 32-year-old clergyman had been on a book-buying spree, but in any event Skinner Row, near Christ Church cathedral, was one of the main centres of the Dublin booktrade, and 'Mr North' was John North, active in the Irish capital from before 1679 right down to his death in 1697. Twenty-five years later, and Brett was still up to his old tricks; in an odd volume of Lewis Ellis Dupin's *Compendious History of the Church from the Beginning of the World to this Present Time* (London, 1715–16) can be found Brett's motto 'Guarda me Dios', and the flyleaf inscribed 'From Mr Sam Fairbrother Skinner Row

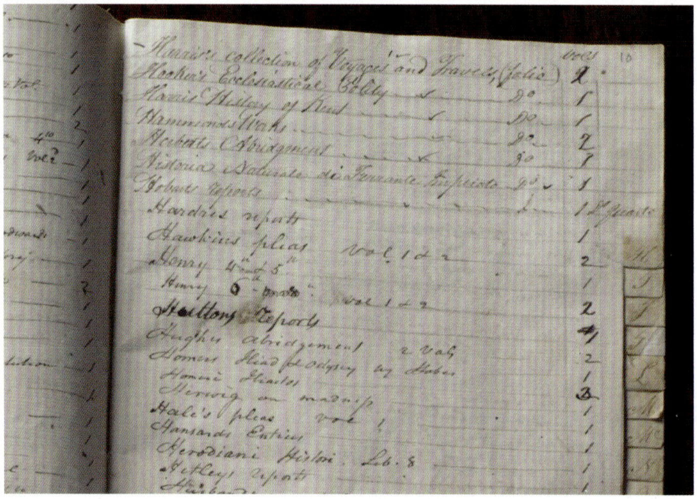

Above
The 1813 library catalogue (Castle Ward)

Dublin'. Fairbrother, too, was a well-known figure, a printer, bookseller, and binder. As King's Stationer in Ireland, it was he who commissioned the famous series of Parliamentary bindings, often described as the finest set of bindings ever made, and tragically lost in the destruction of the Four Courts in Dublin in 1922.[39] But occasionally, at least, Jasper Brett seems to have found books closer to home, notably his copy of Guicciardini's *Historiarum sui Temporis* (Basel, 1566), in an early gold-tooled centrepiece binding with manuscript waste from what looks like a fifteenth-century English legal manuscript. This is inscribed 'Bought from Mr Alex. Adair Mercht. in Belfast', perhaps the man of that name who was Master of the sloop *William* – based in the County Down port of Killough, where the Wards had substantial interests – in 1737.[40]

Of the nineteenth century at Castle Ward there is rather less to say. In the first place, the well-known decline of the Irish book-trade after the Act of Union in 1801, and the eventual coming of railways and steam packets, inevitably had a very visible impact on the contents of the shelves. Books like Duplessi-Bertaux's *Tableaux historiques de la Révolution française* (Paris, 1817), or the magnificent set of hand-coloured Regency costume books, many of them associated with the author William Alexander (1767–1816), are undeniably very handsome and appealing, but in truth they are indistinguishable from the sort of books that might be found in any other aristocratic library in Great Britain or Ireland. But more particularly, Castle Ward itself was at the centre of a bitter family quarrel during the protracted lunacy of the 2nd Viscount Bangor – once a promising undergraduate at Christ Church, Oxford and a troublesome young tourist in French-speaking Geneva. The dispute was resolved only in 1827, on the succession of Edward Southwell Ward as 3rd Viscount, and when the Ordnance Survey visited in the 1830s, the surveyors described the demesne as still 'totally out of order'.[41] These events plainly had a serious impact on the library, which was inventoried in 1813, and valued in 1817, most probably at the instigation of Robert Ward of Bangor Castle, the 2nd Viscount's uncle, accused by other members of the family of stripping Castle Ward of most of its contents.[42] More generally, nineteenth-century Castle Ward seems to have been fairly quiescent, and it is very striking that while many Irish aristocrats featured prominently in the political and social columns of contemporary Dublin and Belfast newspapers, apart from the occasional advertisement (usually placed by John Glen, the Land Steward) the Wards are rarely mentioned. Some books may even have been removed from the house during this period. There was once, for example, a copy of Mark Catesby's *Natural History of Carolina, Florida, and the Bahama Islands*. One of the grandest illustrated books of the eighteenth century, originally published in 1731 (and reissued in 1754), it is certainly not in the collection today: at present it is difficult to say whether it was removed between 1813 and 1827, or sold in the twentieth century, before the National Trust took over.[43] We also

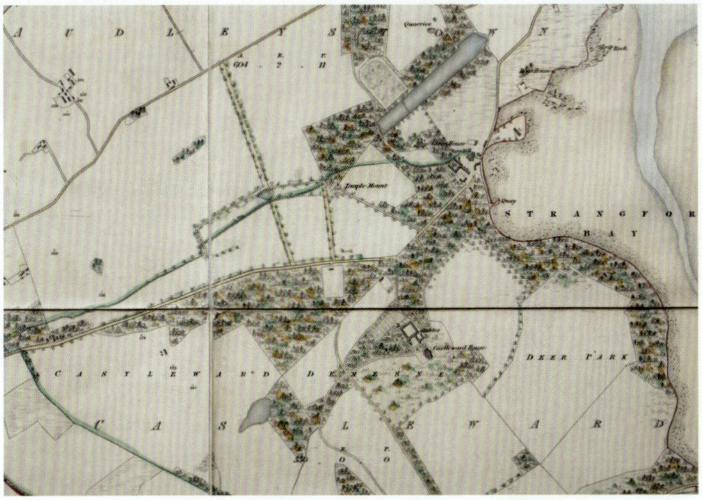

Above
A sheet from the *Ordnance Survey of Ireland: County Down* ([Dublin, 1835]) (Castle Ward)

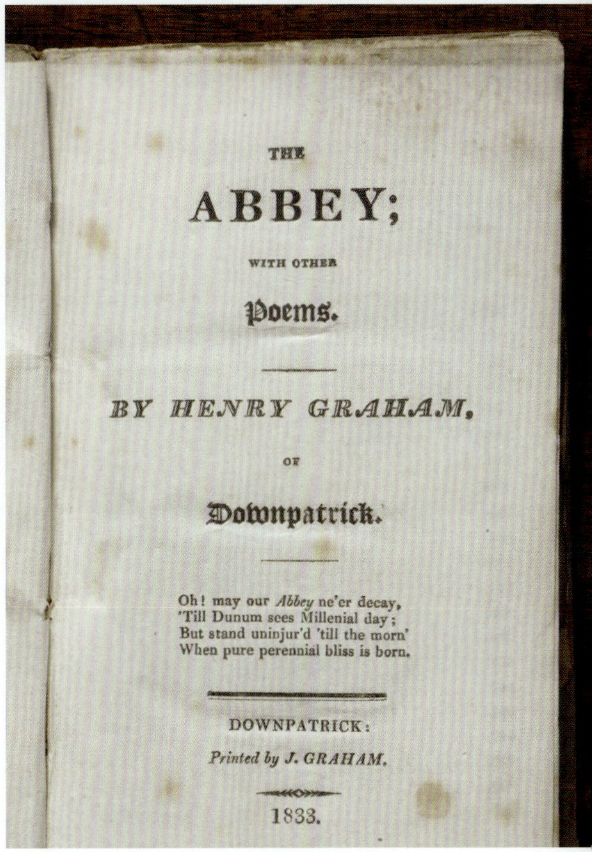
THE

ABBEY;

WITH OTHER

Poems.

BY HENRY GRAHAM,

OF

Downpatrick.

Oh! may our *Abbey* ne'er decay,
'Till Dunum sees Millenial day;
But stand uninjur'd 'till the morn'
When pure perennial bliss is born.

DOWNPATRICK:

Printed by J. GRAHAM.

1833.

Right
Henry Graham, *The Abbey* (Downpatrick, 1833) (Castle Ward)

have evidence of at least one theft – which speaks tellingly of the neglect and confusion at early nineteenth-century Castle Ward – in the form of an incomplete copy of Pierre de Ronsard's *Les Quatre Premiers Livres de la Franciade* (Paris, 1630), with a slip of paper inside, rather touchingly inscribed:

> The enclosed books with some old prints were stolen more than fifty years ago from a heap of books lying on the floor of a room during repairs to Castleward house. One of the books was taken by a lady and the other by a school boy aged about twelve. They are now returned and a pound which is more than the value of the old prints enclosed. The thefts have long since caused regret and repentance.[44]

A happier nineteenth-century legacy is the considerable collection of books in boards at Castle Ward, some of them from London; others issued much more locally, including works like Henry Graham's *The Abbey; with Other Poems*, published in Downpatrick in 1833. The magnificent set of nineteenth-century Ordnance Survey maps of County Down is just as interesting, and considerably more splendid. Sumptuously coloured and in its original boxes, it is surely one of the finest copies extant. Since the Wards owned much of the land depicted in it, one might have expected the maps to have been heavily used, but in fact many are almost pristine and some of the sheets have probably rarely, if ever, been opened. The numerous school text books – some English, and others from Dublin – are also worth noting; so too is the small crop of Irish provincial printing. Most of these books will have entered the house in the time of Edward Southwell Ward, 3rd Viscount Bangor (1790–1837), who created the present sober Library, each press secure with locks and a latticed brass grille, the books within, of all vintages, with a standard family bookplate.

There are also books associated with the pioneering woman scientist Mary Ward (1827–69).[45] The wife of Henry William Crosbie Ward (1828–1911), Mary never lived at Castle Ward, but her husband, the second son of the 3rd Viscount, succeeded to the estate in

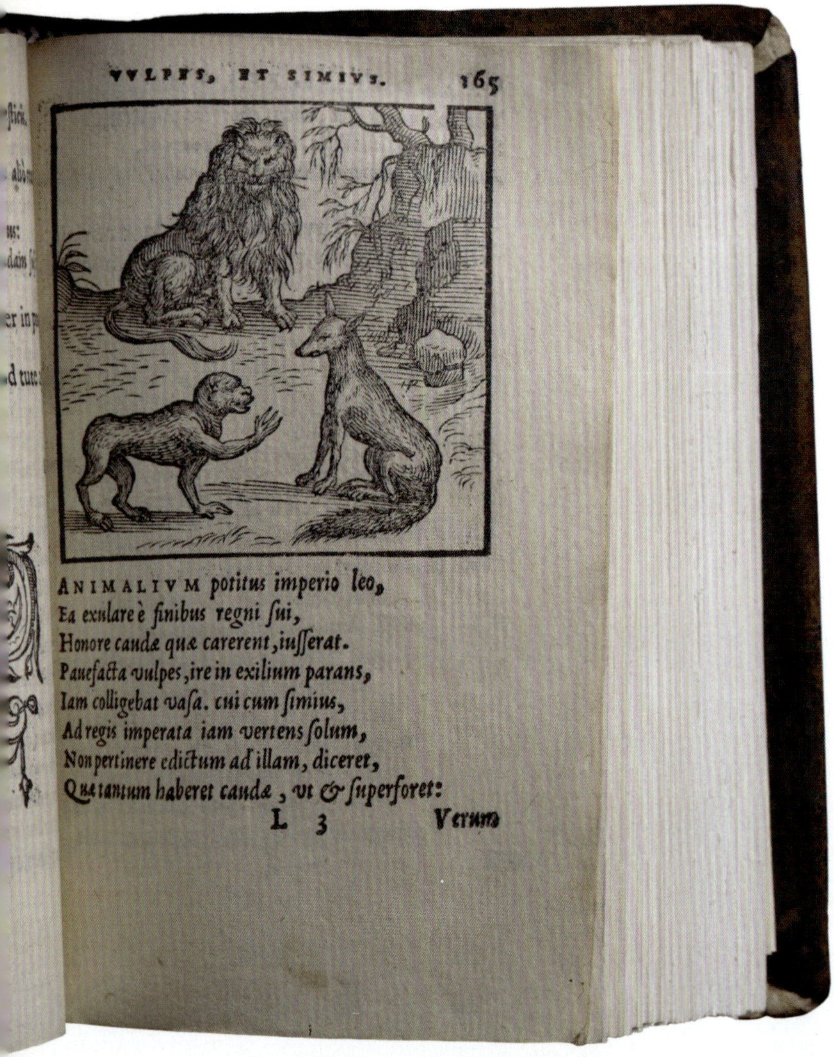
VVLPES, ET SIMIVS. 165

ANIMALIVM potitus imperio leo,
Ea exulare è finibus regni sui,
Honore caudæ quæ carerent, iusserat.
Pauefacta vulpes, ire in exilium parans,
Iam colligebat vasa. cui cum simius,
Ad regis imperata iam vertens solum,
Non pertinere edictum ad illam, diceret,
Quæ tantum haberet caudæ, ut & superforet:
L 3 Verum

Above
Aesop, *Fabulae*
(Lyon, 1580)
(Castle Ward)

1874, five years after her death, crushed under the wheels of an experimental steam locomotive at Birr Castle, County Offaly. Mary's childhood had been spent at Ballylin, near Ferbane, County Offaly, 'a fine example of an Irish gentleman's house', and the home of her parents, the Revd. Henry and Mrs Harriet King. She was given an expensive microscope by her father when she was eighteen years old, and must have acquired her copy of John Quekett's *Practical Treatise on the Use of the Microscope* (London, 1848) not long afterwards. Her married home was Bellair, at Moate, in County Offaly, but she was a frequent visitor to Birr, home of her cousin, the 3rd Earl of Rosse.[46] She was keenly interested in the vast six-foot-diameter reflecting telescope which he constructed there, completed in 1845, on the eve of the Famine, while her own *Sketches with the Microscope* (1857) was privately printed at Birr (then Parsonstown, King's County), and includes fourteen coloured plates executed by the Dublin lithographer Hendrick based on the author's original drawings. The copy surviving at Castle Ward, one of 250 printed, was presumably Mary Ward's own. Well received by critics, it was republished in London the following year under the title *The World of Wonders*. Perhaps rather curiously, one of the Castle Ward books which Mary Ward certainly owned is a miniature edition of Aesop, in Latin and Greek, printed in Lyon by Jean de Tournes in 1580, bought before her marriage, when she was still living at Ballylin. This is one of the oldest books in the collection (the earliest is a 1552 Lyon edition of the late Roman historian Ammianus Marcellinus), and the only sixteenth-century book at Castle Ward which bears any evidence to indicate that it did not belong to the Ward family's Hamilton ancestors. Mary also owned a variety of quite ordinary eighteenth- and nineteenth-century books, presumably brought to Castle Ward when her husband inherited it in 1874; there is perhaps more than a suspicion that a fair number of the unmarked nineteenth-century books on the shelves could also have come from the cultured household of the Kings of Ballylin.

By contrast, most of the later Ward books are anything but intellectual, ranging from pot-boiling novels like Lew Wallace's *Ben Hur* and the imperial derring-do of *Bulldog Drummond*, through to the inevitable books on hunting which were so popular in Irish houses in Edwardian times. Many of these books were relegated to attic stores by the National Trust in the early days of its occupation of Castle Ward, but now clearly have a social and historic interest of their own which it would have been impossible to envisage in the 1950s. A first edition of Captain Scott's *Last Expedition* (London, 1913) sits alongside others of a more strictly practical nature, whether devotional manuals and gardening books, or George Fowler's war-time *How to Bottle Fruit, Vegetables, Game, Poultry, Milk, Tomatoes, Jams, Pickles, etc.* (Reading, 1942) – a book whose purpose would have been readily apparent to earlier generations who strove for self-sufficiency on their estates. But more charming – and certainly more personal – than any of these are the yachting books of Castle Ward's last private owner, Mary Ward's long-lived son, Maxwell Ward, 6th Viscount Bangor, born in 1868, long-time President of the Strangford Lough Yacht Club, and a stickler for the rules, who was never afraid to rebuke even the most well-connected for misdemeanours on the water.[47] With his burial at sea in 1950, Castle Ward was sold to the Northern Ireland government to allow the payment of death duties of £80,000, and was handed over to the National Trust in 1953 with an additional endowment of £35,000.[48] In 1976 the remaining contents of the house which had not been transferred in the 1950s were sold, lock, stock and barrel to the Trust, and 350 years of private libraries round the Lough – first at Killyleagh, then in Bangor Castle, finally in three successive houses at Castle Ward itself – came to an end.

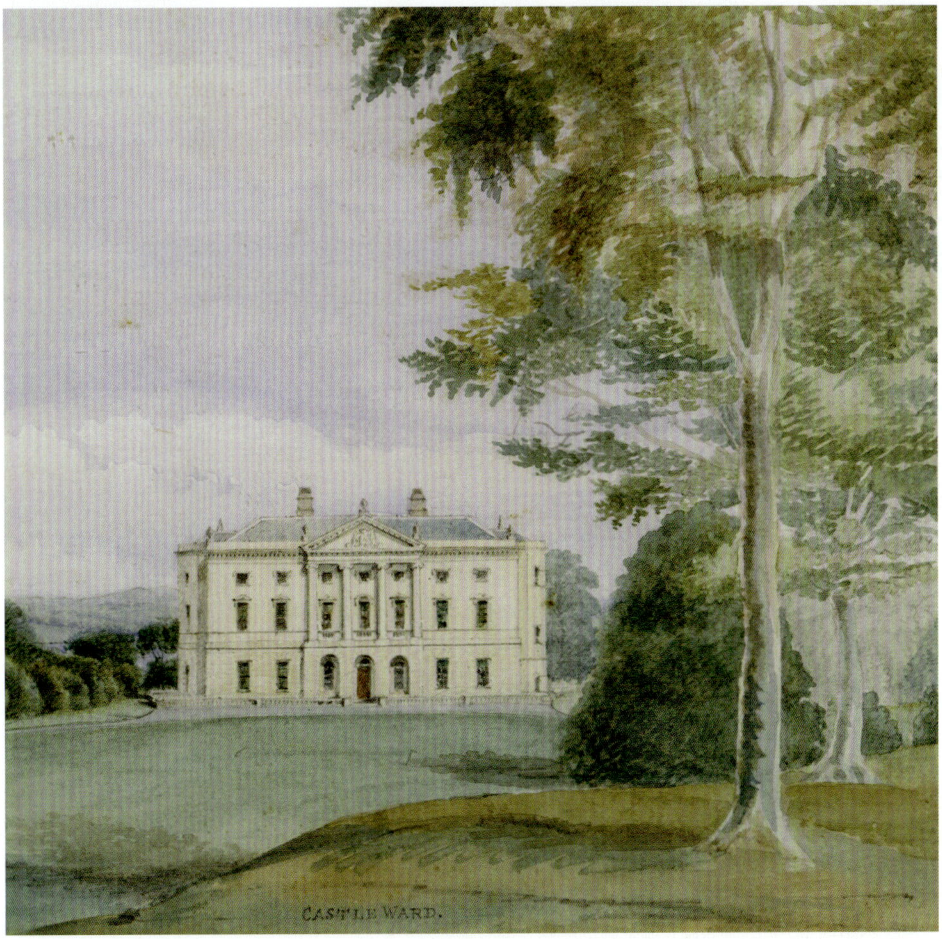

Below
Castle Ward: a watercolour sketch by Mary Ward (Castle Ward)

3 A Convenient Dwelling House of Lime and Stone

Springhill, County Londonderry, 1680–1816

Right
William 'Good-Will' Conyngham (d. 1721), English school, *c.*1700 (Springhill)

Below
Springhill, County Londonderry

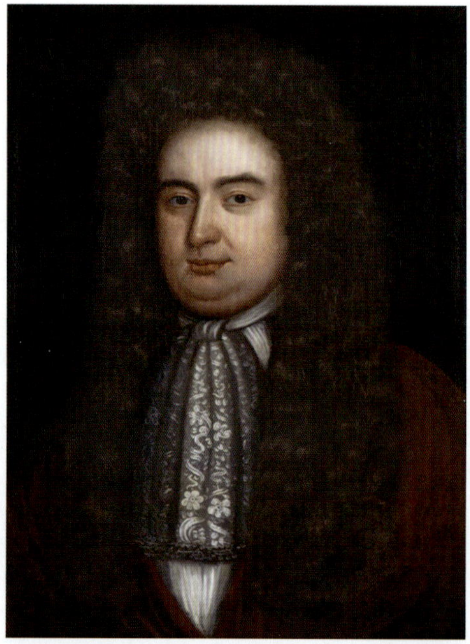

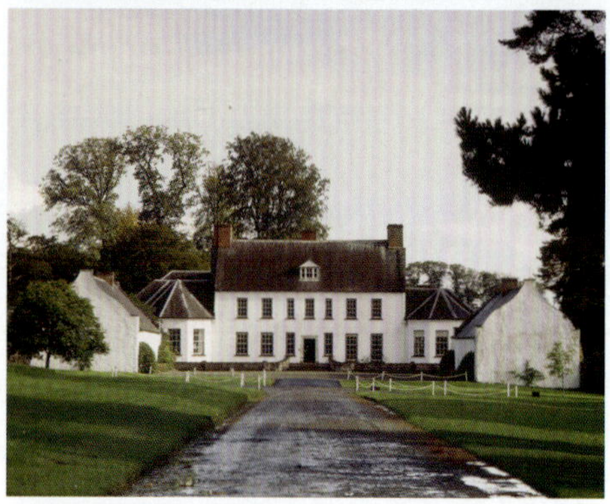

In 1680, three years before the birth of Michael Ward, William 'Good-Will' Conyngham (d.1721) married the sixteen-year-old Anne Upton, the daughter of Arthur Upton of Castle Upton in County Antrim. The groom was descended from a family of Scots Presbyterians who had settled in Ulster in the reign of James I, and the marriage contract drafted by his father-in-law stipulated that he should put up 'a convenient dwelling house of lime and stone, two stories high, with necessary office houses, gardens and orchards'.[1] The choice of wording was clearly no accident. Rather like the County Louth lawyer who in 1635 had exhorted his brother to build 'a good English house of lime and stone slated', so William Conyngham's new father-in-law clearly bought into the notion that the style of houses, and the material from which they were built, was important, a sign of what he would no doubt have seen as the arrival of civility and civilised ways in the north of Ireland.[2] The result was Springhill, a T-shaped house with a decidedly Scottish air, with its associated assembly of estate buildings, and – originally – two bawns, or defensive stockades, a characteristic and very necessary feature of many Plantation houses. The outbuildings which survive so well there make a further point, the desire to tame the surrounding countryside, to create a series of controlled enclosures, stocked with elegant and useful flowers, fruit and vegetables (especially apples and pears – good for eating and for cider) as well as an appropriate setting for a genteel residence.[3] Standing a mile or so south of the little Plantation town of Moneymore, the territory of the Drapers' Company and 40 miles south-east of the walled city of Derry, the Springhill demesne is an attractive place, reckoned in 1802 to have 'the best trees in the county', well-wooded and sheltered in the fertile land between the bleakness of the Sperrins to the west and the flat muddy shores of Lough Neagh five miles east.[4] Yet the history of Springhill, described in 1862 as 'among the most beautiful residences in Ulster', is anything but uncontentious.[5] The area round about had been seized in the early seventeenth century from its original owners, the O'Cahans, O'Neills and O'Mullans. Not surprisingly, the workmen who built Moneymore for the Drapers in 1615 did so – as the then mayor of Derry wrote to the Company – 'as it were wth the Sworde in one hand and the Axe in thother.'[6] Three hundred and fifty years later, Mina Lenox-Conyngham (1867–1961), the chatelaine of Springhill, an unashamed champion of 'the Ulster tradition as the Conynghams understood it', who made no bones of her view that before the Plantation 'the North of Ireland was a wild half civilized region largely covered with forests and overrun by septs [clans]', still recognised the 'bitter animosity seething in the minds of the dispossessed'.[7] Yet for all this, the house survives, and though built more than six decades after the Plantation, it remains one of the oldest large houses in Ireland. Its owners were among the Protestant protagonists of the great siege of Derry in 1689, and two centuries later their descendants welcomed Sir Edward Carson in April 1914, fêting him with flags, illuminations and the cheers of local Unionists while the house was guarded by armed sentries. The Ulster Volunteers drilled on the lawn during the Home Rule Crisis, and the house was raided for arms by Republicans in November 1919, with the help of 'a clever maid from Dublin' who 'proved to be an agent of the I.R.A.', though it escaped the fate of nearby Shane's Castle and Antrim Castle, both burned in 1921.[8]

Though the Conynghams and Lenox-Conynghams who succeeded them were never proprietors of the first rank, they figured prominently in the interrelated network of gentry families who ran County Londonderry right through the eighteenth and nineteenth centuries. When Vaughan Sampson's *Statistical Survey of the County of Londonderry* listed its principal inhabitants in the year after the Act of Union, it divided the better sort into three categories: those worth more than £2500 per year, those worth up to £1000, and those whose property produced up to £500. The owners of Springhill fell into the third category, well behind the absentee Marquess of Donegall, and worth less than a fifth of the greatest proprietors, among them Thomas Conolly of Castletown, and the Earl-Bishop of Derry: the one based in County Kildare, and the other then living in Italy. But unlike these grandees, the Conynghams and Lenox-Conynghams were resident landlords, and this gave them considerable clout. Though they may not have had the metropolitan connections of a Dublin judge like Michael Ward, they were freeholders rather than perpetual tenants, and they and their agents dominated the nearby towns of Cookstown and Moneymore, described as 'neat' the year after the Union, well supplied with fine houses in lime and stone, and the residence of the agents of the various local estates.[9] When the Irish Land Commission reported in 1876, the Lenox-Conynghams had 943 acres. Less than a tenth the size of the Castle Ward estate, and a tiny minnow when sent against the Viceregal grandeur of the Marquesses of Londonderry (50,000 acres, 27,000 of them in Ireland, and with mineral rights a total income in excess of £100,000 a year), it was still enough to make them prominent figures in local society.[10] As recently as the 1940s it was William Lowry Lenox-Conyngham (1903–57), who, as HM Lieutenant for County Londonderry, was in command of the Home Guard in the county.[11]

The owners of Springhill were distinguished from the grandees in several other key respects. Though they intermarried with other local gentry families, including the Uptons of Castle Upton, the Staples of Lissan, and the Stewarts of Killymoon, they also had strong mercantile connections, and when the main Conyngham line failed, the estate was twice inherited by families who had made their money in trade. Good-Will Conyngham himself was succeeded in 1721 by his nephew George Butle (d. 1765), who took the name and arms of Conyngham in the traditional way, but was himself the son of the Belfast merchant David Butle.[12] When in 1784 the male line failed again with the death of George Butle Conyngham's son, William Conyngham, the estate passed to George Lenox (1752–1816), eldest son of William's sister Anne (d. 1777), who assumed the name George Lenox-Conyngham. He was not only married to his uncle's stepdaughter Jane ('Jenny') Hamilton, but was also the grandson of Good-Will Conyngham's brother-in-law John Lenox, and great-grandson of the Derry merchant James Lenox (1652–1723), who was twice mayor of the city in the 1690s, and MP for the County of Londonderry between 1703 and 1713.[13] The Conynghams and the Lenoxes had been closely connected since the late seventeenth century, when James Lenox and Good-Will had both fought in the siege of Derry, and relations were cemented with the marriage in 1707 of Lenox's son John to Rebecca Upton, the younger sister of Good-Will's wife Anne, both women also (confusingly) being aunts by marriage to George Butle Conyngham, whose wife Anne Peacocke was the daughter of their sister Mary.[14] Possessing only six great-grandparents instead of the usual eight, George Lenox-Conyngham was therefore simultaneously nephew and stepson-by-marriage to his predecessor at Springhill, great-nephew of his predecessor's father George Butle Conyngham both in blood and by marriage, and a great-great-nephew of Good-Will Conyngham by blood through his mother and his great-nephew by marriage through his father Clotworthy Lenox (1707–85) and grandfather John Lenox.

Unsurprisingly, this complex extended family of country squires and city merchants was in close contact, and there were constant comings and goings between Moneymore and Derry. Good-Will's widow Anne spent the winters in the city with her sister Rebecca in the 1720s, while his nephew George Butle Conyngham was corresponding with his brother-in-law Clotworthy ('Tatty') Lenox about the importation of wine through the port of Derry four decades on in 1760.[15] In the late 1770s, George Butle Conyngham's son William Conyngham arranged for his four young step-daughters to lodge at his Uncle Tatty's house – perhaps, as Mina Lenox-Conyngham supposed, so that he could have his new wife Jean Hamilton to himself – but perhaps because Derry, cheaper than Dublin but still possessed of sociable entertainments like cock fights and horse racing, was considered a more appropriate place for the finishing of young ladies than Moneymore.[16] At any event, the Hamilton sisters seem to have been well provided for there, being kitted out with fashionable accoutrements like riding habits and apparently riding around in a carriage with two smartly-hatted postilions. The practical arrangements being made by Uncle Tatty's son George Lenox (the future heir of Springhill, who was also the agent for their widowed mother's estate in County Donegal), Miss Bess Hamilton took out a subscription to the city's Assembly Rooms and learned the guitar with a teacher called John Shannon. Her sister, Miss Jenny Hamilton, was provided with a year's tuition with a Mr Flanagan in the fashionable accomplishment of dancing, at the not-inconsiderable cost of £4 11s. Evidently the lessons did the trick, as she married George Lenox in 1779.[17]

Springhill was also distinctive in its religious tradition, and though they eventually conformed to the Church of Ireland, the Conynghams were Scots by descent, and the Lenox-Conynghams' Presbyterian sympathies are fairly clear. James Lenox was an Elder of the Kirk

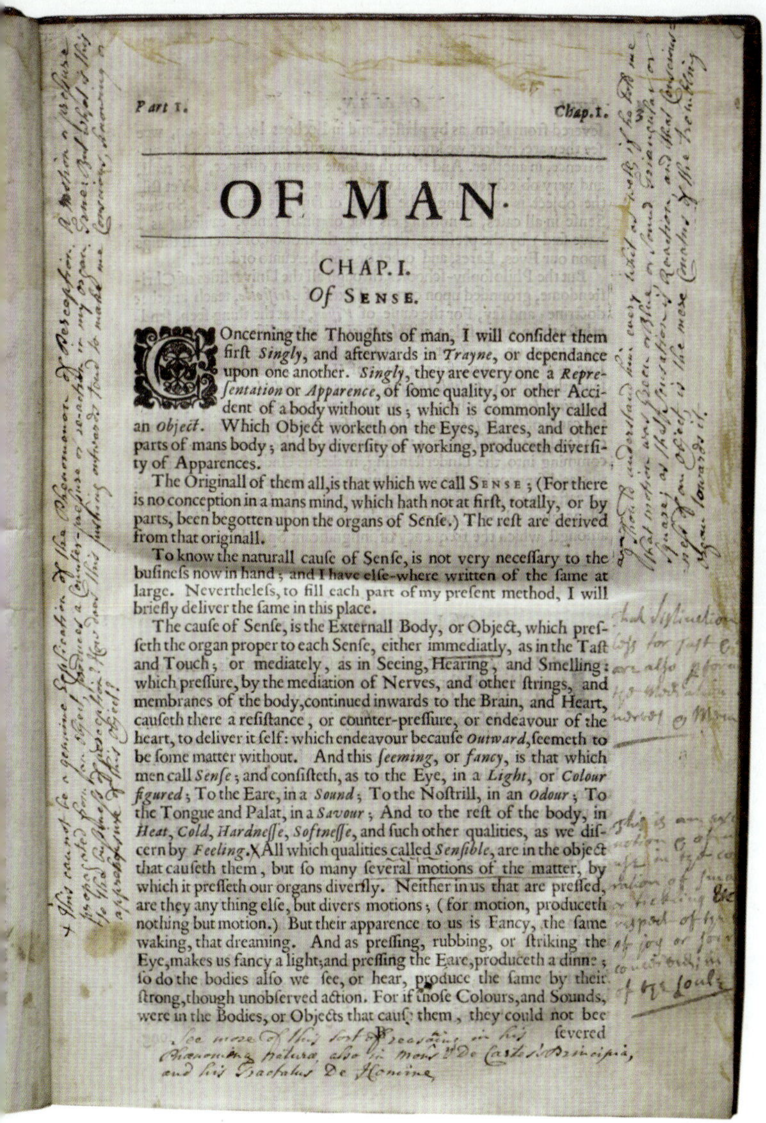
Part I. Chap. I.

OF MAN.

CHAP. I.
Of Sense.

Concerning the Thoughts of man, I will consider them first *Singly*, and afterwards in *Trayne*, or dependance upon one another. *Singly*, they are every one a *Representation* or *Apparence*, of some quality, or other Accident of a body without us; which is commonly called an *Object*. Which Object worketh on the Eyes, Eares, and other parts of mans body; and by diversity of working, produceth diversity of Apparences.

The Originall of them all, is that which we call Sense; (For there is no conception in a mans mind, which hath not at first, totally, or by parts, been begotten upon the organs of Sense.) The rest are derived from that originall.

To know the naturall cause of Sense, is not very necessary to the business now in hand; and I have else-where written of the same at large. Neverthelesse, to fill each part of my present method, I will briefly deliver the same in this place.

The cause of Sense, is the Externall Body, or Object, which presseth the organ proper to each Sense, either immediatly, as in the Tast and Touch; or mediately, as in Seeing, Hearing, and Smelling: which pressure, by the mediation of Nerves, and other strings, and membranes of the body, continued inwards to the Brain, and Heart, causeth there a resistance, or counter-pressure, or endeavour of the heart, to deliver it self: which endeavour because *Outward*, seemeth to be some matter without. And this *seeming*, or *fancy*, is that which men call *Sense*; and consisteth, as to the Eye, in a *Light*, or *Colour figured*; To the Eare, in a *Sound*; To the Nostrill, in an *Odour*; To the Tongue and Palat, in a *Savour*; And to the rest of the body, in *Heat*, *Cold*, *Hardnesse*, *Softnesse*, and such other qualities, as we discern by *Feeling*. All which qualities called *Sensible*, are in the object that causeth them, but so many severall motions of the matter, by which it presseth our organs diversly. Neither in us that are pressed, are they any thing else, but divers motions; (for motion, produceth nothing but motion.) But their apparence to us is Fancy, the same waking, that dreaming. And as pressing, rubbing, or striking the Eye, makes us fancy a light; and pressing the Eare, produceth a dinne; so do the bodies also we see, or hear, produce the same by their strong, though unobserved action. For if those Colours, and Sounds, were in the Bodies, or Objects that cause them, they could not bee severed

Above
Thomas Hobbes, *Leviathan* (London, 1651), Wing H2246, with manuscript notes perhaps written by David Conyngham (Springhill)

in Derry, and was much involved in power struggles between Anglicans and Presbyterians on the city Corporation in the 1690s.[18] When his brother-in-law Good-Will Conyngham died in 1721, one of the beneficiaries in his will was the Revd. William Boyd (d. 1772), a young dissenting minister at Macosquin, County Londonderry, just a little to the south of Coleraine.[19] In 1737 the merchant's son George Butle Conyngham was an occasional conformist, taking the Sacrament according to the rites of the Church of Ireland in order to qualify for public office, though his own religious disabilities do not seem to have deterred him from persecuting Catholics; and he was involved in 1739 in the arrest at nearby Toome Bridge of Fr John Fottrell, Provincial of the Dominicans in Ireland.[20] As late as 1812, George Lenox-Conyngham's son William (1792–1858) was sent to the solidly Calvinist environment of Glasgow University to complete his education, and the family library still contains at least one of his textbooks.[21] George himself had earlier been involved in the Volunteer movement, in the official enquiry which followed the 1798 Rising, expressing the view that 'the Presbyterians and Papists never did cordially unite and from the first they were jealous of one another'. Had they succeeded in introducing 'a Republick on the very same plan' as in France, he opined, 'I am clearly of the opinion that the Protestant traitors never intended that the Papists should derive any benefit from a Revolution; they only wanted their assistance to bring such a measure about and afterwards crush and trample on them.'[22] For all this, the purchase of a heavily annotated copy of the first edition of Hobbes's *Leviathan* (1651) from Samuel Fuller in Dublin in 1733 is perhaps suggestive that previous generations might sometimes have had a more ambivalent attitude towards the civil power.

Given its distinctive religious and social history, it is not surprising that Springhill should have acquired an equally distinctive library. In 1816, when George Lenox-Conyngham 'in a very melancholy state of mind … put an end to his existence by a pistol shot', the house already contained substantial numbers of books from two quite distinct strands: those acquired by the Conynghams at Springhill, and a probably rather larger assembly of printed matter which had originally belonged to their Lenox relations in Derry, and which presumably came to Moneymore when George had inherited in 1788.[23] Many of the books

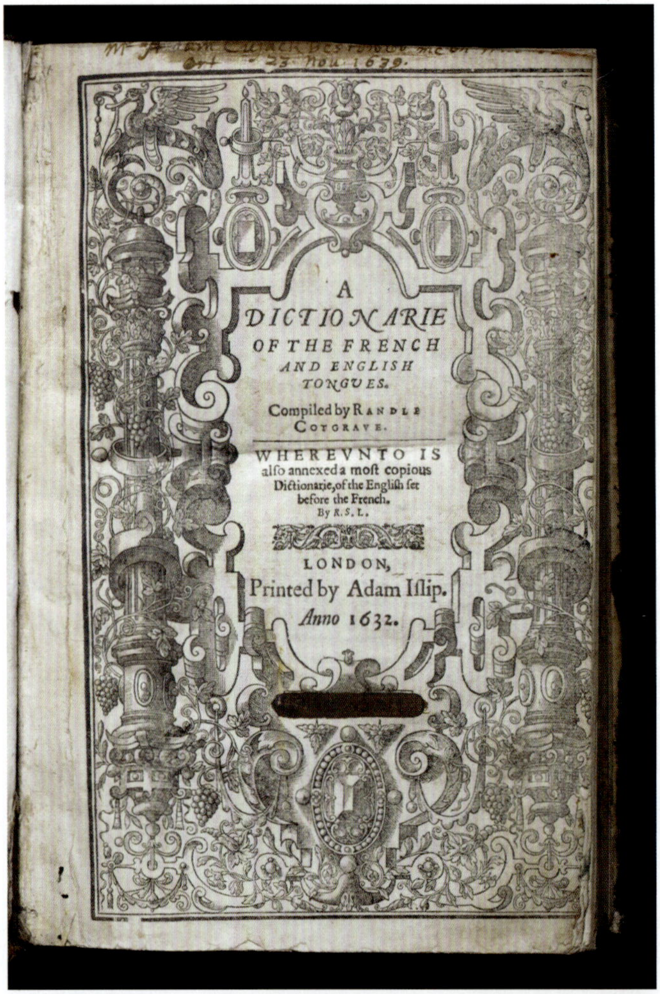

A DICTIONARIE OF THE FRENCH AND ENGLISH TONGUES.

Compiled by RANDLE COTGRAVE.

WHEREVNTO IS alſo annexed a moſt copious Dictionarie, of the Engliſh ſet before the French. By R. S. L.

LONDON, Printed by Adam Iſlip. *Anno* 1632.

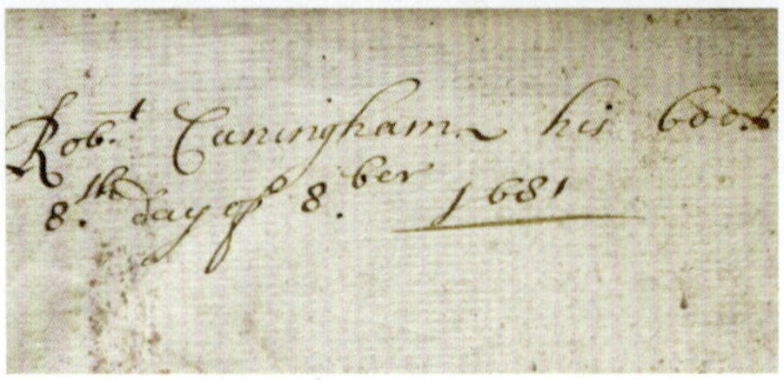

Above
Randle Cotgrave, *A Dictionarie of the French and English Tongues* (London, 1632), STC 5831 (Springhill)

Right
Inscription by Robert Conyngham in Cotgrave's *Dictionarie* (1632) (Springhill)

are inscribed, making it perfectly clear where they came from, though others are without any ownership marks at all, in the absence of any further documentation making it impossible to be sure of their history. Other books are annotated or marked in a way which shows that they have been read, even though in truth we cannot be sure who the readers actually were. No more than a handful of these books appears to have been in the area prior to the building of the present house in 1680, though many were printed earlier in the seventeenth century, and in some cases in the sixteenth century as well. (This seems to provide at least some corroborative evidence for the family legend that the previous house at Springhill was burned in the 1641 rising, and its title deeds lost.)[24] The few exceptions are generally predictably mundane, like John Cowell's *The Interpreter* (London, 1658), a legal reference book which contains the signature of Good-Will's father William Conyngham, who died in 1666. Writing in 1946, Mina Lenox-Conygham also mentioned a Bible, at present untraceable; either it has left the house or the signature in it was – not unreasonably – misread for that of his son during the recent cataloguing of the collection.[25] Both are precisely the sort of books which one might expect to find in the hands of a seventeenth-century country squire.

The earliest book with an obvious family connection is a copy of Randle Cotgrave's *A Dictionarie of the French and English Tongues* (London, 1632), which is marked 'Robt. Cunyngham his booke this 8th day of 8.ber 1681.' This seems to refer to Robert Conyngham (d. 1685), Good-Will Conyngham's brother, a figure only known through inscriptions in books. Robert was also the owner of John Goodman's *A Serious and Compassionate Inquiry into the Causes of the Present Neglect and Contempt of the Protestant Religion* (London, [1684?]), 'bought in Northampton price 2s 6d ex dono Wm Conyngham', though who was actually in Northampton in 1684 or 1685 (the wording perhaps implies that both brothers were there together), and what they were doing there is a matter for speculation. One or other may perhaps have been either on the way to or from London from the Irish boats at Chester. Rather more interesting, perhaps, is a copy of Richard Baxter's *The Life of Faith* (London, 1670) – a conventional enough devotional book by one of the most influential of Nonconformist divines – which belonged to Good-Will Conyngham's Presbyterian mother-in-law Dorothy Upton ('faith is the practical Believing in God as promising and Christ as procuring justification and salvation').[26] Though it seems like an obvious book for a mother to give to her daughter, Anne Upton had already been married to Good-Will Conyngham for nineteen years when her mother Dorothy acquired the book in 1699, a gift from Letitia, widow of the great magnate Arthur Chichester, 1st Earl of Donegall (1606–74/5), owner of the two greatest houses in seventeenth-century Ulster.[27] She had had it in turn from a Mr Samuel Bryan.[28] Assuming that it eventually found its way to Springhill on Dorothy Upton's death, it was a keepsake which, although printed only in 1670, was already fourth-hand, and curious in now containing, slipped between its pages, a pressed leaf. Presumably inserted in the nineteenth century, this sort of re-use illustrates in a rather graphic way the changing perception of books in dynastic libraries which have remained undisturbed over several centuries. A seventeenth-century theological book which had passed through the hands of three well-bred gentlewomen was no longer of much interest to a Victorian squire's wife, but preserving it was an act of family piety, and it provided a useful place to press botanical specimens. In a rather similar way in the Edwardian period, Elizabeth, Countess of Fingall found the old books in the top-floor Library at Killeen Castle 'not very interesting, being mostly religious and medical', but nonetheless they provided a useful foil to the expensive new bookcases installed when she and her friend the connoisseur Hugh Lane rearranged the castle, and 'some of the bindings were beautiful and decorative'.[29]

There are considerably more books which can be very clearly associated with Good-Will Conyngham himself, and a suspicion that he may have owned more than just the books which he inscribed. A number of Springhill volumes have characteristic white paper spine labels, now rather battered, but there are several on books which certainly did belong to him. This sort of label is not unusual in seventeenth-century private libraries, and it is tempting to speculate that they

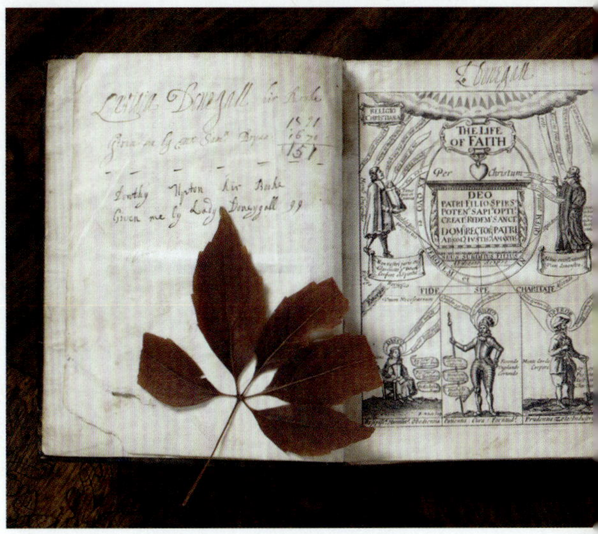

Right
Richard Baxter, *The Life of Faith* (London, 1670), Wing B1301, with the ownership inscription of Dorothy Upton and a pressed leaf, probably inserted in the nineteenth century

may be indicative of books acquired in his lifetime.[30] If this is correct, then this too suggests that, like his younger and smarter contemporary Michael Ward, Good-Will was up-to-date enough to be shelving his books spine-outwards, though again, as at Castle Ward, we have little notion as to precisely how and where they were actually kept. Certainly those surviving are not suggestive of any particular desire to put on the sort of show recommended by the London bookseller John Brotherton (d. 1775), who advertised that he 'Gilds or Letters Gentlemens Studies, or any other Books' in a ticket pasted into a Springhill book of 1701. Of the inscribed books, there are at least two examples bought in London during the Williamite wars. The first is *Jus Divinum Ministerii Evangelicii: Or the Divine Right of the Gospel-Ministry* (London, 1654), written by the noted Dissenting divine Edmund Calamy the Elder (1600–66), in which was proved – no doubt to the full

JOhn Brotherton, at the Bible and Star in Threadneedle-ſtreet, over againſt Merchant-Taylors-Hall, Bindeth all ſorts of Books in Turkey, Calf, or Sheeps-leather, and Gilds and Letters Gentlemens Studies, or any other Books: He

Above
Bookbinder's ticket of John Brotherton pasted into Louis Moreri's *A Supplement to the Great Historical, Geographical, Geneaological and Poetical Dictionary* (London, 1701), ESTC C145458 (Springhill)

satisfaction of the Conynghams and their Presbyterian neighbours – 'that a Bishop and Presbyter are all One in Scripture; and that Ordination by Presbyters is most agreeable to Scripture-Patern.' This is inscribed 'Wm: Conyngham empt: London Augt: 89 2s', evidently bought within weeks of the lifting of the siege of Derry on 31 July 1689, events in which Good-Will was a prominent participant. Presumably he was among the delegates immediately sent from Derry to London to negotiate compensation for the financial privations of the siege, though buying a book seems undeniably a very human response to the terror and boredom of long-term confinement within the walls of a besieged city.[31] The second is inscribed 'Wm: Conyngham empt: Londini 3s. Dec, 89', again in a book redolent of the Conynghams' attitudes to the religious disputes of the day, a copy of Baxter's *A Treatise of Episcopacy* (London 1681). There are also examples of books which Good-Will acquired a little later, for example, Sir Richard Bolton's *A Justice of Peace for Ireland* (Dublin, 1683) – another distinctly practical and useful book, this time with a more specifically Irish slant – acquired in June 1697. But none of this seems to suggest that Good-Will Conygham was a particularly discriminating or voracious collector of books, and his library of humdrum practical and religious books was modest indeed by comparison with the enormous and wide-ranging collection which had been accumulated by Edward Conway, 2nd Viscount Conway and 2nd Viscount Killultagh (1594–1655) of Lisburn Castle, County Antrim since he came from England in 1629 to live on his Irish estate. The books were shelved in his dining room there and from 1635 were being listed in alphabetical order under subjects. The huge catalogue survives in Archbishop Robinson's Library in Armagh and contains 9,900 titles contained in well over 10,000 volumes arranged under no less than 87 subjects. The largest categories include history and biography (3000 titles), literature and romances (2000) and science, medicine and agriculture (1200), but there are also more unusual topics such as demonology and hieroglyphics. Unhappily much of this must have perished when the castle and Brookhill, a house just outside Lisburn occupied by Conway's agent, were burned during the 1641 rising, but there must have been survivors, as well as books in his various English houses, amounting to no less than 3000 titles when the Parliamentary Committee for Sequestrations confiscated his property in London in 1643. These were restored to him on payment of a fine in 1647.[32]

Books that clearly belonged to Good-Will's nephew and successor George Butle Conyngham (d. 1765) are not uncommon at Springhill, and certainly more often found on the shelves than books signed by his uncle. One example which appears to reveal similar religious preoccupations is Peter, Lord King's *An*

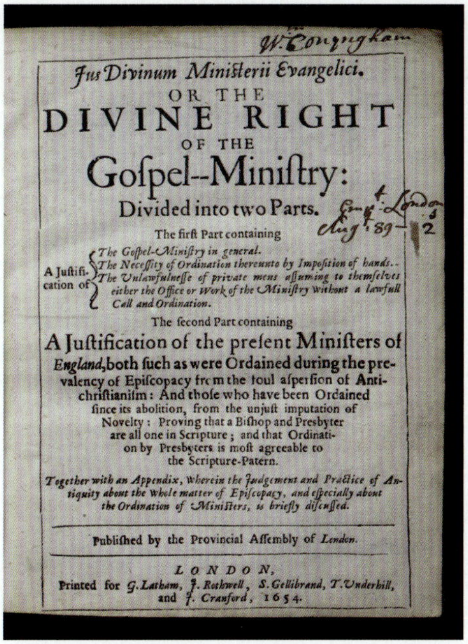
W. Conyngham

Jus Divinum Ministerii Evangelici.
OR THE
DIVINE RIGHT
OF THE
Gospel--Ministry:
Divided into two Parts.

The first Part containing

A Justification of
The Gospel-Ministry in general.
The Necessity of Ordination thereunto by Imposition of hands.
The Unlawfulnesse of private mens assuming to themselves either the Office or Work of the Ministry without a lawfull Call and Ordination.

The second Part containing

A Justification of the present Ministers of *England*, both such as were Ordained during the prevalency of Episcopacy from the foul aspersion of Antichristianism: And those who have been Ordained since its abolition, from the unjust imputation of Novelty: Proving that a Bishop and Presbyter are all one in Scripture; and that Ordination by Presbyters is most agreeable to the Scripture-Patern.

Together with an Appendix, wherein the Judgement and Practice of Antiquity about the whole matter of Episcopacy, and especially about the Ordination of Ministers, is briefly discussed.

Published by the Provincial Assembly of *London*.

LONDON,
Printed for *G. Latham, J. Rothwell, S. Gellibrand, T. Underhill,* and *J. Cranford*, 1654.

Right
Edmund Calamy,
Jus Divinum Ministerii Evangelici
(London, 1654),
Wing J1216
(Springhill)

Enquiry into the Constitution, Discipline, Unity and Worship of the Primitive Church (London, 1713). Another is James Ussher's *A Body of Divinity or: A Sum and Substance of Christian Religion* (London, 1702), similarly signed, and evidently already secondhand, since a previous owner's name has been crossed out on the title-page. More interesting, perhaps, is George's copy of William Molyneux's *The Case of Ireland's being Bound by Acts of Parliament in England, Stated* (Dublin, 1698), a subject of pressing concern to many, and evidently bought by George as a young man, and before he succeeded to the Springhill estates in 1721.

Like many Irish gentry, George's son William Conyngham (1723–84) was a professional soldier who fought for the king in the Seven Years War, and left a number of books behind, including several on the conduct of warfare. His copy of Quincy's *L'art de la guerre* (Paris 1740) is inscribed 'Wm. Conyngham Springhill', and there are other examples of similar books in the library.[33] It is not impossible that William's regular forays to the Continent to fight for king and country – he was at the battle of Minden in 1759 – could explain the presence of some of the more curious Continental books still on the shelves; equally they may have come from other sources, and like other Irish tourists, more than one generation of the Lenox-Conynghams appears to have passed through the Low Countries.[34] William clearly had slightly more intellectual aspirations, reading Ovid's *Epistolarum Heroidum Liber* (Dublin, 1730), proudly noting that he had begun it in April 1733 – when he would have been ten years old – and signing his name in Latin. When he died in 1784, he left his widow a life interest in his personal chattels – 'all rings & ornaments of dress whatsoever … with use for life of all my pictures, plate, books, and household furniture with full power to remove the same', with the careful proviso that 'no part thereof should be sold or disposed of, but should remain for the use of such persons respectively after her death as shall be entitled to the possession of my real estate'.[35]

The most striking thing about the books added during the long reign of George Lenox-Conyngham is that all of the books which contain his signature and initials were actually published in his own lifetime, or just a little before it. They are surprisingly varied in outlook, ranging from firmly orthodox works like *Revelation Examined with Candour* (Dublin, 1732), by the fashionable Tory preacher (and later Dean of Down) Patrick Delany, through to Swift, the Whig bishop Gilbert Burnet's *History of his Own Time* (Dublin, 1734), and Locke's *Essay Concerning Human Understanding* (London, 1735).

And if these seem to speak of an outlook reaching beyond the walls of the demesne, other books perhaps give a better sense of the everyday preoccupations of a family of eighteenth-century country squires. The development of the linen industry was always important in the north of Ireland, and the original connections between Moneymore and the Drapers' Company

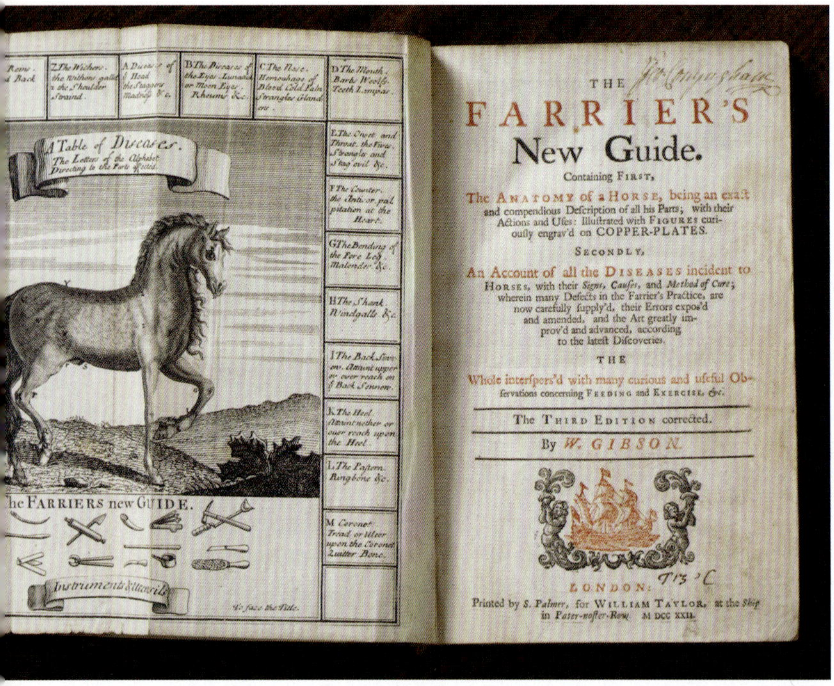

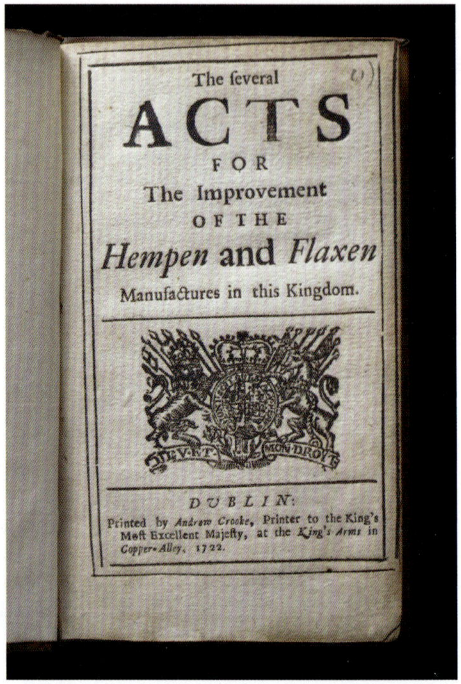

Above
William Gibson, *The Farrier's New Guide* (London, 1722), ESTC N1574, with the ownership inscription of George Butle Conyngham (d. 1765) (Springhill)

Above right
The Several Acts for the Improvement of the Hempen and Flaxen Manufactures in this Kingdom (Dublin, 1722 [i.e. 1735]), ESTC N70554 (Springhill)

no doubt reinforced this. Based on the contemporary belief that a nation might spend a quarter of its national income on cloth and clothing, eighteenth-century Ireland saw successive Acts of Parliament underpinned by a patriotic impulse to encourage the industry, with the establishment of a Linen Board in 1711.[36] Small-format printed editions of the legislation, most now known in only a handful of copies, were issued by Dublin printers to summarise the legal position. Though we do not know precisely who it belonged to, the fact that two of the three known copies of a 1735 reissue of the 1722 *Several Acts for the Improvement of the Hempen and Flaxen Manufactures in this Kingdom* are on the shelves of Ulster houses – at Springhill and Castle Ward – is suggestive of the seriousness with which the local landowners viewed the issue.[37] It is clearly no coincidence that George Butle Conyngham wrote in 1744 to Judge Michael Ward, probably no more than a nodding acquaintance, to lobby on behalf of 'the Linnen Drapers of this country'.[38] Farriery and horses were another serious matter at Springhill, with Thomas Wallis's *The Farrier's and Horseman's Complete Dictionary* (Dublin, 1766) purchased by the 43-year-old William Conyngham in the year of its publication, an appropriate purchase for a former cavalry officer. The interest clearly ran in the family, as William's father George Butle Conyngham had earlier acquired William Gibson's *The Farrier's New Guide* (London, 1722), a very elegant little book, which would have served an obviously practical purpose in a world in which horses were valuable and required expert handlers. It would also have carried an additional resonance in eighteenth-century Ireland, where horses – like libraries – denoted rank, social status, and political inclusion. Not only for daily use, they could be used for sociable – and socially exclusive – activities like hunting and racing, but since 1695 Irish Catholics had been disbarred from owning a horse worth more than £5. They also marked their owners out as full members of the body politic.[39] Old ways of thinking died slowly, as just before the First World War – fully five generations on from George Butle Conyngham and his farriery book – an elderly cottager could still tut-tut at the sight of Mina Lenox-Conygham on a bicycle, crossly informing her that her husband's grandmother 'never went out of doors except in a coach with four grey horses'.[40]

The Lenox books from Derry perhaps speak of rather more cosmopolitan and wide-ranging interests. They presumably came to Springhill following the final union of the two families with the marriage of George Lenox to William Conyngham's step-daughter Jenny in 1779, and the couple's eventual inheritance of the Conyngham estates in 1788. They are also interesting precisely because they represent the surviving books not of a family of country landowners, but of four generations of a mercantile dynasty, starting with Alderman James Lenox (1652–1723) and continuing with his son (and Good-Will Conyngham's brother-in-law) John Lenox, his grandson Clotworthy Lenox (1707–85) – the 'Uncle Tatty' with whom the Hamilton stepdaughters had lodged in the 1770s – and ultimately with George Lenox himself. Books were not the only Lenox family relics which came to Moneymore from Derry, with the Springhill gun room still housing a long gun with its barrel inlaid with silver, supposedly given to James Lenox during the siege.[41] Only two books on the shelves carry inscriptions which show beyond doubt that they belonged to James Lenox, and since both were clearly inscribed for quite specific reasons there is an obvious need for caution in inferring too much from this. The first is a presentation copy from Scotland, William Steuart's *Collections and Observations Methodiz'd* (Edinburgh, 1709), carefully inscribed 'To Alderman James Lennox LndnDerry January 30th 1709/10', as befitting a gift from the author in a handsome gold-tooled binding with gilt edges. The second, also from Scotland, is a copy of David Calderwood's *The True History of the Church of Scotland* ([Edinburgh?], 1678), inscribed 'James Lenox is the Right Owner of this Book Ano Domini 1700', the careful wording being perhaps because the book also contains the 1682 ownership inscription of one William Lenox, perhaps James's father. The same man's name is also to be found in M. de Saint-Réal's *A Conspiracy of the Spaniards Against the State of Venice* (London, 1679). Several further books seem to have belonged to specific members of the family, including James Lenox's son John, who owned *The Prince's Cabala: or Mysteries of State* (London, 1715). John's wife Rebecca Upton ('Beckse'), younger sister of Good-Will Conyngham's wife Anne, owned and wrote her name into copies of William Sherlock's *A Practical Discourse Concerning a Future Judgement* (London, 1699) and William Payne's *Practical Discourse on Repentance* (London, 1708), both rather similar books to the volume of Richard Baxter which Letitia, Lady Donegall had given to her mother Dorothy Upton some years before.

Most of these works seem to address purely local concerns, which is perhaps no more than might be expected, particularly as it is precisely these sorts of devotional and personal books into which owners are most likely to have wished to write their names. However, the Lenoxes were prosperous merchants and ship owners, operating out of the principal port in the north of Ireland at a period which saw a great increase in the number of books coming into the country from abroad. These connections had a very visible effect on the sort of books which seem to have found their way onto the shelves. By the 1690s 'old

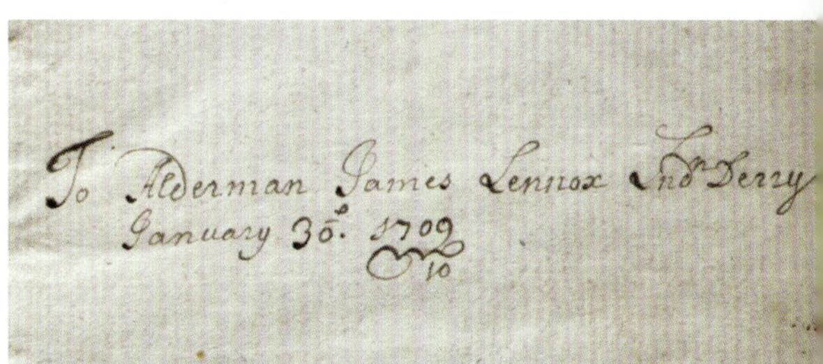

Right
Presentation inscription to Alderman James Lennox (1652–1723) in William Steuart's *Collections and Observations Methodiz'd* (Edinburgh, 1709), ESTC T153281 (Springhill)

books' – presumably secondhand – were routinely being imported into Derry from the port of Bristol. At about the same time William King, from 1691 to 1703 Bishop of Derry, but later Archbishop of Dublin and owner of one of the grandest Irish libraries of the day, was using a Huguenot bookman called Francis le Jau to procure books directly from the Continent, a task for which the members of the French Protestant *diaspora* with their international contacts and linguistic skills were especially well-suited.[42] Could the Marianne Devassey who signed her name into a very imperfect copy of d'Urfé's *Astrée* now at Springhill (probably printed in about 1650) perhaps herself have been a Huguenot refugee?

Whether the Lenoxes were themselves engaged in the booktrade in any very serious way, or whether – as seems more likely – they were among the general merchants who either on their own account or through intermediaries sporadically imported small numbers of books into Ireland on a more *ad hoc* basis, is more difficult to say.[43] Certainly, the merchant David Butle, whose son inherited Springhill in 1721, is known to have imported a Bible and a variety of luxury goods into Belfast at wholesale prices in 1698. Equally, there are many books at Springhill today which hint at direct contacts with the Continent.[44] In the 1680s the Irish student Thomas Molyneux (1661–1733) had gone to study medicine at Leiden, from where he kept his brother back at home supplied with academic gossip and books.[45] The evidence for the Lenoxes is somewhat more elusive, and though there is no obvious record of any member of the family studying in the congenial religious environment of the Netherlands, it seems possible that something similar might have been afoot in Derry in the very early years of the eighteenth century.[46] A copy of Jean-Nicolas de Parival's *Les Delices de la Hollande* (Amsterdam, 1697) seems to have belonged to John Lenox (written 'J..n L…x' on the title-page), but the date of its arrival in Ireland is hinted at by the ownership inscription of a Dutch owner in Rotterdam in 1701. Whether it was purchased in the Netherlands by an Irishman, or sent back to Ireland as a secondhand book remains open to question, but like any guidebook of this kind it was probably purchased in the place that it described. Then there is a Greek New Testament printed in Rotterdam in 1710, a book which by its ownership inscription in French – 'Acheté de Henry Riboleau le 10 Fevr. 1715/16 coste £1s13d00' – clearly reached Derry via London. Finally and perhaps most intriguingly of all is a *Sammelband* of two works by Descartes, his *Meditationes de Prima Philosophia* (Amsterdam, 1685), and *Principia Philosophiae* (Amsterdam, 1685), which belonged to a Leiden philosophy student of French extraction named Daniel Morel. Both works are copiously annotated with the notes that he took down verbatim in 1686 at the lectures of Professor Burcher de Volder (1643–1709), the leading Dutch exponent of Cartesian philosophy, and a key figure in the teaching of natural philosophy at Leiden. They then passed through the hands of at least one Dutch owner before ending up in Ireland, though the identity of their Irish owner unfortunately remains mysterious. He may have been the same man responsible for the two seventeenth-century English-Dutch dictionaries on the shelves at Springhill.

One of the frustrations of dealing with the Springhill library is the all-too-common impossibility of knowing for certain which are Lenox books and which belonged to their Conyngham cousins. Another is the question of use, and while some books certainly betray obvious evidence of this – either by marginal notes or other forms of inscription – others are more difficult to interpret. A copy of Cardano's *De Subtilitate* (Basel, 1611), was demonstrably read by someone, as it has occasional

Right
René Descartes, *Meditationes de Prima Philosophia* (Amsterdam, 1685), annotated with notes taken in 1686 at lectures given in Leiden by Professor Burcher de Volder (1643–1709) (Springhill)

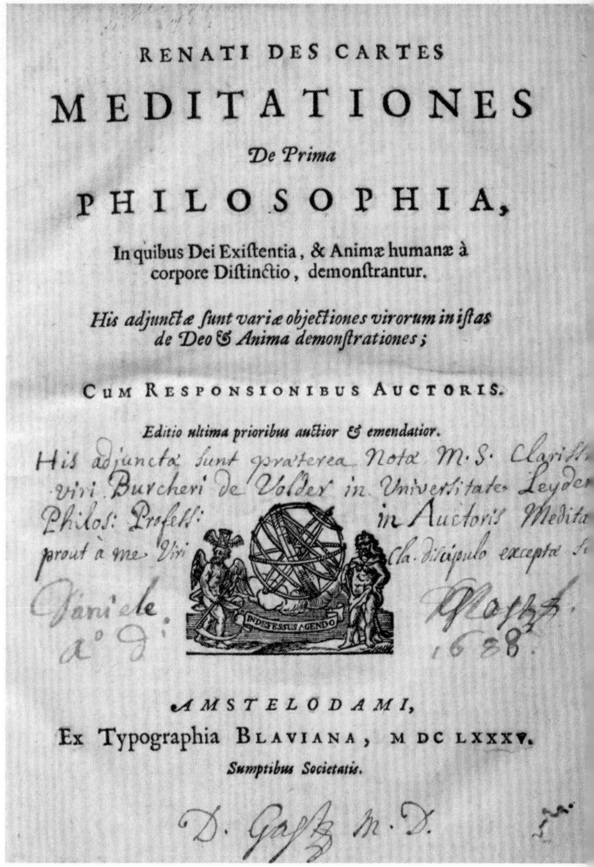
RENATI DES CARTES

MEDITATIONES

De Prima

PHILOSOPHIA,

In quibus Dei Exiſtentia, & Animæ humanæ à corpore Diſtinctio, demonſtrantur.

His adjunctæ ſunt variæ objectiones virorum in iſtas de Deo & Anima demonſtrationes;

CUM RESPONSIONIBUS AUCTORIS.

Editio ultima prioribus auctior & emendatior.

His adjunctæ sunt præterea Notæ M.S. Clariss. viri Burcheri de Volder in Universitate Leyden. Philos: Profess: in Auctoris Medita... prout a me Viri Cla. discipulo excepta ...

1686.

AMSTELODAMI,

Ex Typographia BLAVIANA, M DC LXXXV.

Sumptibus Societatis.

D. Gast M.D.

pencil marks written into it; but who was reading it, what they thought of it, and whether it was read in Ireland at all, is now impossible to say. Other books give a general sense of having been handled and presumably read over the centuries, just as surely as some of the books in certain libraries – Dr Edward Worth's in Dublin is a good example – are so beautifully bound and in such pristine condition that it is reasonable to assume simply from their physical state that they have rarely, if ever, been opened.[47] But since the Lenoxes and Conynghams had far less money at their disposal than a fashionable Dublin physician like Dr Worth, and since most of their books are comparatively plainly and simply bound, it seems reasonable to infer that for the most part their books were purchased to be read – or at least with the aspiration to do so – rather than for reasons of display or conspicuous consumption.

However, certain general themes emerge which probably apply both to country squires and city merchants, and given the close connections between the Conynghams and the Lenoxes, and the distinct possibility that the two strands of the Springhill library may well have had sources in common, this is perhaps not too surprising. The most obvious of these is the comparative lack of classical Anglican theology of the seventeenth and early eighteenth centuries, books which could be found in some numbers in most English libraries of the period, and which can still be found on the Ward shelves at Castle Ward. There is a single volume of Archbishop Tillotson's sermons printed in 1707 (which could very well have come to Springhill later), but strikingly few copies of the usually ubiquitous *Book of Common Prayer*, only one of which could even conceivably have been in the house in Good-Will Conyngham's day. By contrast, there are numerous books with a distinctly Calvinist flavour, including Huguenot books from Saumur and Charenton, several early Geneva imprints, including Jean Crespin's *Histoire des Martyrs* ([Geneva], 1582), books by the Scots theologian George Buchanan, as well as a 1634 edition of Calvin's *Institutes*. These stand alongside books addressing more specifically Irish concerns. One of the most striking of these is a copy of a weighty polemic, William Atwood's *The Superiority and Direct Dominion of the Imperial Crown of England, over the Crown and Kingdom of Scotland* (London, 1705). It clearly interested its Irish owner – no doubt intrigued not only by its implications for the future of the Kingdom of Scotland, but perhaps by the parallels for the governance of the Kingdom of Ireland. He – and we can only assume that the owner was a man – made copious notes on its back pastedown, together with another long note at the front explaining that the work had been condemned to be burned by the Edinburgh Parliament in the year of its publication. Again

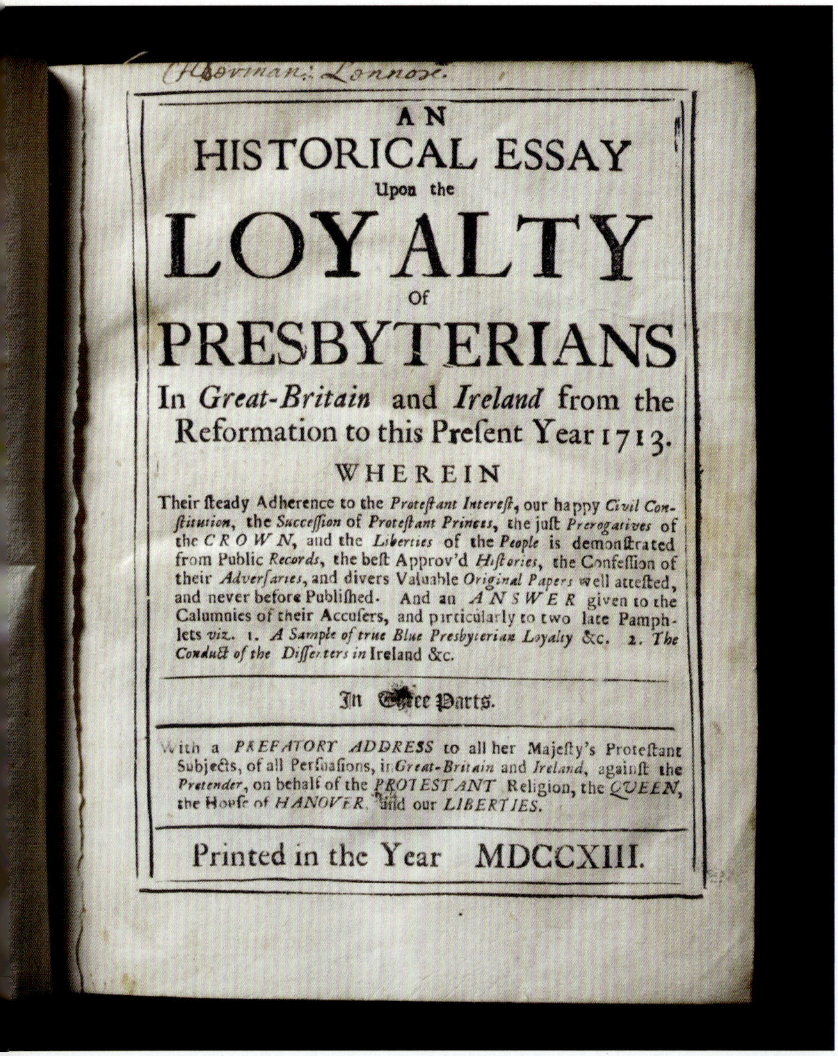

AN
HISTORICAL ESSAY
Upon the
LOYALTY
OF
PRESBYTERIANS
In *Great-Britain* and *Ireland* from the Reformation to this Prefent Year 1713.
WHEREIN
Their ftеady Adherence to the *Proteftant Intereft*, our happy *Civil Conftitution*, the *Succeffion* of *Proteftant Princes*, the juft *Prerogatives* of the *CROWN*, and the *Liberties* of the *People* is demonftrated from Public *Records*, the beft Approv'd *Hiftories*, the Confeffion of their *Adverfaries*, and divers Valuable *Original Papers* well attefted, and never before Publifhed. And an *ANSWER* given to the Calumnies of their Accufers, and particularly to two late Pamphlets *viz.* 1. *A Sample of true Blue Presbyterian Loyalty* &c. 2. *The Conduct of the Diffenters in* Ireland &c.
In Three Parts.
With a *PREFATORY ADDRESS* to all her Majefty's Proteftant Subjects, of all Perfuafions, in *Great-Britain* and *Ireland*, againft the *Pretender*, on behalf of the *PROTESTANT* Religion, the *QUEEN*, the Houfe of *HANOVER*, and our *LIBERTIES*.
Printed in the Year MDCCXIII.

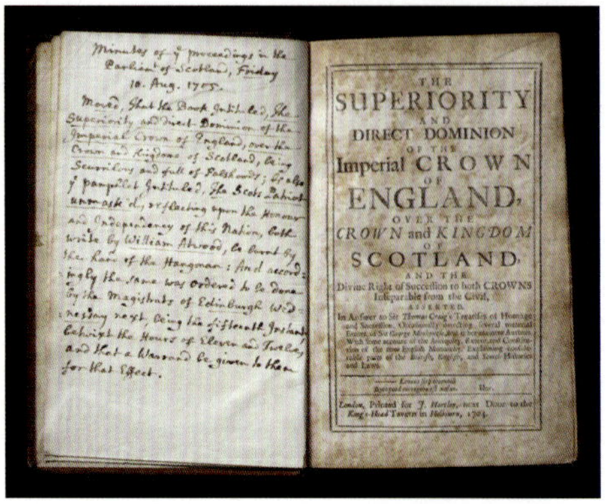

indicative of questions relating to Ulster Dissenters – and ultimately the question of whether their loyalty was to the Kirk or the Crown – is James Kirkpatrick's *An Historical Essay on the Loyalty of Presbyterians in Great-Britain and Ireland from the Reformation to this Present Year 1713* ([Belfast], 1713). This, the earliest piece of Belfast printing at Springhill, was issued by James Blow, the successor of Patrick Neill, who had set up shop as the city's first printer in 1693–4.[48] It appears from a smudged ownership inscription to have belonged to a member of the Lenox family – firm Presbyterians – in Derry.

One final volume, a set of twelve pamphlets bound together, starting with a 1685 edition of Thomas Browne's *Religio Medici* hints at a further way in which books, valuable pieces of real estate, could pass from hand to hand by sometimes less than straightforward means. It belonged eventually to Clotworthy Lenox – Uncle Tatty – but prior to that appears to have been pawned by a man called Robert Ward for 8s. 6d. Today we have little or no idea of the string of events that led to this, and in its own way this is perhaps a microcosm of the early history of the Springhill library, a history which remains alive and vivid simply because so many of the books have survived to tell their own story. Had they vanished, having been sold, burned or simply scattered, there would be little evidence indeed that either the Lenoxes or the Conynghams had owned a substantial number of books in the late seventeenth and early eighteenth centuries.

Above right
William Atwood, *The Superiority and Direct Dominion of the Imperial Crown of England, over the Crown and Kingdom of Scotland* (London, 1705), ESTC T99914, annotated with notes describing the burning of this book on the orders of the Scottish Parliament in 1705 (Springhill)

Above
James Kirkpatrick, *An Historical Essay upon the Loyalty of Presbyterians* ([Belfast?], 1713), ESTC T145486 (Springhill)

The Lenox-Conynghams of Springhill

(1) William Conyngham (d. 1666); Cromwellian Commissioner in County Antrim; purchased land at Ballydrum (Springhill) in 1653

Arthur Upton of Castle Upton (1623–1706) = Dorothy Beresford

Alderman James Lenox, Mayor of Derry, 1693, 1697; MP for the city, 1693–1703 (1652–1728)

Robert Conyngham (d. 1685)

Anne Conyngham (d. 1712) = David Butle, merchant in Belfast (d. 1714)

William 'Good-Will' Conyngham (d. 1721) = Anne Upton (b. *c.* 1664)

Mr Peacocke = Mary Upton

Rebecca Upton = John Lenox

George Butle Conyngham (d. 1765) = Anne Peacocke m. 1721

(2) Colonel William Conyngham (1723–84) = Jean Hamilton = (1) John Hamilton of Castlefinn, County Doncgal (d. 1774)

Mary Conyngham

David Conyngham (1727–88) = Anne Saunders

John Conyngham

Anne Conyngham (d. 1777) = Clotworthy Lenox ('Uncle Tatty') (1707–85)

Elizabeth Hamilton ('Bess')

(1) Jane Hamilton ('Jenny') = George Lenox-Conyngham (1752–1816) = (2) Olivia Irvine of Castle Irvine, County Fermanagh

4 others

Richard 3rd Viscount Molesworth (1680–1758) Field Marshal = Mary Ussher (d. 1763); killed in house fire, Brook Street, London

2 others (d. in 1763 fire)

Elizabeth Molesworth = James Stewart of Killymoon, County Tyrone (1741–1821)

Henrietta Molesworth (1745–1812) = John Staples of Lissan, County Tyrone (1736–1820)

Charlotte Melosina Staples (1786–1847) = William Lenox-Conyngham ('Wims') (1792–1858)

Sir William Lenox-Conyngham ('Billy') (1824–1906) = Laura Arbuthnot (1830–1917)

John Lenox-Conyngham

Harriett (Hazzy) Lenox-Conyngham (d. 1900) = Marcus Gage of Streeve Hill, Limavady, County Londonderry

James David Beresford of Learmont Castle, County Londonderry = Charlotte Lenox-Conyngham

William Arbuthnot Lenox-Conyngham (1857–1938) = Mina Lowry of Rockdale, Tullyhogue, County Tyrone (1867–1961)

10 others

William Lowry Lenox-Conyngham (1903–57); gave Springhill to the National Trust

2 others

4 The White Presses in the Library

Springhill, County Londonderry, 1816–1961

Right
Harriet Staples (née Molesworth); painted by Francis Cotes (Springhill)

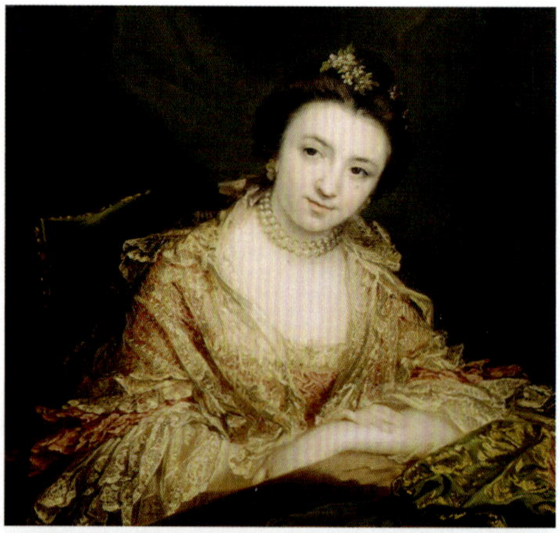

Right
John Staples (1736–1820), by Pompeo Batoni (Springhill)

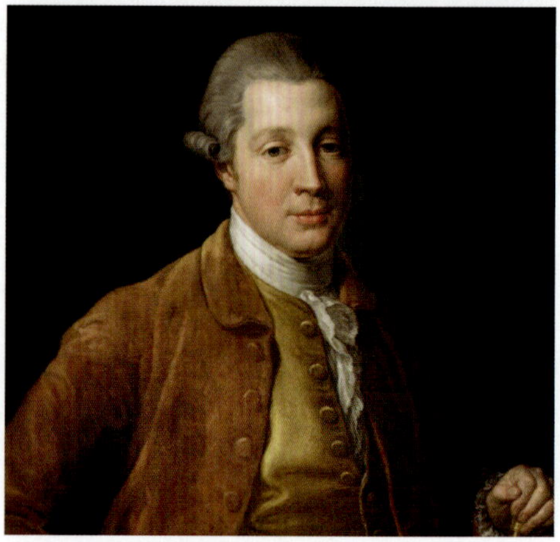

Opposite
Mary, Viscountess Molesworth, who died in a house fire in 1763; pastel by William Hoare of Bath (Springhill)

On 6 May 1763, a terrible fire took light in the London townhouse of the Dowager Lady Molesworth. Lady Molesworth had been widowed five years previously, the second wife of Richard, Viscount Molesworth (1680–1758), a British Field Marshal who had ended his career as Commander-in-Chief in Ireland. His family's chief residence was at Breckdenstown, near Swords, in north County Dublin, particularly known for its magnificent landscape gardens, but the Molesworths also owned some of the smartest streets in Dublin, and were well-known in London society as well, keeping house at 49 Brook Street, near Hanover Square.[1] As Horace Walpole rather gleefully reported, Lady Molesworth, along with her daughters Mary and Melosina, burned to death, along with six of her servants, including a French governess who jumped from a garret 'and was dashed to pieces'. Two other daughters survived. The suspicious pointed the finger of blame at two black slaves who had belonged to Lady Molesworth's brother, Captain Usher, visiting from Jamaica. They died in the fire, but the true culprit was later discovered to have been another servant, who had then taken advantage of the confusion to steal some of the Molesworths' silver.[2] Nine years later, in 1772, Elizabeth Molesworth, the younger of the two surviving sisters, married Colonel James Stewart (1741–1821), 'a gentlemanlike young man', thought the 2nd Duke of Leinster. Her new husband had been elected MP for County Tyrone four years previously in 1768, and remained in the Commons until 1812: first in Dublin, and then in London. Well-known to the Prince Regent, he later commissioned John Nash to rebuild the family seat, Killymoon Castle, and had been painted by Pompeo Batoni in 1767. Two years further on, Elizabeth's elder sister Henrietta Molesworth (1745–1812) – usually known to her family as Harriet – who had broken her right leg escaping from the fire and, as Walpole put it, 'has had it cut off', was married to another Tyrone landowner, John Staples (1736–1820). MP for Clogher in County Tyrone, he lived at Lissan House, near Cookstown, and was a client of his former brother-in-law Thomas Conolly of Castletown (1738–1803).[3]

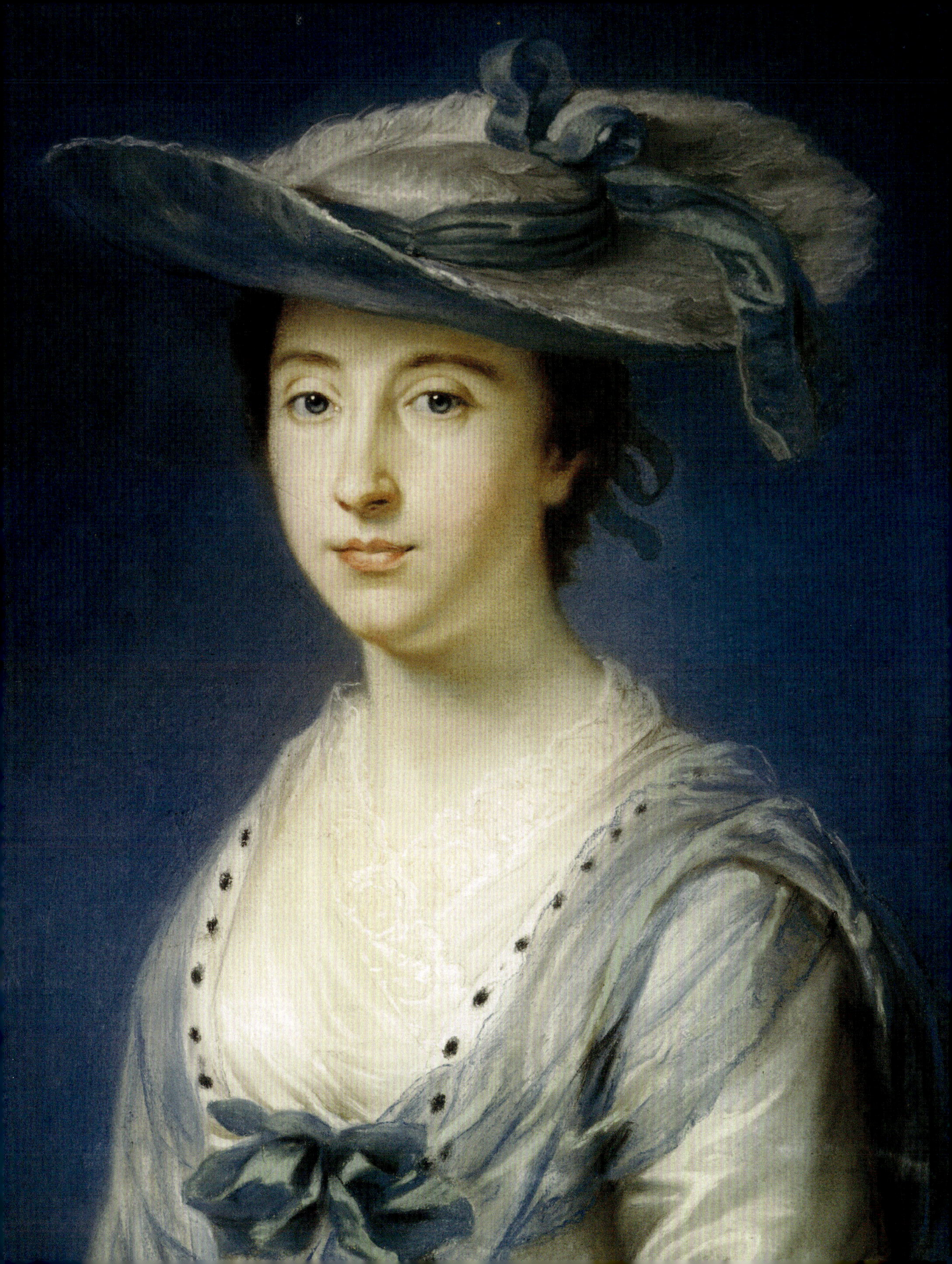

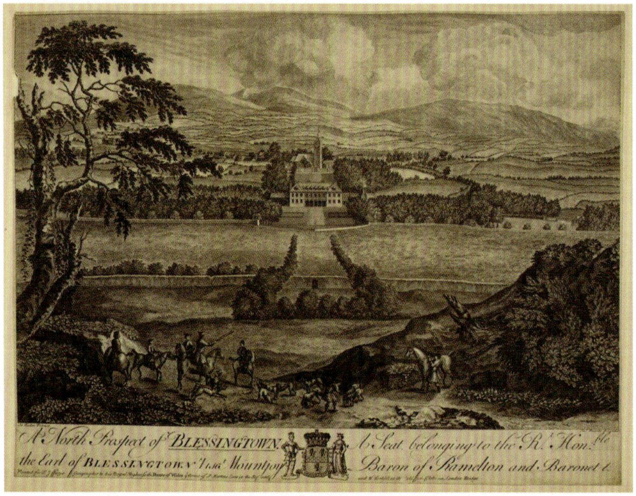

Above
An eighteenth-century print of Blessington House, County Wicklow, engraved by John Brooks after Joseph Tudor (d. 1759) (British Library)

Harriet Molesworth's ivory walking stick is today on display in the Drawing Room at Springhill, but the Brook Street fire might appear to be fairly tangential to the matter in hand. In fact it is critical in explaining how it is that a modest gentry house in the far southern corner of County Londonderry has ended up with one of the largest surviving country-house libraries in Ireland, a library filled not only with books acquired locally by the Lenoxes and Conynghams, but with several hundred books assembled by one of grandest families in mid-eighteenth-century Dublin, the property of an aristocratic couple who would surely have thought Springhill to be a house lived in by people much below their sphere.

Harriet Molesworth was a particular favourite of her godmother, Eleanor, Countess of Blessington (*c.*1712–74), daughter of Robert FitzGerald of Castle Dod, County Cork, and the wife of William Stewart, Viscount Mountjoy (1709–69), created 1st Earl of Blessington in 1745.[4] After the death of Harriet's mother in the fire, the by then elderly Countess seems to have taken the eighteen-year-old orphan under her wing, and Harriet went to live with her. With the death of her husband in 1769, Lady Blessington took possession of most of his property, though gossip had it that the couple had debts of some £35,000, and this resulted in the sale of estates in England and in County Donegal.[5] Nonetheless, when she in turn died seven years later, Harriet was generously provided for in Lady Blessington's will. The first and perhaps most valuable legacy was a diamond necklace – an elegant adornment for a grand lady, but like gold or silver plate easily turned into hard cash should need arise – but Harriet received other personal possessions as well, among them a set of prints, 'a white box', and a silhouette portrait of Lady Blessington's 'dear' husband, which the widowed Countess commended 'to her particular care'.[6] There was then a cash bequest of £5000, a colossal sum equivalent to perhaps ten years' income for a small-fry country landowner like George Lenox-Conyngham, and even more astonishing at a period when perhaps 70% of the population of Ireland subsisted on less than £10 a year, and £5 might be sufficient for a frugal but respectable existence.[7] Finally, there were Lady Blessington's books, which, since she had no living children, seem to have constituted neither more nor less than the family library from Blessington House, County Wicklow. Originally built in 1673 for Lord Blessington's great-grandfather Michael Boyle (*c.*1610–1702), Lord Chancellor of Ireland, and Archbishop of Armagh for 25 years from 1678, this was one of the largest and most magnificent seventeenth-century houses in Ireland, blessed with glasshouses, 'a very handsome noble garden wilderness … and a noble large park'.[8] Visiting in 1709, the astronomer and County Kildare landowner Samuel Molyneux (1689–1728) thought it 'one of the finest seats in Ireland', and 'much beyond any seat in all respects that I have seen in this Kingdom'.[9] A century later, the topographer Samuel Lewis noted that the demesne was 410 acres, and the adjacent deer-park 340, the whole surrounded by a wall.[10] The Blessingtons were nothing if not smart, and their house contained choice things.[11] There was also a house at Silchester in Hampshire, and in 1750 the couple also held the tenancy of a house in Hampstead, and the year before at 24 St James's Square in London.[12] Blessington himself had been a leading light in the Dublin Florists' Club, the first organization devoted to the promotion of ornamental horticulture in Ireland, which met from 1746 to 1766. Restricted to 30 members, the Club was in effect a smart dining society, and each member was enjoined in 1757 'to bring with him to this Clubb some flower otherwise the penalty of paying a half a Crown English for such a default will be enforced against him'.[13]

A very wealthy man, Lord Blessington had inherited not only the Boyle acres through his mother Lady Anne Boyle when that family became extinct with the death of Lord Blessington's brother-in-law in Paris in 1732, but also the ancestral lands of his father's family, the Viscounts Mountjoy, originally from County Tyrone. His distant ancestor Charles, Lord Mountjoy, had been the Lord Deputy who had defeated the Great O'Neill for Queen Elizabeth, and publicly and symbolically smashed the O'Neills' crowning stone at Tullyhogue – some four miles south of Springhill – in 1601.[14] One of Ireland's leading Freemasons, bullish in his Whiggish politics, and cock-sure of his own social status, Lord Blessington himself had caused offence at a public reception in 1748 by strutting around Dublin Castle in the gaudy livery of Frederick, Prince of Wales, and snubbing the Speaker of the Irish House of Commons.[15]

The couple's library appears to have been appropriately smart to match, the books housed in 'White Presses', which, since there is little evidence of grand Library rooms in Irish houses much before about 1730 and Blessington himself died in 1769, were probably both recent and of their own creation.[16] Evidently, the books kept in this room went back several generations, since the only books not bequeathed to Harriet Molesworth were a set of 'Books of Devotion with a Gold Cypher or Coronet upon them' which had belonged to 'the Old Lady Blesinton' – presumably her husband's grandmother Anne, Viscountess Blessington (*c.*1658–1725). Why these books were excluded from the main bequest is unclear. It may have been for reasons of family politics, as their intended recipient, 'Mrs Dunbar', was a descendant of her late husband's aunt Lady Mary Boyle, and some of the family estates were entailed on her husband. It could be that Lady Blessington did not think that ancient religious books – even ones with gold stamps on their spines – a suitable bequest for a well-educated young goddaughter, and judged them better bestowed elsewhere. Equally, the bequest from Lady Blessington to Harriet does not appear to have included the library which Archbishop Michael Boyle had purchased whole from Bishop Seth Ward of Salisbury in the late seventeenth century; it may be that these books had already left Blessington House by the time that Lady Blessington's husband took over the estate in 1732, or they may have been associated with the couple's secondary Irish residence, Monkstown Castle in south Dublin. At any event at least one of Archbishop Boyle's books – an annotated copy of William Bedell's 1685 edition of the Old Testament in Irish – eventually passed by descent to the Marquesses of Downshire at Hillsborough Castle, and is today in the parish church at Hillsborough.[17]

Somewhat less than a hundred of the books at Springhill today are actually inscribed by one of the Blessingtons (who usually spelt the name 'Blesinton'), but it seems clear that this can represent no more than a small proportion of the

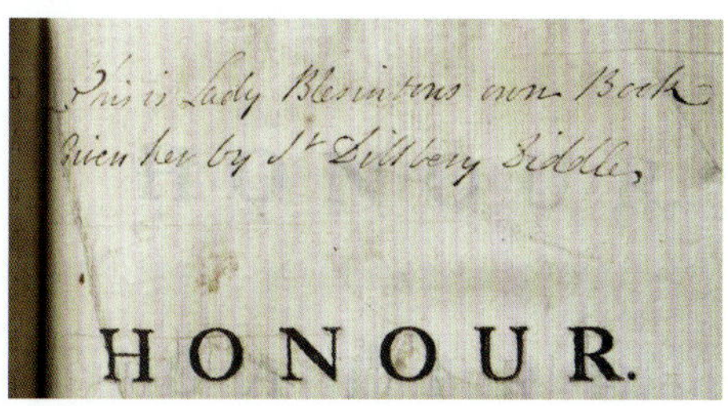

Right
Lady Blessington's whimsical ownership inscription in Paul Whitehead, *Honour: A Satire* (London, 1747), ESTC T54332 (Springhill)

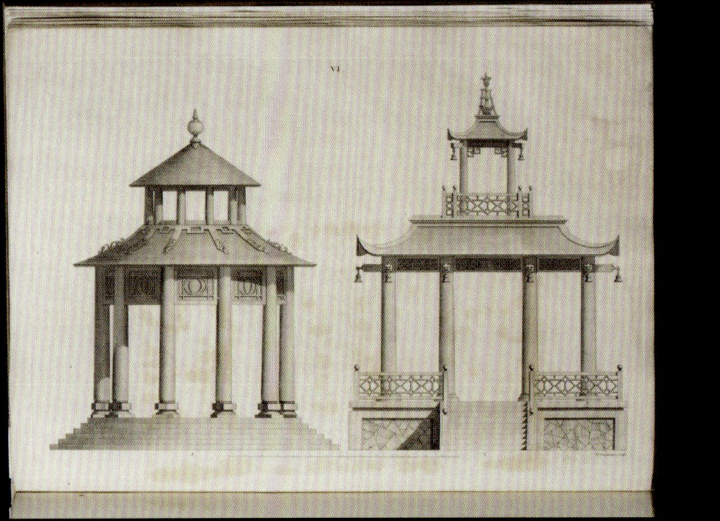

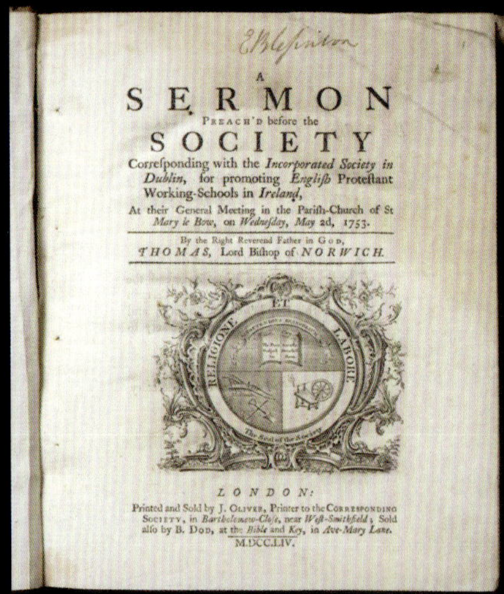

A

SERMON

PREACH'D before the

SOCIETY

Correſponding with the *Incorporated Society in Dublin*, for promoting *Engliſh* Proteſtant Working-Schools in *Ireland*,

At their General Meeting in the Pariſh-Church of St *Mary le Bow*, on *Wedneſday*, May 2d, 1753.

By the Right Reverend Father in GOD,

THOMAS, Lord Biſhop of *NORWICH*.

LONDON:

Printed and Sold by J. OLIVER, Printer to the CORRESPONDING SOCIETY, in *Bartholomew-Cloſe*, near *Weſt-Smithfield*; Sold alſo by B. DOD, at the *Bible* and *Key*, in *Ave-Mary Lane*.

M.DCC.LIV.

Above
Plate from William Chambers, *Designs of Chinese Buildings* (London, 1757), ESTC T31726 (Springhill)

Above right
Thomas Secker, *A Sermon preached before the Society for Corresponding with the Incorporated Society in Dublin* (London, 1757), inscribed by Lady Blessington, ESTC T47821 (Springhill)

library inherited by Harriet Molesworth. Mostly printed in the Earl and Countess's lifetimes, they include a fair sprinkling of London and Continental books, but comparatively few from Ireland. Lord Blessington's books include grand architectural books like Colen Campbell's *Vitruvius Britannicus* (London, [1722 ?]), and inevitably one wonders whether he was also the original owner of unsigned books like the 1721 London edition of Palladio, Charles-Étienne Briseux's *Architecture Moderne* (Paris, 1728) – priced £4–10–0 in an eighteenth-century hand – and, most splendid of all, William Chambers's magnificently-illustrated *Designs of Chinese Buildings* (London, 1757). Standard works of history like Rapin de Thoyras's *Histoire d'Angleterre* (The Hague, 1730) sit alongside plays, Ovid and Dryden, a 1742 Bible in French, political pamphlets, Swammerdam's *The Book of Nature* (London, 1758), splendidly illustrated, and *An Account of the Ceremonies Observed in the Coronations of the Kings and Queens of England* (London, 1760).

Lady Blessington's own books are no less varied, including French novels, some, like Mme Leprince de Beaumont's *La Triomphe de la Verité* (Nancy, 1748) in the original French, and others – like Le Noble's *Ildegerte, Queen of Norway* (London, 1721) – in English translation. Her copy of Sir William Keith's *An Essay on the Education of a Young British Nobleman* (London, 1730), a pamphlet which must have been acquired before 1745 – when she was still 'E. Mountjoy' – has a certain poignancy, as Lady Blessington's only child William, Lord Mountjoy died at the age of 19 in 1754. As revealing is the extensive collection of bound sermons printed for the Corresponding Society, an assembly of Irish Protestants resident in London which, like its Dublin counterpart the Incorporated Society, raised funds by means of an annual sermon, usually preached by an English divine. Ostensibly a charitable organisation whose purpose was to promote the Protestant interest in Ireland, the Society's annual gathering in London provided Irish gentlefolk resident in England with a useful opportunity for sociability and social networking, and the Blessingtons were enthusiastic supporters, the Earl subscribing £10 in 1754.[18] Lady Blessington and her goddaughter appear to have shared a taste in music, and a large group of oratorio programmes – like fashionable sermon-going, another way in which the well-to-do could simultaneously be entertained and indulge a taste for public philanthropy – remains on the shelves at Springhill. Though signed by Harriet, many date from the 1740s and

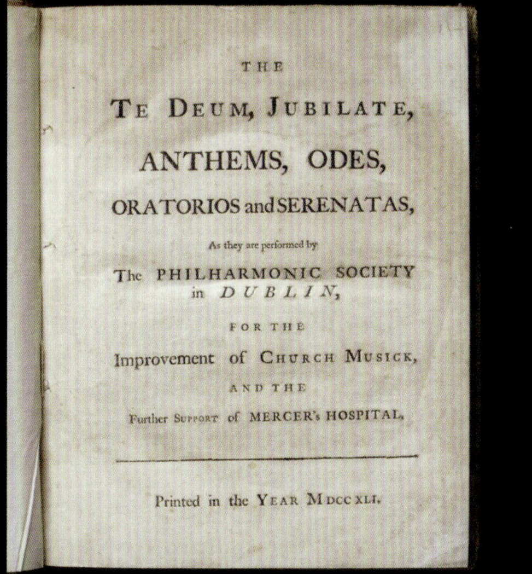
THE

TE DEUM, JUBILATE,

ANTHEMS, ODES,

ORATORIOS and SERENATAS,

As they are performed by

The PHILHARMONIC SOCIETY in *DUBLIN*,

FOR THE

Improvement of CHURCH MUSICK,

AND THE

Further SUPPORT of MERCER's HOSPITAL.

Printed in the YEAR MDCCXLI.

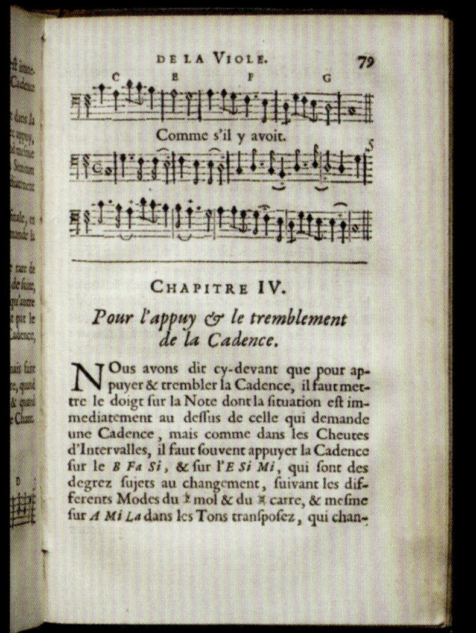
DE LA VIOLE. 79

Comme s'il y avoit.

CHAPITRE IV.

Pour l'appuy & le tremblement de la Cadence.

NOus avons dit cy-devant que pour appuyer & trembler la Cadence, il faut mettre le doigt ſur la Note dont la ſituation eſt immediatement au deſſus de celle qui demande une Cadence, mais comme dans les Cheutes d'Intervalles, il faut ſouvent appuyer la Cadence ſur le *B Fa Si*, & ſur l'*E Si Mi*, qui ſont des degrez ſujets au changement, ſuivant les differents Modes du ♭ mol & du ♮ carre, & meſme ſur *A Mi La* dans les Tons tranſpoſez, qui chan-

Above
Title-page of the Dublin Philharmonic Society's *The Te Deum, Jubilate, Anthems, Odes, Oratorios and Serenatas* ([Dublin], 1741), ESTC T213588 (Springhill)

Above right
Jean Rousseau, *Traité de la Viole* (Paris, 1687) (Springhill)

1750s and presumably belonged to Lady Blessington. There are London-printed libretti for several of Handel's finest works, including *Theodora* (1750), *Belshazzar* (1751), *Israel in Egypt* (1756) and *Deborah* (1744), as well as a programme for one of the Dublin Philharmonic Society's annual concerts for the support of the city's Mercers' Hospital. Though this was one of the most popular events in the Dublin social calendar, attended by the Lord Lieutenant and known to cause traffic jams in the vicinity of the city's St Andrew's church, very few programmes now exist.[19] That for 1741 is known in only three copies, and the one at Springhill is the only example which is complete and undamaged.[20] Several of the oratorio programmes are hardly less rare, indicative not only of the poor survival rate of such ephemeral publications, but of the fact that this sort of printed matter is disproportionately likely to have survived in a private and domestic library like that at Springhill – precisely the sort of collections least likely to have survived in Ireland. Another and almost equally unusual book, a *Traité de la Viole* (Paris, 1687) compiled by the French virtuoso Jean Rousseau (1644–99), probably also has a Blessington provenance. In five parts, it includes a basic treatise for beginners, a defence of the melodic and expressive possibilities of the viol, instructions on ornamentation and bowing, and a discussion of the need for players to be able to transpose their music at sight.[21] The survival of all these books is due entirely to the quirks of inheritance, as Blessington House was (as the Marquess of Downshire's agent wrote to his employer) 'completely destroyed' by the insurgents in 1798, to the consternation of the local parish priest Fr Miley, who wrote to the Catholic Archbishop of Dublin to deplore the 'anarchy, confusion, plunder and burning.'[22]

Harriet Molesworth became Mrs John Staples of Lissan in 1774, a little while after the death of her wealthy godmother. Both the Molesworths and the Blessingtons had historic connections with County Tyrone, and Harriet's new husband was among the leading landowners in the county. A visitor in 1802 thought Lissan – a rambling house in the foothills of the Sperrins – 'neat and commodious', and commended Staples as a man of taste, who had 'not only decorated a secluded recess of mountainous territory, but seems even to have caused an imitative emulation, in a way proportionate to their situations, among the neighbouring gentlemen, and even in the poor mountaineers'.[23] Nonetheless, there is perhaps a slight suspicion that Harriet's friends and family may have regarded

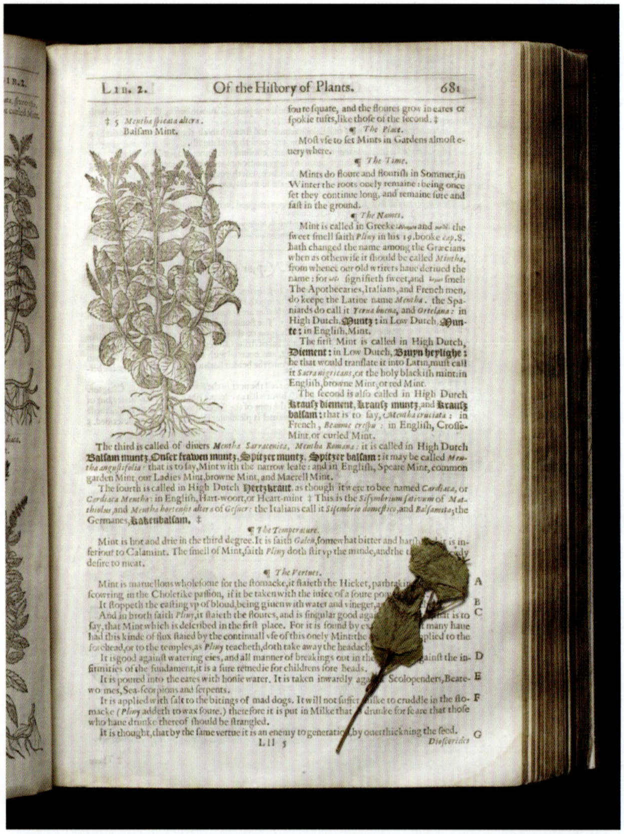

Above
John Gerard, *The Herball or General Historie of Plantes* (London, 1633), STC 11751, showing the Balsam Mint and a pressed leaf of the herb (Springhill)

the match as a slight *mésalliance* to be tolerated only because the 29-year-old bride had lost a leg. At the very least, they appear to have been determined to prevent her considerable personal fortune from coming under the control of her husband, a widower of nearly 40. The marriage settlement was carefully worded to ensure that Harriet and her family retained control of the 'divers sums of money and other particulars' which she had inherited both from Lady Blessington and from her mother's family. On her own death in 1812, a carefully-drafted codicil she had added to her will came into force, excluding her eldest son from inheriting her personal property, which was specifically allocated to the younger children. It seems that her third child, Charlotte Melosina Staples (1786–1847), who became *châtelaine* of Springhill on her marriage to William Lenox-Conyngham ('Wims') in 1819, inherited all or most of her mother's books, and much else besides.[24] Like her mother, there is perhaps a slight sense that her family may have thought Charlotte – 33 when she came to Springhill and perhaps considered in danger of being left 'on the shelf' – had, in marrying a country squire, married beneath her (her sisters Grace and Frances had carried off far grander prizes in the persons of the Marquess of Ormonde and Henry Ponsonby, Bishop of Derry).[25] This may conceivably explain why so many personal chattels came into her possession, and consequently ended up at Springhill after 1819; perhaps her grander sisters simply did not need them.

The Blessington-Staples strand of the Springhill library is self-evidently extremely remarkable, and seems if anything even more interesting with the discovery that so many of the books within it had belonged successively to three generations of gentlewomen, and had passed by inheritance through the female line on two separate occasions as the result of a deliberate decision on the part of their women owners. The clear implication, perhaps, is that women used to strong and well-read female role-models had no difficulty themselves in following in the family tradition, and certainly Harriet Staples was no mere passive recipient of Lady Blessington's library, but bought – and presumably read – books on a surprisingly prolific scale, as her signature on so many Springhill title-pages shows. They range from her copy of Gerard's *Herball* (1633), bought in 1774, just after she married, through to standard works like Burnet's *History of his Own Time* (London, 1724), and even a splendidly-illustrated Italian edition of *Ossian* (Padua, 1772), the great pseudo-Celtic literary fraud of the eighteenth century, given to her by Lord O'Neill of Shanes Castle in 1800. Perhaps too, her godmother may quite self-consciously have encouraged an interest in books – and bequeathed a library – precisely because the loss of Harriet's leg made it difficult for her

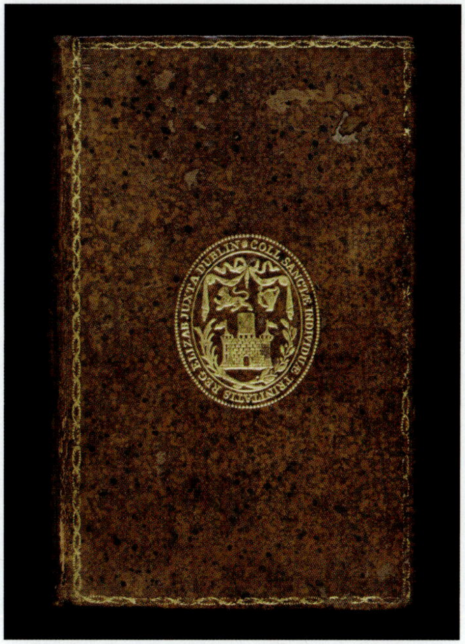

Right
A Trinity College, Dublin prize binding on Adam Smith's *An Enquiry into the Nature and Causes of the Wealth of Nations* (London, 1799), ESTC T95382 (Springhill)

to participate in fashionable pleasures like riding and dancing. She comes across as a bookish figure with up-to-date tastes, buying considerable numbers of books in French, as well as the occasional antiquarian purchase.

Charlotte Melosina herself seems to have shared some of her mother's tastes. As a young women she received as gifts from her father 'duplications' from the library at Lissan – in 1818, for example, he gave her a 1739 edition of Samuel Butler's *Hudibras*, and she may well have ended up with entailed books which should properly have stayed at Lissan as well. Some of these are quite mundane, and include a 1793 Dublin edition of Hugh Blair's *Lectures on Rhetoric and Belles Lettres*, in a Trinity College prize binding, presented to Charlotte's father in 1796. Equally puzzling is a 1653 edition of Ussher's *Body of Divinitie*, which appears to have been at Lissan for a considerable time; one wonders why Charlotte might have wanted it. One of the most intriguing of all the former Lissan books is *The English Irish Dictionary. An Focloir Bearla Gaoidhelige* (Paris, 1732), the first Irish dictionary to appear in print, edited by Conchubhar Ó Beaglaoich, and Aodh Buidhe Mac Cruitín, which was acquired in 1827.[26] Another is a copy of the first edition of the New Testament in Syriac, edited by Johann Albrecht Widmanstatt (1506–59) and printed in Vienna under the patronage of the Emperor Ferdinand in 1555; on the face of things an unlikely find on the shelves of a small gentry house in mid-Ulster.[27] On the title-page is the signature of the Revd George Walker (1645?–90), Rector of Donoughmore, near Dungannon, and joint governor of Derry during the great siege.[28] It would be easy enough to assume that this book might have been a relic collected by a member of the Lenox family in early eighteenth-century Derry, but as members of the Kirk they are unlikely to have venerated George Walker, who was no friend to Presbyterians, speaking against them 'with a good deal of warmth' in audience with William III in Belfast in June 1690.[29] In fact it seems to have come from Lissan and to have ended up there because the Staples family was distantly related to Walker by marriage. The other books in oriental languages may have a similar source, and they include a copy of Buxtorf's *Lexicon Chaldaicum et Syriacum* (Basel, 1622),

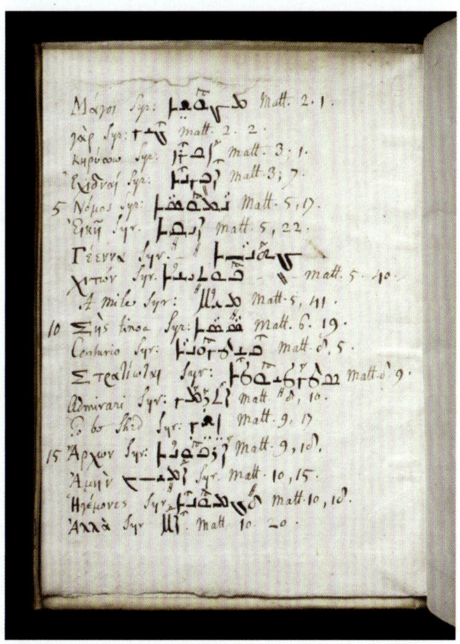

Right
Annotations in Latin and Hebrew in Johannes Buxtorf's *Lexicon Chaldaicum et Syriacum* (Basel, 1622) (Springhill)

massively annotated by a contemporary reader in both Latin and Hebrew, and an Arabic grammar by Thomas Erpenius (1584–1624), printed in Leiden in 1656. Elusive as all this is, these books are an interesting pointer to the interconnections between the worlds of the country gentry and clerical learning in seventeenth- and eighteenth-century Ireland.[30] But even more unexpected is a Hebrew manuscript of the *Book of Common Prayer*, signed by the 'old man, Abraham bar Ya'akov, prayer-leader, begun on the fifteenth day of the month of May 1717 according to the Christian calendar here in the community of Dublin'. Abraham bar Jacob (1656–*c.*1725) was a Polish Jew who converted to Christianity in Dublin in 1706, and the translation of the Prayer Book was commissioned by Archbishop William King. Three manuscripts of it have long been known, in Trinity College Library and Marsh's Library, and King's own copy at the Diocesan Library in Cashel. The Springhill manuscript is a fourth, previously unrecorded; how it came to Springhill will probably remain a matter of conjecture.[31]

Twenty-first-century visitors to Springhill see a series of rather safe Irish Georgian interiors, created by the National Trust – in tune with the spirit of the times – in the late 1950s and early 60s. Reflective of the contemporary horror of Victoriana, and in Ireland perhaps also of the successful propagandising of the Irish Georgian Society (founded in 1958), they bear only a limited resemblance to the clutter of the house in Victorian and Edwardian times. The modest little Library room, just to the right of the front door, has not altered all that much since the nineteenth century, though it has certainly been repainted and the furnishings probably thinned out. The books themselves still stand on their plain and undecorated shelves – the seven presses probably installed in the first half of the nineteenth century, perhaps when books arrived from Lissan after 1819 – but almost certainly rearranged, as they do not fit especially well, with long rows of small volumes on shelves which are patently too big from them. In the circumstances it is perhaps fortunate that the library survived at all, with Robin Fedden, the Trust's then Historic Buildings Secretary, deciding in consort with its chairman

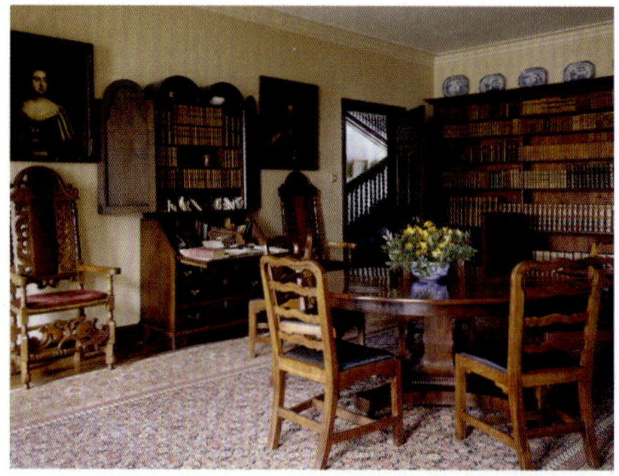

Right
The Library at Springhill

Lord Antrim that only the '*leather bound* books' needed to be retained and 'properly arranged', the 'other books to be stored away or sold' (fortunately, none was sold).[32] In the adjacent Drawing Room, the two low bookcases which were there at least as far back as 1839 are still where they were, and contain the small-format 'polite' books – many in French – which they have probably always contained, many of them also Staples books from Lissan. The Drawing Room itself, once kitted-out with vivid Victorian wallpaper and comfortably cushioned chairs, is barely recognisable as that shown in early photographs, carefully done over in 1959 by a Chelsea interior designer to make it 'look as if people were living in the house'.[33] These two rooms are the only show rooms which contain books today, but it is clear that Springhill was positively overflowing with books in Edwardian times, distributed on shelves and tables throughout the house. There would have been books in the Nursery, 'for many years' the domain of Mrs Meighan, the nanny, who was still remembered at Springhill in 1946.[34] Further books were to be found in the Smoking Room, a lean-to at the back of the house demolished by the National Trust in the early years of its ownership, and in various spaces subsequently converted for office or staff accommodation. Almost all these books are still in the house, closely packed in racking in the attics, unseen by visitors, but a potent reminder of the last phase of Springhill's history as a private house.

This tremendous profusion of books needs an explanation which goes beyond the bookish tendencies of a family which had been acquiring (and probably only rarely discarding) books since the late seventeenth century. In the first place, of course, it was due to the great inheritance from the libraries at Lissan and Blessington, but the Lenox-Conyngham talent for marriages continued into Victorian times. During the course of the nineteenth century, the daughters of the house intermarried, much as they had always done, with the sons of other Ulster gentry families, and a further series of historical accidents brought yet more books back to Moneymore. In 1853 Marcus Gage of Streeve Hill, a Big House near Limavady, County Londonderry, proposed to Charlotte Melosina's daughter Harriett ('Hazzy') Lenox-Conyngham in the Library at Springhill. The couple married in January 1854, but despite the magnificence of the ceremony, attended by 'the gentry of the county … in splendid equipages', and judged a 'brilliant assembly of rank, beauty and fashion', the young man made a poor impression on his in-laws, family tradition remembering him as 'genial, foolish and very extravagant'.[35] The couple subsequently set up home at Ballinacree, a grand new residence built for them near Ballymoney in County Antrim. The Gage family themselves were closely related to the neighbouring family, the McCauslands, who lived nearby at Fruit Hill, a splendid house rebuilt by Charles Lanyon in 1836, and now known as Drenagh.[36] Marcus Gage's grandfather, also called Marcus Gage (b.1755), was born Marcus McCausland, and changed his name to Gage to inherit another nearby demesne, Bellarena, which had originally belonged to his uncle Hodson Gage.[37] After her husband's death Hazzy lived on in genteel poverty at Coleraine, a childless widow, and it seems that the couple's library came to Springhill after her own death in 1900.[38] It included books which had belonged not just to them, but to Marcus's Gage and McCausland ancestors, as well as to Robert Gage, Rector of Desertoghill, who had predeceased his older brother. Some of the Gage books are on the face of it fairly mundane, with *The Agriculturist's Calculator: a Series of Tables for the Use of All Engaged in Agriculture or the Management of Landed Property* (Glasgow, 1851) speaking quite eloquently of the trials and tribulations of running a landed estate in hard times; it may be no coincidence that Marcus Gage himself was by 1859 acting as agent for at least two local landowners.[39] Other Gage books contain a characteristic family bookplate, probably from the early nineteenth century, with the rhyming injunction to borrowers to return the book to its proper owner – interesting in itself, since if books had not habitually been lent to friends and neighbours, there would have been no need for it. Others contain the ticket of Eccles, a binder in Coleraine, again saying something of the practicalities of buying and binding books in a provincial corner of Ireland in the middle of the nineteenth century.

Hazzy's younger sister Charlotte Lenox-Conygham also married another local squire, James David Beresford, a younger son of Learmont Castle, a castellated neo-Elizabethan mansion of 1830, in the uplands of the Sperrins about a dozen miles north-west of Moneymore. The couple, married for only ten years, later moved to Moneymore, and at least some of their books too may have ended up at Springhill. Beresford, descended from a younger brother of the Marquesses of Waterford, of Curraghmore, County Waterford, was reckoned the 'handsomest member of the British Army'.[40] He may

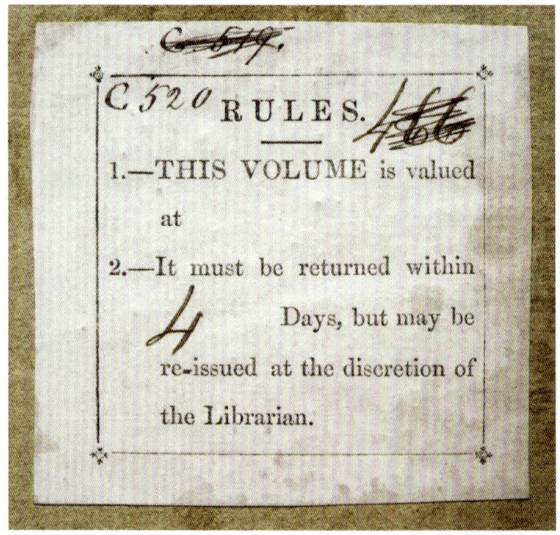
~~C 519~~

C 520 RULES. ~~466~~

1.—THIS VOLUME is valued at

2.—It must be returned within 4 Days, but may be re-issued at the discretion of the Librarian.

Right
Label of the Londonderry Military Library pasted into Baron de Jomini's *Précis de l'Art de la Guerre* (Paris, 1838) (Springhill)

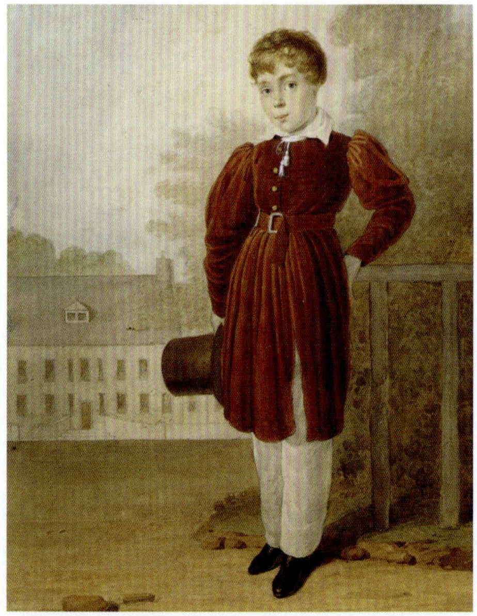

Right
William Lenox-Conyngham in the uniform of the Royal School at Dungannon

well have been the owner of the Baron de Jomini's *Précis de l'Art de la Guerre* (Paris, 1838), a book formerly in the otherwise unrecorded 'Londonderry Military Library', presumably associated with the British garrison in the city, with the library's rules ('must be returned within 4 days') pasted into the front.

In addition to the books which came in from two younger sisters, the Springhill attics also include many acquired during the reign of their long-lived brother Sir William Lenox-Conyngham (1824–1906), known to his family as Billy. In old-age a sombre patriarch with a great white beard, he is more memorably portrayed at Springhill in a portrait showing him as a boy of ten, in the distinctive uniform of the Royal School at Dungannon. It may be significant that he and his family were frequently away from Ireland, living in Edinburgh during the schooling of the children, and for several years from 1882 Springhill was let to tenants while Sir William – then in the employ of the Drapers' Company – went to live in their manor house in Moneymore. There was a further lengthy stay in England during Sir William's last years, and by the time of his death the Springhill demesne was clearly in a bad way. Billy Lenox-Conygham's chief pastime was coursing with his greyhounds, and he does not appear from the evidence of the surviving books to have been much of a reader.[41] The same certainly cannot be said of his even longer-lived daughter-in-law Mina Lenox-Conyngham (née Lowry), who first came to Springhill for country house theatricals in the 1880s, married Sir William's son and heir in 1899, and died at Springhill in 1961, in her 94th year.

Born at Rockdale, Tullyhogue in County Tyrone, Mina was a *grande dame* who saw the sale of the family estates to the Land Commission in 1906, the Easter Rising, the Partition, the First and Second World Wars, the death of her eldest son, and the acquisition of Springhill by the National Trust in 1957, and she lived on into the era of the Beatles and John F. Kennedy. As in late Victorian times, members of the Lenox-Conyngham family were frequently away from Springhill. Following family tradition, Mina's husband fought in the Boer War, and three of her brothers-in-law were colonels in the British Army, one of them killed on the Somme in 1916. Staunch supporters of the Unionist cause, the family were involved in gun-running for the Ulster Volunteer Force in 1914, and they were forced to withdraw to Dublin in the dangerous years after the First World War.[42] With the subsequent restoration of relative calm, the family returned, but the inter-war years saw lengthy visits to London and to South Africa. Then, between 1940 and 1944, Springhill was requisitioned by the military, though its *châtelaine* managed to 'reserve a corner of the house as a pied-à-terre' to keep an eye on proceedings, and was entertained in her own dining room, first by British, and later American, troops.[43]

The attic stores at Springhill are still packed with books which, in themselves, provide ample evidence of Mina Lenox-Conyngham's long and active life. The family historian, her *Old Ulster House* was published in 1946, when she was already 79 years old. A rambling and discursive yarn with a taste for ghost stories and spectacular set-piece narratives, on publication it was admired by some, and derided by others, but quite apart from its gleanings from the Lenox-Conyngham archive, it says much about the passage of events which were still within living memory in 1946. The most trenchant criticism of the new book, perhaps, came in the columns of *Irish Historical Studies*, when Edward MacLysaght (1887–1986), the first Chief Herald of Ireland, poked fun at Mina's historical technique, and airily dismissed the Ulster landed gentry as 'a section of society not Irish and only superficially British', and Springhill and its owners as 'humdrum'. MacLysaght – the English-born son of a Cork father, who came to Ireland in 1909, quickly became passionately interested in the Celtic revival, learned Irish, was a backer of Sinn Féin in County Clare during the War of Independence, and became a Free State Senator in 1922 – was hardly a figure calculated to think well of Springhill and the Lenox-Conynghams. What now seems remarkable about his comments is less the predictable failure to realise (or to care) that his preferred version of Irish history was just as one-sided and eccentric as Mina's own, but the use of the word 'humdrum'. In one sense undeniably fair, at least for the events of the twentieth century, with the benefit of 60 years of hindsight what is perhaps most striking is how little ultimately this seems to matter.

Despite occasional flashes of eccentricity – did Mina really read the 1940 edition of the memoirs of Maxim Gorky? – the most striking thing about the more recent books at Springhill is not only their sheer ordinariness, but at the same time that such a vivid picture of gentry life in mid-Ulster emerges from them. The carefully annotated copy of William R. Young's *Fighters of Derry* (London, 1932), the Dorothy L. Sayers and the *Hercule Poirot Investigates* (1932), wartime propaganda about the use of manure, or the biography

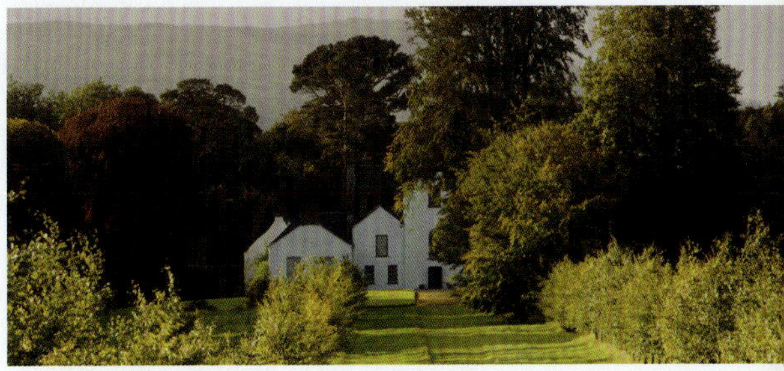

Right
The rear façade of Springhill

of General Smuts (whom Mina had met in South Africa in 1922) – even the Army and Navy Store catalogues from the 1950s – all speak for themselves.

Mina's studied ambivalence towards the future ('the era of communistic destruction and of the atomic bomb') comes across clearly in *An Old Ulster House*, and it is clear she had mixed feelings too about the wartime troops who took over the house which had already been hers for nearly half a century. Nonetheless, despite her apparent misgivings – about ice-cream, Deep South cooking, black GIs and Mass in the front court at Springhill – she followed her instincts in trying to make the best of the situation.[44] Enlightened nineteenth-century chatelaines had provided books for the amusement and edification of their servants. In the rather different circumstances of total war, Mina rolled up her sleeves and set up the 'Springhill Library for Troops' for her not entirely welcome visitors. Some of its books, at least, still survive alongside her own.

5 The Exhilarating and Invigorating Air of the Downhill

Downhill, County Londonderry, 1783–1803

Exactly a month before the American Declaration of Independence John Wesley attended morning service at St Columb's Cathedral in Derry. It being Whit Sunday, the city's bishop was in the pulpit. The 73-year-old evangelist enjoyed a 'judicious and useful sermon on the blasphemy of the Holy Ghost', and was impressed with the liturgy: Bishop Hervey had, he thought, 'celebrated the Lord's Supper with admirable solemnity'. Two days later, Wesley was invited to a good solid dinner at the Bishop's Palace – 'a piece of boiled beef and an English pudding', he recalled, served unfashionably early, his host accommodatingly remarking 'I know you do not love our hours, and will therefore order dinner to be on the table between two and three o'clock'. The Bishop of Derry was good company, and John Wesley was charmed. 'The Bishop is entirely easy and unaffected in his whole behaviour', he confided to his diary, 'exemplary in all parts of public worship, and plenteous in good works'.[1] It was a view shared by some – his friend the agronomist Arthur Young thought him possessed of 'an uncommon vein of pleasantry and wit' – but others were rather less enamoured, and even Young was forced to admit that 'he lived in a manner not very episcopal'.[2]

Some years earlier, this exemplary bishop – then simply the Revd Mr Hervey – had made an equally good impression on Voltaire. Visiting Ferney in 1766, the youthful clergyman (an excellent linguist who 'spoke all modern languages fluently') and the aged *philosophe* indulged in a little banter.[3] In the version later recounted by Lady Holland, Voltaire gestured to the church and the theatre which he had recently built, and asked: *'Où joue on la plus grande farce?'* His guest's reply – *'C'est selon les auteurs'* ('it depends on the authors') would have scandalised the pious churchgoers of Derry.[4] Appalled by his later dalliance with the Volunteers, George III agreed, describing the Bishop as a 'wicked prelate'.[5] The Volunteer leader Lord Charlemont (1728–99) was more damning still, denouncing him as a 'Deist' and a 'blasphemer'.[6] Lady Holland herself thought the Earl-Bishop 'an abominable, wicked old fellow'.

When John Wesley visited Derry in 1776, Frederick Augustus Hervey (1730–1803) had already been a bishop of the Church of Ireland for nine years. The younger son of an aristocratic family – his father had been a favourite of George II

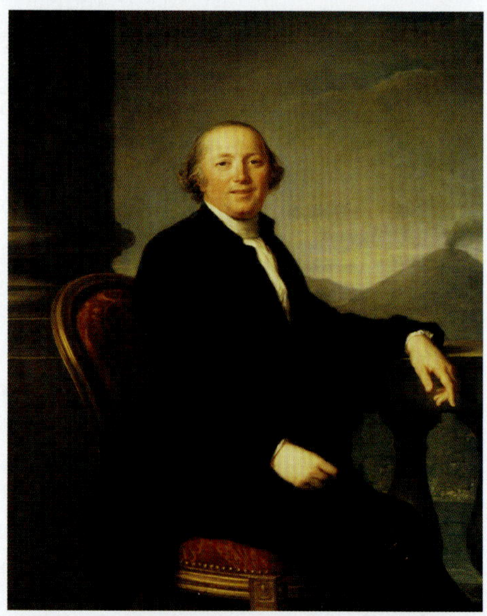

Right
Frederick Hervey (1730–1803), 4th Earl of Bristol and Bishop of Derry, painted in Naples in 1790 by Elisabeth Vigée-Lebrun (National Trust, Ickworth)

and Queen Caroline – he was educated at Westminster School and Corpus Christi College, Cambridge. Bright, possessed of quick wits and an easy good temper, he was always intended for the Church, and was ordained at the age of 25, but his great chance came with the appointment of his eldest brother, the 2nd Earl of Bristol, as Lord Lieutenant of Ireland in the autumn of 1766. Within five months the 37-year-old Hervey had been advanced to the episcopal bench, becoming bishop of the impoverished southern diocese of Cloyne early the following year. Cloyne, no more than a village and worth only £2500 a year, was not one of the more desirable preferments in Ireland, and the new bishop did not stay in County Cork for long. After just over a year he was elevated to the walled city of Derry, moving from one of the poorest sees in Ireland to the very richest, with its 70,000 acres of land, a plum worth £7000 a year in 1767, a figure which by careful management the new bishop more than doubled during his 36-year episcopate. Visiting in 1802, the Secretary of the Honourable Irish Society was scathing: 'I wish his lordship's conduct authorised me to say he paid equal attention to his spiritual duties.'[7] Matters did not rest there, and with the unexpected death of two elder brothers, in 1775 the Bishop of Derry became 4th Earl of Bristol, inheriting the Hervey family lands in Suffolk, as well as the ancestral estate, Ickworth. This curious junction of the sacred and the secular left the Earl-Bishop (the first since Odo of Bayeux in the twelfth century, it was said) with a vast income and seats in the House of Lords in both Dublin and London. It was a far cry from the annuity of £100 allocated to him in his father's will in 1743.[8]

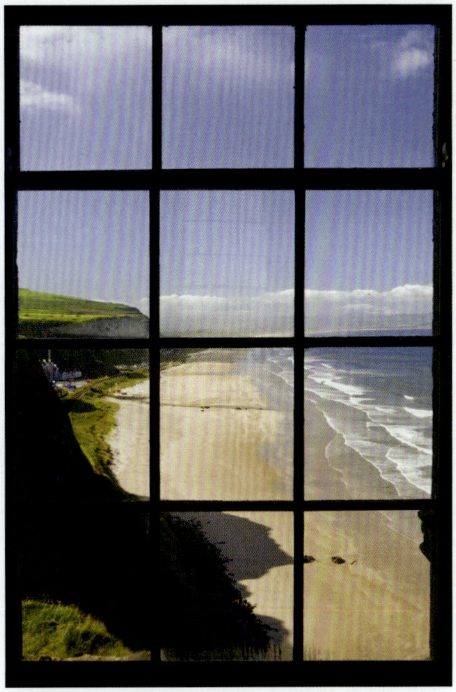

Right
View from the Mussenden Temple looking west onto Magilligan Strand

The Earl-Bishop rapidly established the reputation of being a great traveller and a great builder – and for being something of an odd bod. Popular in his adopted city of Derry for his noisy refusal to nominate needy English clergy to Irish benefices (and seemingly unaware of any irony in this), he was sighted in Rome in 1771 in 'the dress of an English bishop'. Impressed by the independent-minded Gallicanism of the French church, already in 1768 he was cooking up schemes for a new oath of allegiance which Irish Catholics might square with their consciences. His proposals met with little favour with the authorities and if the Catholic antiquarian Charles O'Conor of Bellanagare applauded the Earl-Bishop's 'Patriotic, and indeed generous Efforts to make all good subjects agree in one Summary of Civil Principles', his lobbying of Archbishop Secker of Canterbury produced an unambiguous response.[9] The Church of Rome 'was peculiarly formidable to Protestant States', and 'any proposals … that could bear but the smallest Appearance of being favourable to Papists, though proceeding from the sincerest purpose … would raise a clamour against us'.[10] Undeterred, the Bishop of Derry took himself to Rome for an interview with the newly-elected Pope Clement XIV.[11] By 1784, the Earl of Abercorn's agent was alarmed by the Bishop's flirtation with the

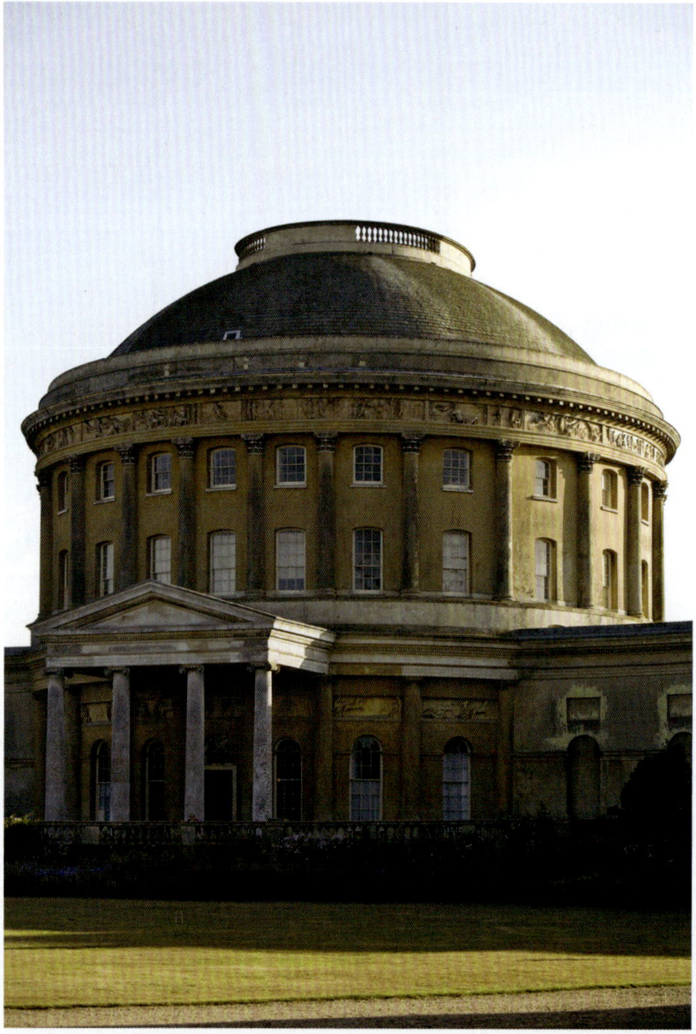

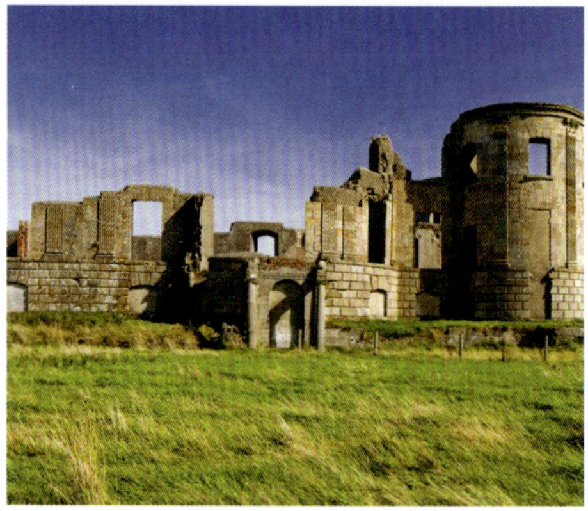

Volunteers, reporting that 'his lordship has volunteered raising different parts of the country, that he expects that there will be a thousand of them, and that they are expected to be called the Bristol rangers'.[12] In tandem with these political activities, in 1771 the Earl-Bishop, inspired by Robert Adam's publication in 1764 of his magnificently-illustrated *Ruins of the Palace of the Emperor Diocletian at Spalatro*, embarked on 'a most delightful jaunt' to Dalmatia and admired the ruins at Split.[13] Having already improved his episcopal palace in Derry, he began to spend lavishly on his estate at Downhill, on the north coast of Ireland, some 25 miles north-east of the city. James Wyatt made designs for a palace there in 1778, and the following year the Earl-Bishop commissioned a mausoleum in memory of his brother the dead Lord Lieutenant, a building designed by the Cork architect Michael Shanahan, whom the Bishop had first met during his brief stay at Cloyne. The Earl-Bishop was prone to wasting the time of established architects with commissions which never came to fruition, but, despite a visit from the young John Soane (inveigled to Ireland in the summer of 1780, and later to complain bitterly of the 'the magnificent promises and splendid delusions of the Lord Bishop of Derry') it was Shanahan who was eventually responsible for most of the building operations at Downhill.[14] The Cork architect evidently found his patron exasperating, in 1783 grumbling about his 'daily memorandums, some of the most frivolous kind'.[15] By then, the Bishop's Palace in Derry, where the Earl-Bishop had already completed 'a delightful summer-house' much admired by John Wesley on a subsequent visit to Ireland in 1787, was forgotten, for, as Wesley put it, 'his lordship has utterly forsaken it for it is no longer new'.[16]

The Earl-Bishop was preoccupied with his grand projects at Downhill for the best part of a decade in the 1770s and 1780s, though from 1787 he was also at work on another palace ('a large and very expensive round house, on a plan as singular as himself', thought Arthur Young) at Ballyscullion, near Bellaghy, in the extreme south-east of his diocese.[17]

Opposite

Left
Ickworth, Suffolk

Right
The ruins of Downhill Palace, County Londonderry

The softer landscape there was much admired by contemporaries, and was 'considered by Lord Bristol not to be inferior to any Italian scenery', but the altogether wilder scenery of Downhill left many baffled.[18] With hardly any trees and facing the full force of the winter gales, it was a fearsomely exposed spot for a great house ('you will think your poor Father raving in a feverish delirium', confided the Earl-Bishop to his daughter), but the Earl-Bishop adored it.[19] An asthmatic, all through his life he had a horror of damp houses, denouncing his birthplace, Ickworth, which he rarely visited, for 'the wetness of the soil'. Downhill, set on top of a huge cliff was altogether better because of its 'exhilarating and invigorating air, or rather ether.'[20] A visitor in 1802 thought the whole scheme completely crazed, observing that the Bishop was said to 'have planted more than a million trees and shrubs' at Downhill, but 'hardly any of them have thriven'.[21] Arthur Young had put the figure at 200,000 trees in Ireland; but the point was unarguable.[22] Another visitor could not forbear to sneer at the eccentric patron's 'mania for building superb palaces in Ireland and England while he lives in ugly rat-holes in the Continent'.[23]

The most remarkable of all the buildings at Downhill is a circular temple – the Mussenden Temple – perched in a location of almost lunatic audacity some 200 feet above the ocean, but lined up on the main axis of Downhill Palace, a building which very sensibly faces inland. Always interested in the theoretical possibilities of architecture, the Earl-Bishop's well-known predilection for circular buildings could be given free reign in the Temple, with none of the inconveniences attendant on a house like Ballyscullion (or indeed the new residence which the Earl-Bishop later commissioned at Ickworth) which the patron might actually have to live in. To stand inside the Temple and look out, even on a fine day, feels curiously like standing on the bridge of a ship, and the urbane classicism of Shanahan's design contrasts strangely with the wildness of its location. Internally, the Temple is today no more than a shell, though fragments of plasterwork reportedly survived into the 1970s, but outside it stands serene and pristine in its extraordinary setting.

The story of the Earl-Bishop's libraries has yet to be written, but the Temple was in fact built as a library. It certainly contained books in 1802, when Arthur

Below
The Mussenden Temple, Downhill, County Londonderry

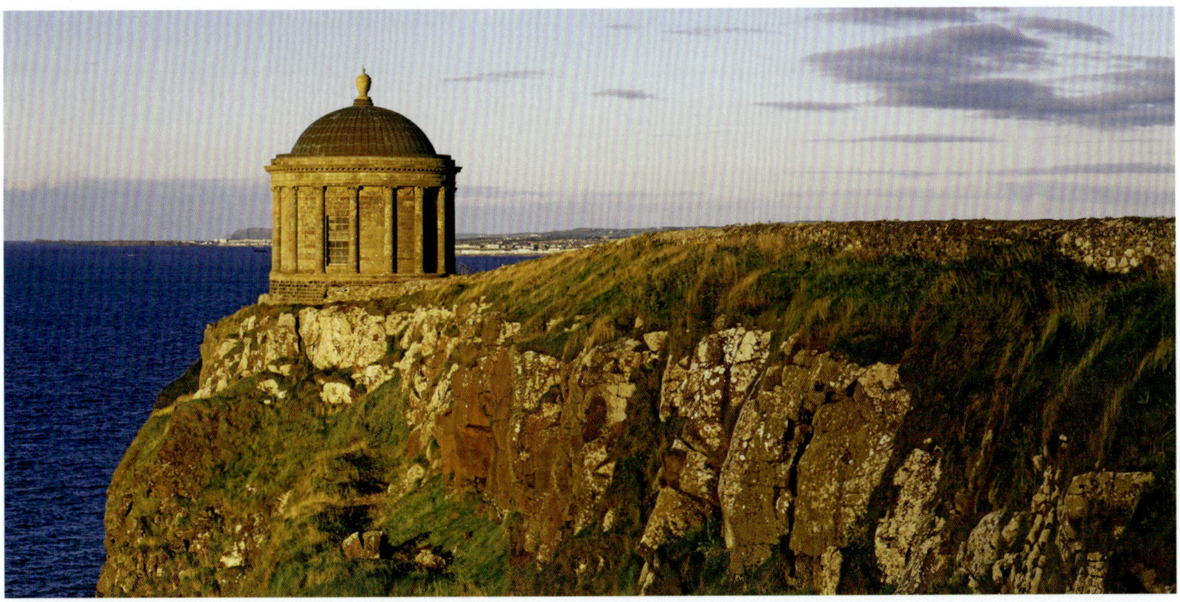

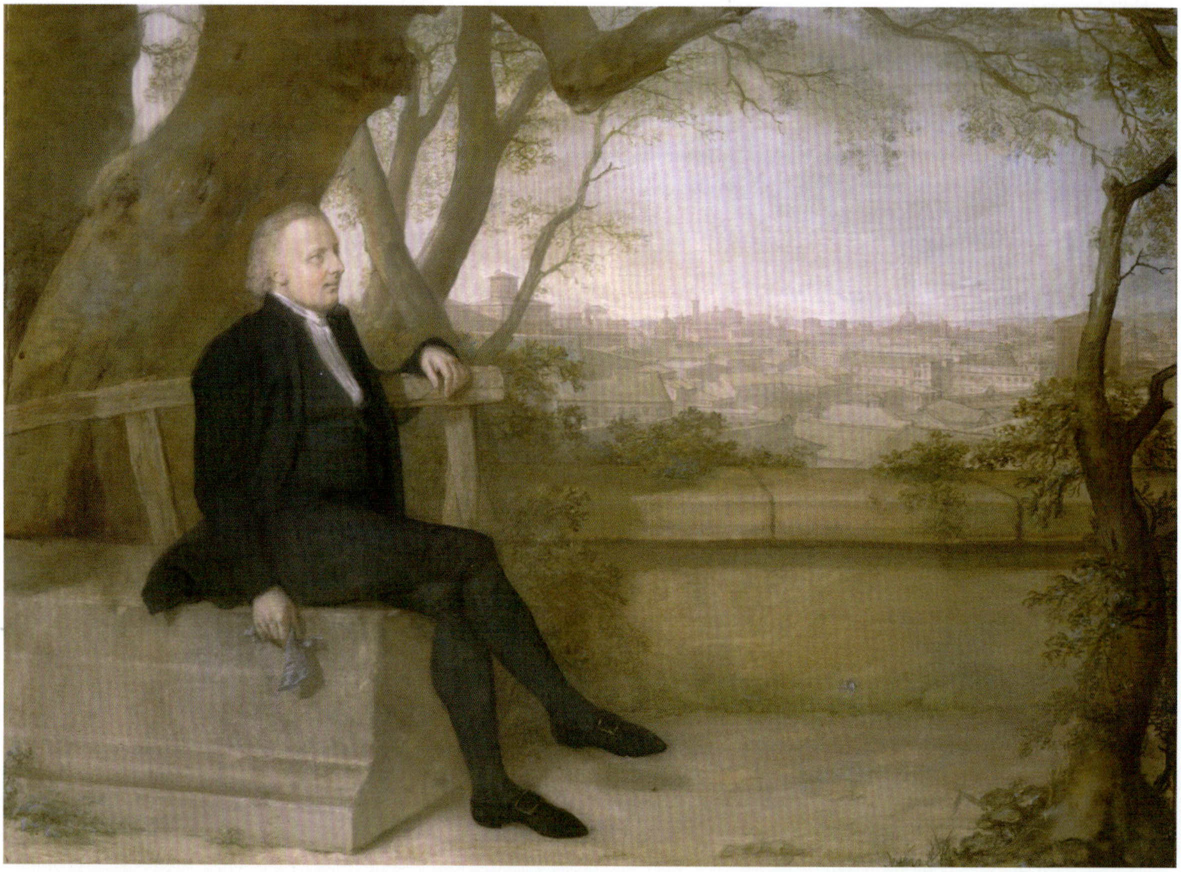

Above
The Earl-Bishop in Rome; painted by Hugh Douglas Hamilton (Ickworth)

McMackin, 'the old man who has taken care of your Lordships Temple at D:Hill this twelve years past', wrote to the errant prelate – who had long since abandoned Ireland for Italy – to complain that he 'never got any wages for cleaning the Books which was done 4 times every year'. Despite his 83 years, he reckoned himself 'still Capable of taking the proper Care of the Books in the Temple', and solicited 'your Lordship's Benevolence' for his labours.[24]

The Mussenden Temple is a remarkable building, but the key to understanding it is the realisation that it was always fundamentally intended as a summer Library which would exist in tandem with the Library in the adjacent Downhill Palace. The Earl-Bishop liked books, though he was sniffy about those he believed collected for reasons of vanity or ostentation.[25] Sometimes referred to as the New Gallery, the palace Library was completed in 1783, and was situated immediately to the north of the Earl-Bishop's Picture Gallery, which contained pictures by Titian, Raphael and Rembrandt.[26] Though there was also a Library at Ballyscullion, and the Hervey family's ancestral books remained at Ickworth Lodge, it seems likely that the majority of the Earl-Bishop's own books – or at least those books which he kept in Ireland – were housed in Downhill Palace. Presumably he had some sort of library in Italy as well. If so, it was probably confiscated along with the rest of his possessions when he was arrested by the French in Milan in 1798.[27] The Temple was evidently no more than an annexe, and one which existed for a variety of not entirely compatible purposes. In the first place it was a temple, dedicated to the memory of his cousin Mrs Frideswide Mussenden (d. 1785), with whom the Earl-Bishop

Right
The Temple of Vesta at Tivoli; by G. del Drago (Florence Court)

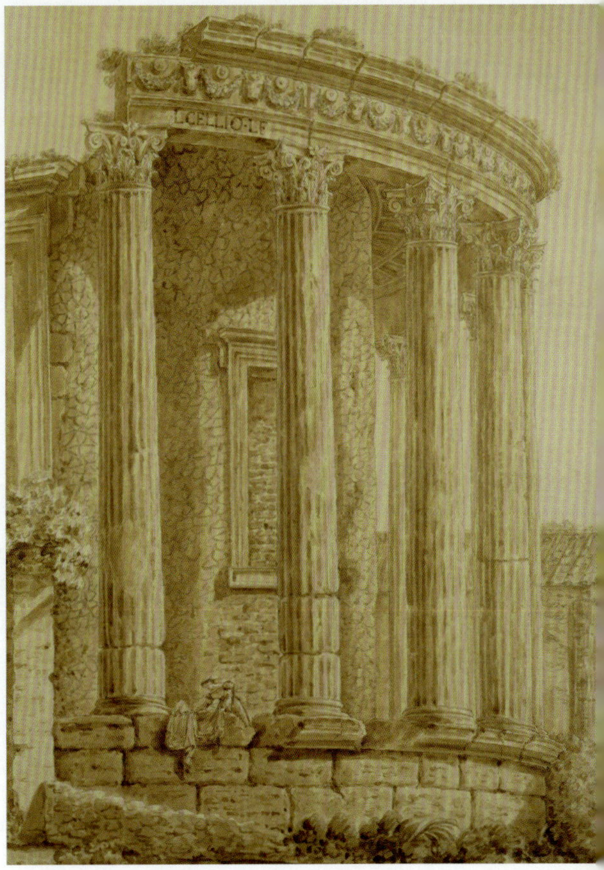

enjoyed a brief and perhaps platonic dalliance shortly before her untimely death at the age of 22, though a French visitor in the 1790s heard that it was dedicated to Eolus, the god of the winds.[28] One of a sequence of broadly similar garden buildings put up in the vicinity of a number of grand Irish houses from the middle of the eighteenth century, architecturally it relates to the other ornamental buildings which Shanahan built for the Earl-Bishop at Downhill. Its architectural form was derived ultimately from the 1st century BC Temple of Vesta in Rome, and from the cliff-top Temple of Vesta at Tivoli. It was later claimed – perhaps not entirely plausibly – that the Earl-Bishop had wished to buy the latter and transport it back to Ireland; certainly, he had discussed the idea of building a copy of it with the young John Soane when the two men met in Italy in 1778.[29] Another prototype, cited as his model by the Earl-Bishop in a letter to another correspondent, was Bramante's Tempietto at the church of San Pietro in Montorio on the Janiculum in Rome:

> I intend to build a Grecian temple in Frideswide's honour. It shall be called the Mussenden Temple. I intend to build it on the edge of a cliff. It will give employment to the poor of the district, and employment, as you know, is one of Ireland's ills … It is to be circular in shape, domed – not unlike Bramante's temple of Mount Gianicolo. Elegant, exquisite, looking towards the sea. Below there will be a drop of hundreds of feet on to the Strand of Magilligan … It is to have a library and a crypt underneath. A luminous idea has just struck me. I might provide a stipend of £10 per year for a priest, and my Roman Catholic workmen could worship in the crypt.[30]

The Tempietto, completed in 1502, was, like the Mussenden Temple, intended to be a commemorative building: not to the paramour of a Protestant bishop, but a martyrium for St Peter himself, crucified, according to tradition, on that very spot. The Earl-Bishop, a frequent visitor to the Eternal City, esteemed by the city's artists and connoisseurs, but capable of disgracing himself with unseemly antics (notoriously he once appeared for Holy Week ceremonies in the Sistine Chapel in his Anglican episcopal garb, for 'which piece of absurdity he was obliged to go down to the lower part of the chapel, among the common people'), cannot have been ignorant of this fact.[31] Despite the eccentric scheme to equip the basement of the Temple with a resident Catholic priest, the idea that the Temple's main function would be to house a library was one that originated early on. The recipient of the degree of Doctor of Divinity from the University of Oxford in April 1770, the Earl-Bishop could hardly have been unaware of the enormous circular library completed there a couple of decades earlier by James Gibbs, which stands right next to his adoptive college, Brasenose. The designs for the Radcliffe Library were published in a magnificent illustrated book issued by Gibbs in 1747, and were themselves ultimately derived from an unexecuted scheme by Hawksmoor for a domed library in Oxford, and they in turn from proposals submitted by Wren in the 1670s for a circular library at Trinity College, Cambridge.[32] The Earl-Bishop's peculiar contribution was to combine the library functions of these great rotundas – themselves the inspiration for the many round library reading rooms which sprang up across Europe and America in the succeeding 150 years – with the form of an ornamental garden building of diminutive scale. It was not, of course, the only element of eccentricity. The phenomenon of the summer library is not wholly unprecedented. There is, for example, a small library in the Chinese Pavilion built in 1766 for Queen Luise Ulrike of Sweden in the grounds of the royal palace at Drottningholm, near Stockholm.[33] The Temple built by Lady Anne Ward at Castle Ward between 1755 and 1760, though not a library, was thought in the 1770s to be 'sweetly calculated for reading and meditation', and recommended as a place to which the studious might 'retire' with a good book borrowed from the Wards' collection.[34] Another possible Irish prototype is the Marino Casino, 'a Dwelling House on a very small Scale' built by Sir William Chambers for the Earl-Bishop's enemy Lord Charlemont between the late 1750s and 1775. Situated just to the north of Dublin in the gardens of the long-vanished Marino House, it too included a small library, being designed not for 'Family Accommodation, but Solitude and Retirement'.[35] The parallels with the Mussenden Temple are obvious, but the Temple's extraordinary conceit is that the Earl-Bishop's place of solitude and retirement was built not in soft and gentle parkland, but on the edge of a 200-foot cliff – in 'a rural and romantic situation', as Shanahan put it – a suitably dramatic venue for the Enlightened reader to sit with his book and contemplate the Sublime as the Atlantic raged below.[36]

The Earl-Bishop was regarded – and clearly liked to regard himself – as an accomplished classical scholar. A pupil of the Latin scholar Vincent Bourne, he embellished more than one of his buildings with a Latin quotation.[37] At Ballyscullion, not far from the point where the River Bann flows north out of Lough Neagh, the frieze was inscribed with an adaptation of a passage from Virgil's *Georgics*:

> Here is a verdant plain;
> I will place a temple of marble
> Besides the waters, where the vast
> Bann strays in sluggish windings,
> And clothes his banks with tender reed.[38]

At Downhill the text ranged in brass letters around the base of the dome was not a traditional *psyches iatreion* ('pharmacy of the soul') found on other libraries, most famously the abbey library at St Gallen in Switzerland, but the couplet which opens part two of Lucretius's *De Rerum Natura*:

> Suave mari magno turbantibus aequora
> Ventis e terra alterius magnum spectare laborem.

In Dryden's translation it reads

> 'Tis pleasant, safely to behold from shore
> The rolling ship, and hear the tempest roar[39]

but more literally: 'It is pleasant to watch from the land the great struggle of another in a sea made great by rushing winds'. A popular quotation cited by authors as varied as St Augustine, Montaigne, Bacon, Archbishop Tillotson, and even by Fielding in his novel *Jonathan Wild* (1725), it carried with it a studied element of ambiguity. At first reading, it seems to imply a callous disregard for the tribulations of others, and no doubt the Earl-Bishop – notorious for practical jokes and for taking pleasure in discomfiting his

Right
The Radcliffe Library, Oxford

guests – took a certain wry amusement if less well-educated visitors read it like that. But Lucretius (c.94–55 BC) had preached Epicureanism, the philosophy that the highest good is pleasure, which is itself identical to the practice of virtue, and the Earl-Bishop's chosen quotation continues (in free translation): 'this is not because one delights from any man's distress, but because it is pleasurable to perceive from what troubles one is oneself free'. Given the elemental grandeur of the Temple's location, it is certainly not surprising that he should have remembered a Latin quotation about the roar of the sea, but the chosen text was entirely appropriate for a place of retreat from the hurly-burly of everyday life. Only by looking down on the seas of ignorance from his Temple on the serene heights of philosophy is it possible for a cultivated man to acquire the lofty detachment which allows the philosopher to see life as it really is.[40]

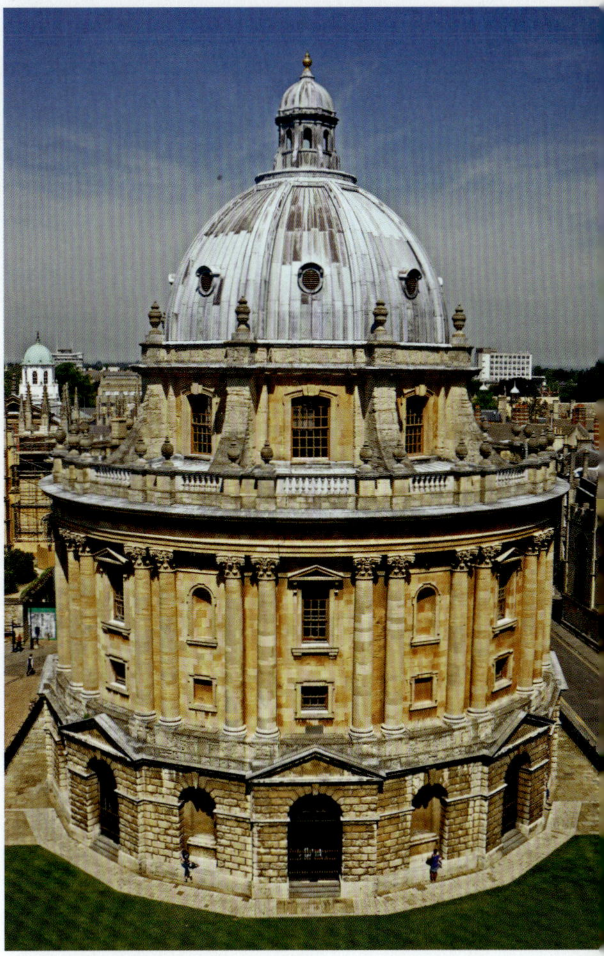

But as so often with the Earl-Bishop, the gap between the Sublime and the absurd was difficult to bridge, and the sheer impracticality of both Downhill and the Temple quickly became apparent. When the Kerry landowner Robert Day passed through Downhill in 1801 he had clambered up the 'elevated abrupt and prominent Cliff' to visit a 'handsome Grecian temple full of valuable but mouldering books, some on shelves and some piled in disorder upon the floor'. Judge Day was 'delighted by the splendid collection of pictures' in Downhill Palace, but critical of the 'misapplication of so much treasure upon a spot where no suitable Demesne can be created, where trees will not grow'. And impressed as he was with 'the costly architecture of the eccentric Mitred Earl', he could not help noticing that 'the salt spray begins already to corrode the sumptuous Pile', and predicting with impressive prescience that 'imagination, anticipating no distant period, weeps over the splendid Ruins, a sad monument of human folly'.[41] In this he was right, as the Palace was burned out in 1851 (deliberately, thought its owner, Sir Henry Hervey Bruce, who offered a reward for information), and though rebuilt by John Lanyon in 1873, it was subsequently unroofed and fell into ruin again in the 1950s.[42] Of the Earl-Bishop's libraries, not a book remains, nor even a catalogue or a list of what was in them. The only remnants are the two books which launched the young John Soane as a collector of architectural books in 1778: a Neapolitan edition of Vitruvius, printed in 1758, and Consul Smith's facsimile of Palladio's *Quattro Libri* issued in Venice in 1767, the first in plain vellum, and the second with the Earl-Bishop's arms in gilt on the covers.[43]

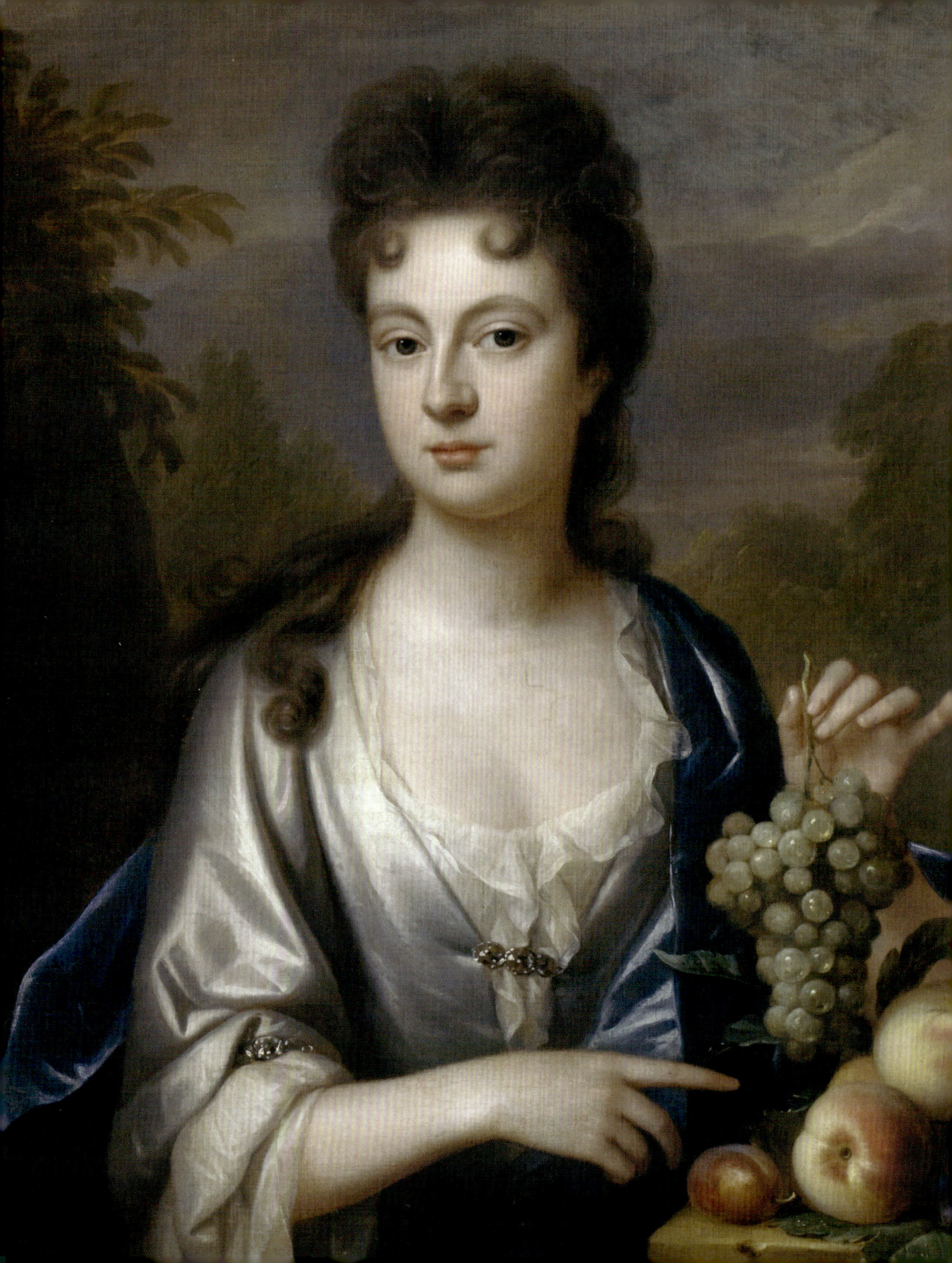

6 Fossils and the Orange Order

Florence Court, County Fermanagh, 1718–2002

Right
Florence Court, County Fermanagh

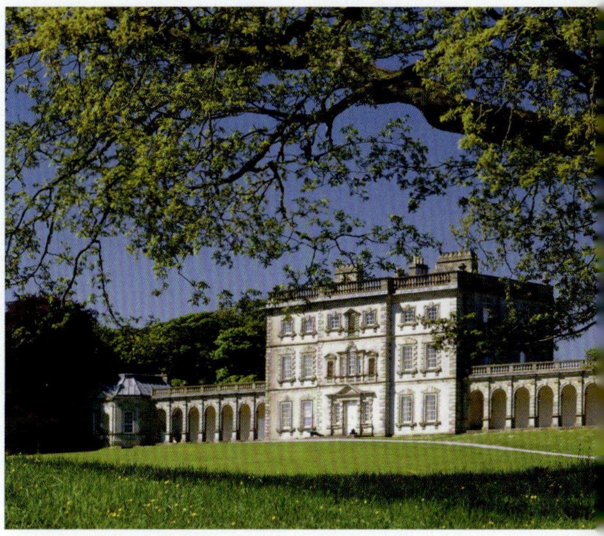

William Cole (1576–1653) arrived in Ireland from Devon in 1600. A professional soldier, by 1609 he was Constable and Governor of Enniskillen, Provost of Enniskillen by 1613, and knighted by James I four years later.[1] The little town had been the royal centre of the Maguires, and standing on an island between Upper and Lower Lough Erne, right in the middle of County Fermanagh, it was of vital strategic importance, commanding one of only three easy routes into Ulster from the rest of Ireland. Plantation Enniskillen was strongly fortified, and Sir William succeeded in holding it for the settlers during the 1641 rising, when most of the surrounding countryside had been recaptured by the Irish.[2] He and his descendants lived on at Enniskillen Castle for almost a century, moving out to nearby Portora only in 1710. Eight years later the Catholic antiquarian John Dolan reported that Sir William's grandson Sir John Cole (1680–1726) – by 1713 worth £1000 a year – had started work on 'very costly and sumptuous buildings on his estate at Clanawley'.[3] Some eight miles south-west of Enniskillen, the new demesne was in a situation of 'majestic wildness', as the Revd William Henry, a local Protestant clergyman, noted with a perhaps surprising degree of approval in 1739.[4] Sir John decided to name it after his wife, the Devonian gentlewoman Florence Bourchier Wrey (1684–1718). Florence Court remains one of the finest surviving Irish Palladian houses, 'a superb and beautiful seat', proclaimed a guidebook in 1784.[5]

Opposite
Florence Bourchier Wrey (1684–1718), English school, *c.*1705–15 (Florence Court)

The architectural history of Florence Court has been the subject of considerable controversy. Traditionally said to have been built between 1756 and 1764 for Sir John Cole's successor and namesake, created Lord Mount Florence in 1760, the house has also been attributed to the German-born Richard Cassels or Castle (1690–1751), who also designed Carton House in County Kildare, Powerscourt, County Wicklow, and Leinster House in Dublin. If this is so, then parts of the present house (including the room which is today the Library) must certainly date from the 1730s.[6] That so grand a house should have been built in a remote corner of south Fermanagh was indicative of the growing confidence of the Protestant Ascendancy in the decades after the Battle of the Boyne. Only a few decades earlier, the mountainous landscape of south-west Ulster had been dominated by tories (*toraidhe* – a raider) and rapparees (*rapaire* – a variety of pike), dispossessed Catholics who had taken to the hills, objects of fear for Irish Protestants.[7]

By contrast, books were seen as part of the apparatus of gentility in Georgian

Opposite
Mottled calf binding and folding plate from Samuel Hayes's *Practical Treatise on Planting* (Dublin, 1794) ESTC N22062 with gold-tooled owner's label

Ireland. If artfully deployed on smart shelves, they might no doubt be useful in putting on a show to impress the neighbours, and indeed at least one Irish house – Newbridge, County Dublin – still has the set of bookbinding tools used to embellish Cobbe family books in the later eighteenth and early nineteenth centuries.[8] Equally, a collection of books provided a focus for sociability and social networking, a reservoir of useful and practical knowledge – from the latest fashions to the administration of the law or the draining of bogs, and of course a place of diversion and amusement; books provided a substitute for company and conversation where none was otherwise to be had.[9] Whether there was a dedicated Library room at Florence Court in the eighteenth century we do not know, though the fact that some members of the Cole family had bookplates printed probably suggests that there was, perhaps in the room to the right of the front hall which still houses the books today. Equally, other books may indeed have been kept in Dublin, where Lord Cole had a residence in Granby Row in 1799, while in later years, reflecting the shift in political gravity after the Union, there was a 'family mansion' in Eaton Square in London.[10] On the face of it, eighteenth-century Fermanagh might perhaps seem an unlikely setting for a fine library, but the county was less of a backwater than might easily be supposed. In 1769 Enniskillen was thought by one visitor to be 'one of the most considerable inland towns in the kingdom'. The small spa at Swanlinbar, four or five miles away in County Cavan, was 'celebrated for its mineral waters' and recommended to Irish patriots in preference to the watery pleasures of Bath or the Continent, while race meetings, with prizes, were held at the nearby town of Belturbet.[11] Belturbet was also the centre of missionary activity, the Church of Ireland rector, Dr John Richardson (1668/9–1747), being a proponent of Irish-speaking preachers and Irish-language books to wean the people away from the old faith – in Protestant eyes a further step on the road to civility.[12] Books were to be found in the residences of the polite right across Fermanagh and Tyrone. Many still survive at nearby Castle Coole, where a homely red-brick house of 1709 – burned out in 1797 – preceded James Wyatt's neo-classical masterpiece.[13] Twenty-five miles away at Clogher, the bibliophile Bishop John Stearne (1660–1745) assembled one of the finest libraries in Ireland, bequeathing his choicer books to Marsh's Library in Dublin 'as a small token of the great regard I have for the bountiful erector and endower of the library', Archbishop Narcissus Marsh (1638–1713). Conscious too of their potential to educate and to improve, after bequests to Trinity College, other books were distributed by lot among the poorer curates of his diocese.[14] Thirty miles away, on the north side of Lower Lough Erne, a library survived at Castle Archdale into the twentieth century, but the Big House there was demolished in 1970, and the books are now long gone. Nonetheless, the surviving Edwardian catalogue reveals a substantial collection deployed in ten large bookcases in the 'Study: to the left of the entrance', with additional books distributed between the Drawing Room and the Morning Room. It seems clear that some at least of these books will have been at

Below
Bookbinding tools from Newbridge, County Dublin (Collection of Alec Cobbe)

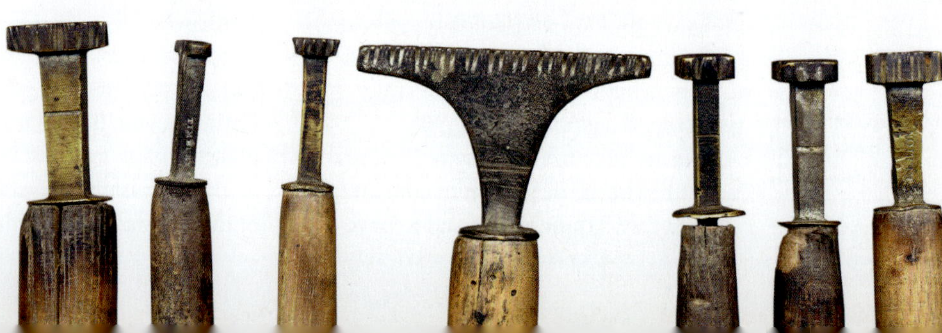

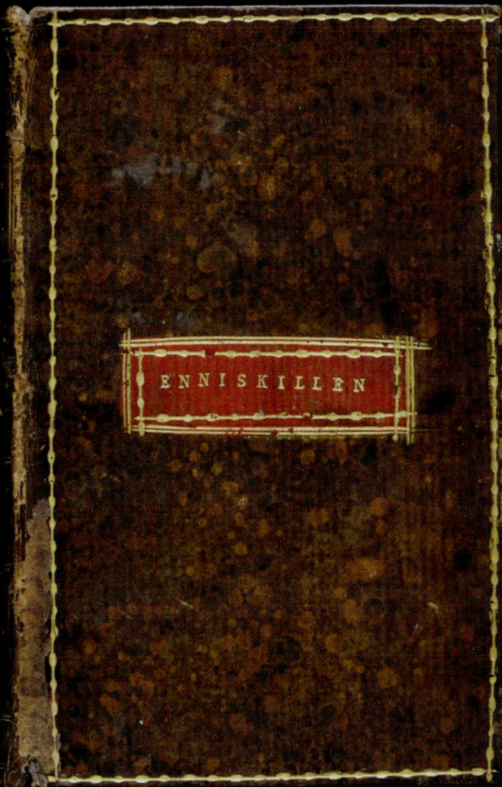

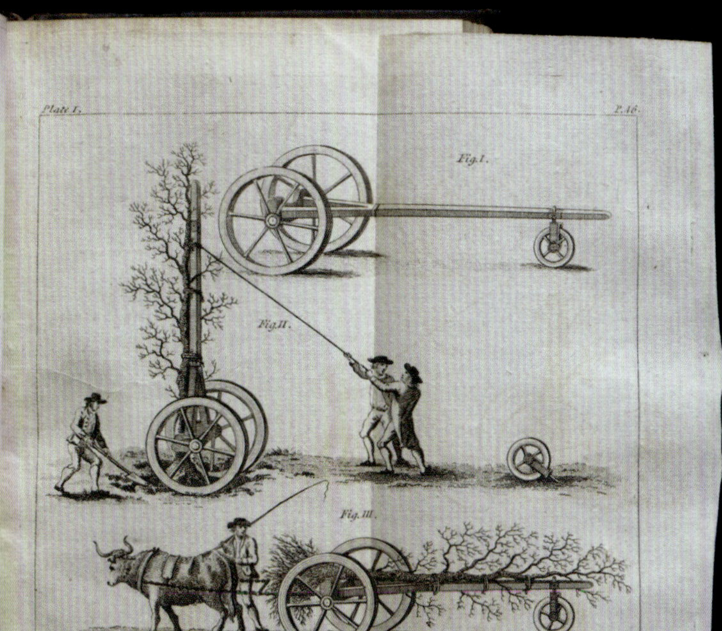

Castle Archdale in Georgian times.[15]

Comparatively few books survive at Florence Court which were demonstrably in the house in the eighteenth century, though the chances of history mean that some of these books are now to be found on the shelves of Cambridge University Library. The earliest family book at Florence Court today is a folio of Archbishop Tillotson's *Works* (London, 1701), which would be unremarkable in itself but for the fact that it originally belonged to Florence Bourchier Wrey. Though her father's bookplate is pasted into the front cover, he cannot have owned it for long, and Florence herself subsequently crossed his name through and replaced it with her own. She was also the owner of a copy of the best-selling devotional book *The Whole Duty of Man* (Oxford, 1704), usually attributed to the Oxford divine Richard Allestree (1619–81). She may perhaps have brought both books when she first came to Ireland from Devon; certainly both are the sort of books which a gentlewoman might have been expected to be reading in the reign of Queen Anne. From slightly later, a handful of books also survives which belonged to Florence's son, John Cole (1709–67), who was created Lord Mount Florence in 1760. Several of these are of specifically Irish interest, ranging from a standard reference book like Lodge's *Peerage of Ireland* (Dublin, 1754) through to the openly polemical such as Archbishop King's *State of the Protestants in Ireland under the Late King James's Government* (Dublin, 1730). More mundane, but of obvious practical utility to an improving landlord, are books like Samuel Hayes's *Practical Treatise on Planting* (Dublin, 1794), illustrated with elegant copperplates, issued under the auspices of the Royal Dublin Society, and smartly bound in mottled calf, with a gold-tooled owner's label on the front cover. This seems to have belonged to Mount Florence's son, the 1st Earl of Enniskillen (1736–1803). A perhaps more surprising find is *Dissertations on the History of Ireland* (Dublin, 1766), by the Catholic antiquarian Charles O'Conor – the very man whom the Earl-Bishop was consulting on Catholic Emancipation at about the same time. Its discussion of ancient Irish history, 'occasional observations on Fingal and Temora', and its fold-out table of the Irish alphabet are none of them topics which one might have expected Lord Mount Florence to find very appealing, but his apparent interest in native Irish history and culture was a theme which was to continue at Florence Court into Victorian times.

By the end of the eighteenth century, the Coles dominated County Fermanagh, exercising a controlling interest in the little borough of Enniskillen. Interestingly enough, the 1st Earl of Enniskillen was not particularly obedient to the wishes of the authorities in Dublin, and was involved in the Volunteer movement. His successor, the 2nd Earl (1768–1840), opposed the Act of Union but for all this was certainly no friend to Irish Catholics. Described by a visitor to Fermanagh in 1801 as 'The Prince of Orange', he presented to the House of Lords a petition against Catholic Emancipation signed by 15,000 Fermanagh Protestants in March 1829.[16] While undoubtedly a man of great wealth when set against his tenants, in 1816 he was grumbling that 'we are horribly poor in this country – no rents. We must all live at home, as we can get no money to go abroad.'[17] And indeed when government officials visited his corner of Fermanagh two decades later, they noted with concern that 'emigration prevails and is increasing'.[18] The books on both agricultural improvement and on foreign travel perhaps reflect these interrelated problems: the one to squeeze more out of difficult terrain, and the other perhaps a substitute for the fashionable Continental tourism which Lord Enniskillen felt his family could not afford.

The career of his son William Willoughby Cole, 3rd Earl of Enniskillen (1807–86), was dominated by twin passions: fossils and the Orange Order. Already an influential politician before the death of his father, he became a prominent public figure in mid-Victorian Ireland, rarely out of the newspapers, and establishing a reputation as a Tory 'ultra' of the most uncompromising views. Serving as Grand Master of the Grand Orange Lodge of Ireland from 1845, the 3rd Earl was Grand Master of the Orange Institution throughout the British Empire from 1866 until his death. The Land League – 'an essentially disloyal organization' as he called it in a public letter to his tenants in 1881 – drew his particular ire; it was, he suggested, 'utterly opposed to the teachings of Christianity and civilization'.[19] Clearly this strong reaction was in part down to the fear that Protestant tenants in Fermanagh might join with their Catholic neighbours in campaigning for land reform, and indeed in 1883 a local newspaper had observed that the whole county, Catholic and Protestant, was 'overrun' by the Land League.[20] Three years earlier, in 1880, the elderly Earl himself had chaired an Orange meeting in Florencecourt village to expel a Protestant farmer from the Order for joining the League.[21] The 3rd Earl's son was, as MP for Enniskillen, the only Tory MP in Ulster to vote against the 1881 Land Act, while in 1885 Lord Enniskillen himself circulated a memorandum to Orange lodges, urging them to organise demonstrations against Gladstone's proposals for Home Rule.[22] As one of the largest landowners in north-west Ireland, with some 30,000 acres, Lord Enniskillen perhaps had more to lose from change than most, and the presence on his shelves of the 1876 official report on land ownership in Ireland surely reflects his concerns for the future.[23] But for all this, his politics were clearly animated by a strong element of religious principle. A staunch supporter of the Church of Ireland, rebuilding nearby Killesher Church in 1883 – a decade and a half after the former state

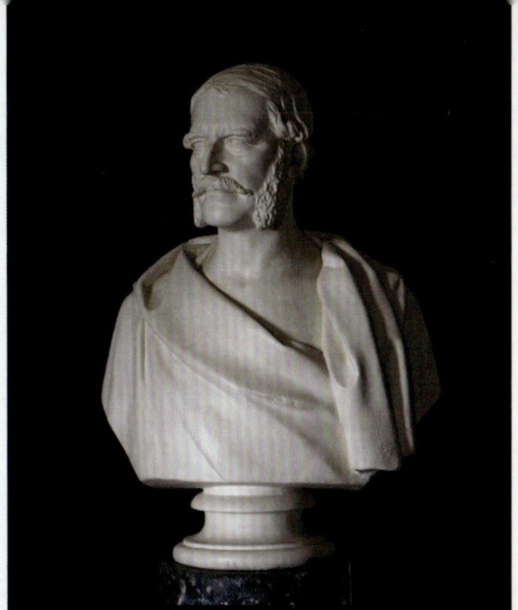

Right
Plaster bust of William Willoughby Cole, 3rd Earl of Enniskillen (Florence Court)

church had been disestablished and partially disendowed in 1869 – Lord Enniskillen was a bitter enemy of the Catholic Church, tabling a petition against government funding of St Patrick's College at Maynooth in 1845.[24] In the aftermath of the so-called Battle of Dolly's Brae – a notorious armed confrontation between Orangemen and Catholics in County Down in 1849, in which at least 30 Catholics were killed [25] – he put his name to the Order's official report on the affair, in which he denounced the Dublin Castle administration for negligence and complacency in the face of the nefarious designs of the Church of Rome:

> It is not that we suppose as yet any definite and positive purpose, on the part of Her Majesty's Government, to betray and crush Protestantism here, but what is more dangerous, that there is a very definite plan to do so, on the part of the Roman Catholic Church body (and, above all, their clergy); and that we look in vain to our rulers for principles, or firmness to resist this constant and powerful pressure.[26]

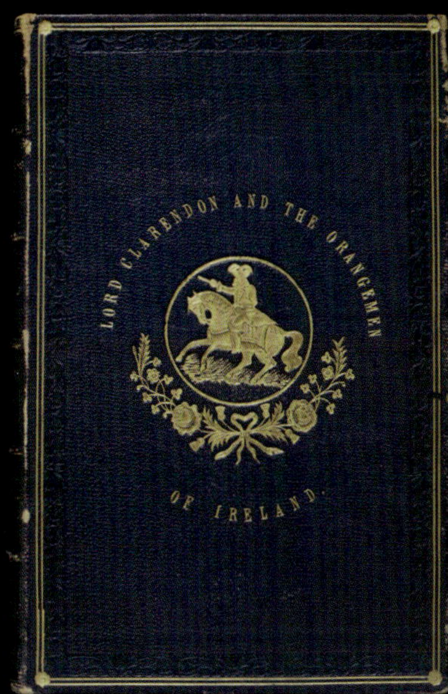

Right
Report of the Special Committee on the Grand Orange Lodge of Ireland (Dublin, 1849), bound with a gold-tooled portrait of King William III (Florence Court)

Lord Enniskillen's own copy of the report is in a special binding, with King Billy tooled in gold on its covers, and is by no means the only piece of Orange memorabilia on the shelves. Among several which speak very powerfully of the more intransigent end of the Irish Protestant spectrum, there are, in particular, many presentation copies. One of the most striking, perhaps, is a Dublin edition of Burnet's *History of the Reformation of the Church of England* (1730–33), a gift from John Leech, Deputy Grand Master of the Orange Order in Scotland, to commemorate 'the anniversary of the proclamation of William + Mary at Edinburg' [sic]. Inside is pasted a contemporary gloss, a small anti-Catholic pamphlet by Robert Leech, *The Secret Monita of the Jesuits* (1858). Another instance is Andrew Hamilton's *Actions of the Enniskillen-Men* (1813), a Belfast reprint of a pamphlet about the defence of the town by Irish Protestants during the Williamite Wars, originally issued in 1690, presented to the 3rd Earl by Robert Jones of Fortland in 1836, who himself bought it at the sale of the 'last bishop of Killalla [*sic*]'. This too would have had a resonance for Lord Enniskillen, not only because of his family's involvement in the battle for Enniskillen, but because the impoverished west coast diocese of Killala, County Mayo, had been abolished by the Irish Church Temporalities Act of 1833. The legislation, tabled by the reforming Whig ministers, alarmed by the profusion of Irish dioceses with minuscule Anglican populations, provoked outrage among Protestants.[27] Lord Enniskillen, who opposed Catholic Emancipation in 1829 and was still opposing Home Rule in 1885, would certainly have viewed the Act as one more betrayal of Irish Protestants by dangerous radicals in London. The bishop in question, James Verschoyle (1750–1837), also a Canon of St Patrick's Cathedral in Dublin, was the descendant of a Dutch family resident in Ireland since the sixteenth century.

Below
The pavilion at the far end of the colonnade housed the 3rd Earl's museum of fish fossils at Florence Court

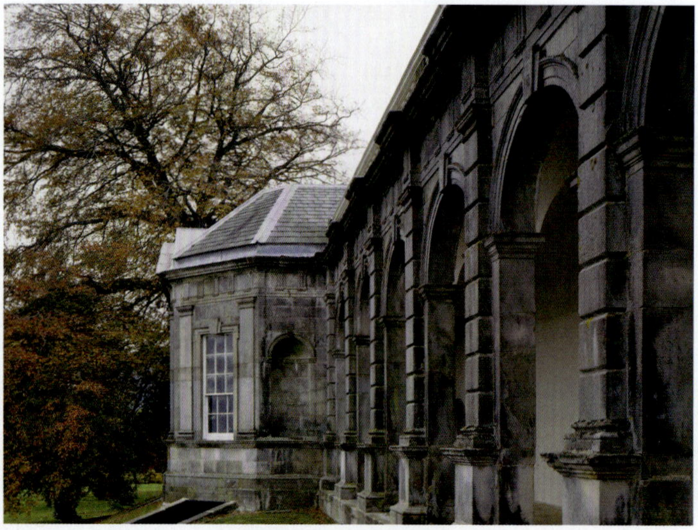

No doubt Lord Enniskillen was as glad to have the book as he would have been appalled by the abolition of ten of the Church of Ireland's 22 bishoprics.

Enniskillen's other great passion was geology. As an undergraduate at Oxford, he had been profoundly influenced by the eccentric William Buckland (1784–1856), the University's first reader in geology, famous for his exotic pets – he owned a tame bear called Tiglath-Pileser – and for his declared intention to eat his way through the entire animal kingdom.[28] Though Enniskillen himself published nothing other than a catalogue of his own collection, he devoted much of his life to amassing an extraordinary museum of fossils, numbering almost 10,000 specimens, which were stored in specially-converted accommodation in the south pavilion of Florence Court.[29] The passion evidently started early in life. By 1830 the fossils were already being described as 'one of the best private geological collections in the United Kingdom, perhaps in Europe.'[30] The Earl went on collecting trips, and in 1835 it was a matter of common gossip that he had taken a house in Lyme Regis, 'that part of the coast of Dorset being particularly rich in … geological curiosities.'[31] Interestingly, the Earl's private museum was not the only one of its kind in Fermanagh, the staff of the Irish Ordnance Survey noting on a visit to nearby Castle Caldwell in the 1830s that 'the drawing room is used as a museum containing stuffed specimens of beasts, birds, fishes of various countries, also a great collection of ancient coins, manuscripts.'[32]

The fossils attracted visitors to Florence Court from all over Europe, though when Lord Enniskillen became blind in old age, the whole collection was sold to the British Museum for £3,500, and now forms one of the foundation collections of the Natural History Museum in London. Some visitors – like the biologist Louis Compton Miall (1842–1921), curator of the Museum of the Leeds Philosophical Society, who came to Florence Court in 1875 – travelled over from England.[33] Others were from further afield, and the Swiss palaeontologist and geologist Louis Agassiz (1807–73) was a particular friend of Lord Enniskillen. A sceptic on evolution, Agassiz was the first man to suggest that there had been an Ice Age, and that the landscape had been shaped by glaciation, but was also a leading proponent of nineteenth-century scientific racism, a belief system which won him many admirers in *ante bellum* America following his relocation to the United States in 1846.[34] Agassiz presented Enniskillen with books and a large number of scientific pamphlets and offprints, including his paper *Glacial Phenomena in Maine* (Boston, 1867), and his *Geological Sketches* (Boston, 1866–76), and the Earl also owned a copy of his *Essay on Classification* (London, 1859). A copy of the first edition of Darwin's *Narrative of the Surveying Voyages of His Majesty's Ships Adventure and Beagle between the Years 1826 and 1836* (London, 1839) is unfortunately no longer at Florence Court, but many books on related subjects have survived. Some seem to have been textbooks from the Earl's youth: books like Sir Henry De La Beche's *A Geological Manual* (London,

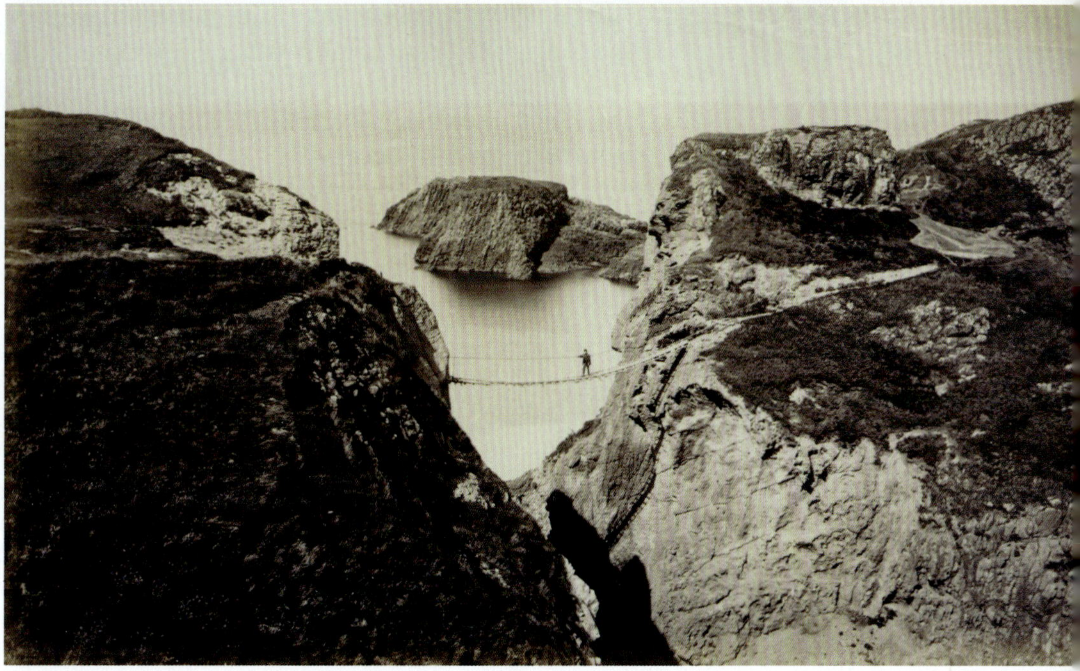

Right
Photographic plate from John Hudson's *Photographs of the Giant's Causeway* (Glasgow, 1867) (Florence Court)

1831) – the author born in the fossil-rich environment of Lyme Regis, and Director of the Geological Survey of Great Britain – Thomas Thomson's *Outlines of Mineralogy, Geology, and Mineral Analysis* (London, 1836) and William Chapman Hewitson's *British Oology* (Newcastle, 1833–42), with lithographic plates of the eggs calculated to whet the appetite of the collector. Others have a very definite local tinge, including most obviously Robert Mallet's *The Dynamics of Earthquakes* (Dublin, 1846) one of the founding texts of seismology, its author the President of the Royal Geological Society of Ireland from 1846 to 1848 – and Joseph Ellison Portlock's *Report on the Geology of the County of Londonderry, and of Parts of Tyrone and Fermanagh* (Dublin, 1843). An employee of the Ordnance Survey of Ireland, Portlock (1794–1864) worked for the Ordnance Office in Ireland from 1825 to 1843, but his volume on these northern counties was the only one of his surveys to make it into print.[35] More striking perhaps than any of these is Lord Enniskillen's volume of *Photographs of the Giant's Causeway* (Glasgow, 1867), a spectacular photographically-illustrated book, with twelve mounted plates of the north coast of Ireland by the Killarney photographer John Hudson.[36]

Something of the full range of Lord Enniskillen's interests comes across from the number of learned societies with which he was associated. In the course of a long and active life he served as Vice-President of the Numismatic Society and Vice-President of both the Geological Society of

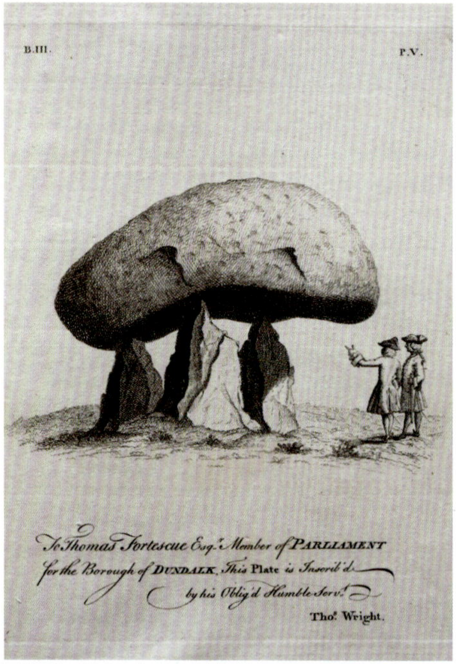

Right
Thomas Wright, *Louthiana: or, an Introduction to the Antiquities of Ireland* (London, 1758), ESTC T145624 (Florence Court)

Dublin and the Archaeological Institute in Dublin. It would be easy to assume from this that these positions were essentially honorific, but press reports make it clear that Lord Enniskillen was sometimes an active participant at meetings. A Fellow of the Society of Antiquaries of London, in 1843, for example, he exhibited an ancient 'brass vessel found in Ireland', said to resemble a coffee pot.[37] Occasionally he seems to have dabbled in more exotic pursuits, presenting a Pali manuscript on ivory to the British Museum.[38] In Ireland, he was a generous donor to the Museum of the Royal Irish Academy (its contents now absorbed into the National Museum in Dublin), presenting antiquities as various as a double comb and a pair of iron manacles discovered in the crannog (ancient lake dwelling) of Lough Laoghaire, near Clogher, County Tyrone (1845), a stone hammer found in County Cavan (1869), and a sepulchral urn (1880) from Belcoo, on the Fermanagh-Cavan border. He also presented a bronze sword found in the Barony of Lurg, in west Fermanagh, to the Museum of Practical Geology in Jermyn Street in London; it arrived at the National Museum with other objects from Jermyn Street in 1901.[39]

These broad-ranging interests are very strongly represented on his shelves, with books on coins and medals, as well as on historical and antiquarian topics, particularly Irish history, architecture and antiquities. At first sight, many of these seem to contrast strangely with Lord Enniskillen's political outlook, but of course his life and career coincided with a period of dramatic changes in Irish intellectual life. Dying in 1886, seven years before the foundation of the Gaelic League in 1893, Lord Enniskillen lived at a time when it was still not only possible but positively conventional for clever Irish aristocrats to combine a passionate political allegiance to the British Empire with an equal passion for the history, antiquities and culture of Ireland, and with the ownership of books like George Petrie's *Christian Inscriptions in the Irish Language* (Dublin, 1871–8). Only with the growing polarisation of the next generation were these two strands to become for many increasingly incompatible. For most, Irishness became equated with Catholicism and political nationalism, and other traditions simply had no place in the new dispensation; for others, mostly Protestant, an interest in the Celtic past and especially the Irish language became so closely associated with the repudiation of the British connection and with disloyalty to the Crown that such enthusiasms could lose their allure.

Lord Enniskillen was particularly associated with research into crannogs, in the very last year of his life buying a copy of W.G. Wood-Martin's *Lake Dwellings of Ireland* (Dublin, 1886), a subject which he had himself investigated in collaboration with the Enniskillen antiquarian William Frederick Wakeman (1822–1900), whose *Archaeologia Hibernica* (Dublin, 1848) is in the library. The pair deposited the antiquities they found in the museum of the Royal Historical and Archaeological Society of Ireland in 1870 and 1871.[40] Some of the

Right
Henry O'Neill, *Illustrations of the Most Interesting of the Sculptured Crosses of Ancient Ireland* (London, 1857) (Florence Court)

Far right
Photographic plate from Arthur Hill's *Monograph of Cormac's Chapel, Cashel* (Cork, 1874) (Florence Court)

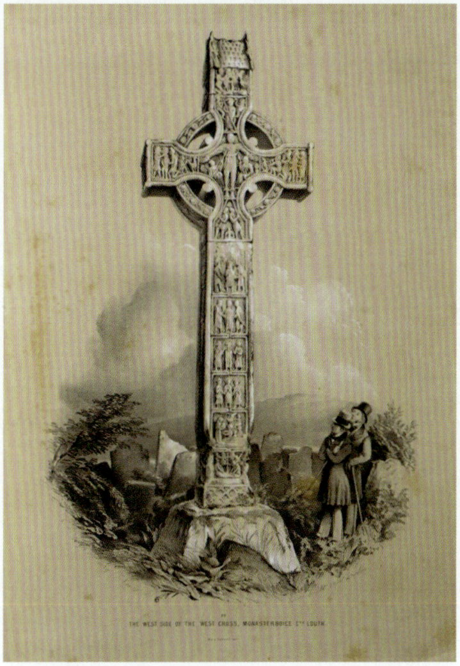

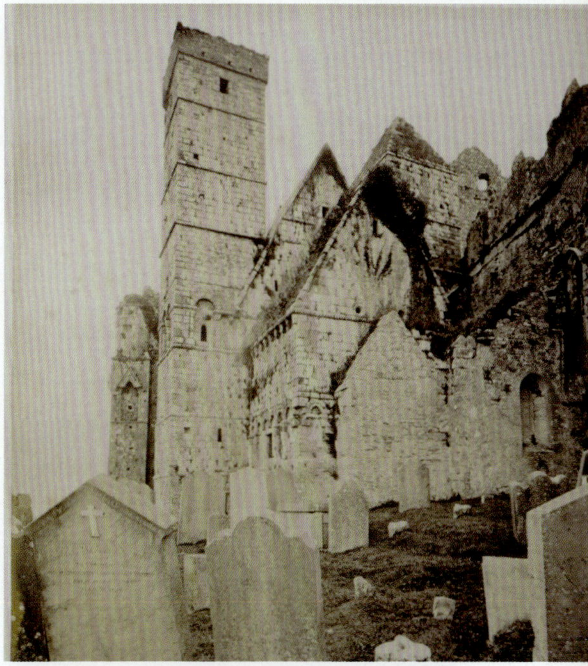

Right
An Augustinian nun, as illustrated in Mervyn Archdall, *Monasticon Hibernicon* (Dublin, 1786), ESTC T145669 (Florence Court)

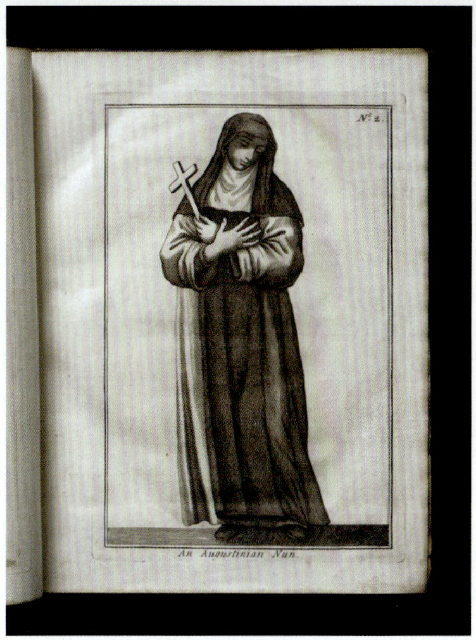

books on the shelves clearly reflect these archaeological interests, though one, Thomas Wright's *Louthiana* (London, 1758) – the first of two intended volumes on the antiquities of County Louth – has a further connection with Florence Court. The author, an Englishman and a native of County Durham, visited Ireland in 1746, moving in polite circles, designing garden features rather in the style of William Kent, and teaching astronomy, surveying and mathematics. He visited Florence Court, where he dined with 'Mr Cole' (the future Lord Mount Florence) and designed a rustic thatched arbour which survived long enough to be photographed in 1860.[41] More predictable staples include ordinary, everyday books like Froude's *The English in Ireland in the Eighteenth Century* (London, 1872–74), but there are also books which are and were more obviously collectable. Henry O'Neill's *Illustrations of the Most Interesting of the Sculptured Crosses of Ancient Ireland* (London, 1857) is one of the larger and more spectacular examples. O'Neill (1798–1880) belonged to O'Connell's Repeal Association and painted the Liberator in Richmond Jail in 1843, but his politics evidently did not deter Lord Enniskillen, who was presumably attracted both by the magnificent lithographic plates and by the subject matter.[42] In rather similar vein is *A Monograph of Cormac's Chapel, Cashel* (Cork, 1874), which again took advantage of new technology with a lithographic title-page, lithographic and photo-lithographic plates, and

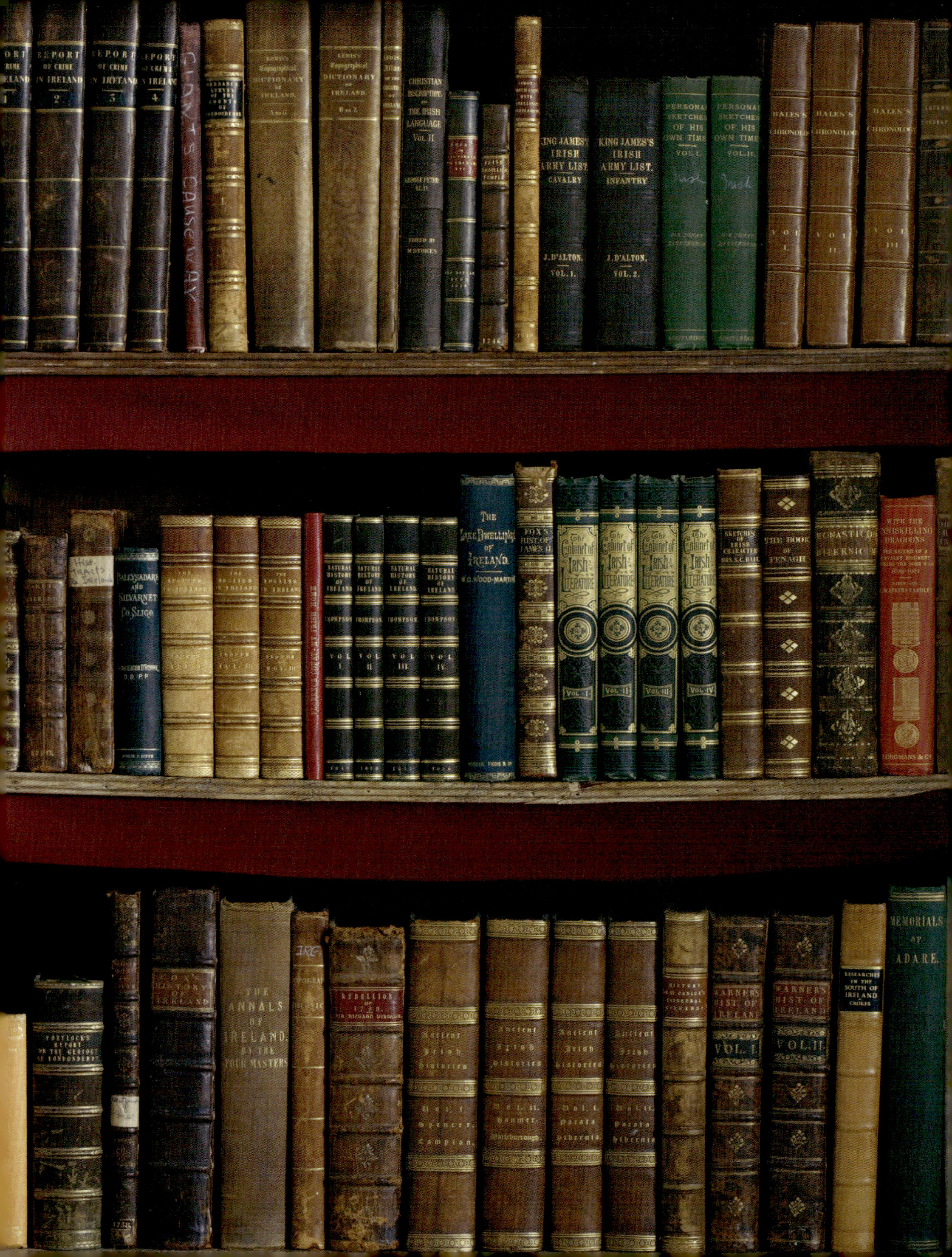
REPORT OF CRIME IN IRELAND 2
REPORT OF CRIME IN IRELAND 3
REPORT OF CRIME IN IRELAND 4
GIANT'S CAUSEWAY
LEWIS'S Topographical DICTIONARY OF IRELAND
CHRISTIAN INSCRIPTIONS IN THE IRISH LANGUAGE VOL. II
KING JAMES'S IRISH ARMY LIST. CAVALRY J. D'ALTON. VOL. 1.
KING JAMES'S IRISH ARMY LIST. INFANTRY J. D'ALTON. VOL. 2.
PERSONAL SKETCHES OF HIS OWN TIME VOL. I.
PERSONAL SKETCHES OF HIS OWN TIME VOL. II.
HALES'S CHRONOLOGY
BALLYSADARE AND KILVARNET CO. SLIGO
NATURAL HISTORY OF IRELAND THOMPSON
THE LAKE DWELLINGS OF IRELAND W. G. WOOD-MARTIN
FOX'S HIST. OF JAMES II
The Cabinet of Irish Literature
SKETCHES OF IRISH CHARACTER MRS. S. C. HALL
THE BOOK OF FENAGH
MONASTICON HIBERNICUM
WITH THE INNISKILLING DRAGOONS
LONGMANS & CO
PORTLOCK'S REPORT ON THE GEOLOGY OF LONDONDERRY
FOX'S HISTORY OF IRELAND
THE ANNALS OF IRELAND, BY THE FOUR MASTERS
REBELLION OF 1798
Ancient Irish Histories
WARNER'S HIST. OF IRELAND VOL. I.
WARNER'S HIST. OF IRELAND VOL. II.
RESEARCHES IN THE SOUTH OF IRELAND CROKER
MEMORIALS OF ADARE

Opposite
The collection of Hibernica at Florence Court

Right
John Ray, *L'Histoire Naturelle, eclairie dans une de Ses Parties Principales, l'Ornithologie* (Paris, 1767), plate 6, drawn and engraved by François Nicolas Martinet (b. 1731) and coloured by Jacques de Seve (1742–88) (Florence Court)

two original photographs of what is one of the most magnificent Irish Romanesque buildings. Lord Enniskillen was a subscriber; the author, the Cork architect Arthur Hill (1846–1921), produced a number of short monographs on similar topics. From more than a century earlier, (and with Fermanagh connections), is Mervyn Archdall's *Monasticon Hibernicon* (Dublin, 1786) – hailed by contemporaries as an Irish counterpart to William Dugdale's *Monasticon Anglicanum* (1655) – with its eighteen fantastical copperplates of Irish monks and nuns a surprising find in the library of a staunch Orangeman.

Despite the substantial array of earlier books at Florence Court, it seems clear that the library there was substantially the creation of the 3rd Earl in the nineteenth century. No documentation survives on the fitting-up of the Library room, but on stylistic grounds there seems to be little doubt that it dates from the first half of the nineteenth century. It is interesting not only that Florence Court was the only Big House in Fermanagh whose library was specifically mentioned in the memoirs submitted by the officers of Irish Ordnance Survey ('about 3000 volumes and contains some very rare works on Irish history and antiquities'), but also that the reports seem to imply that they were shown over the books by the future Earl of Enniskillen, then Lord Cole.[43] Though considerably interfered with in modern times (the original paint finishes appear to have been stripped from the shelves, either by the Enniskillens in the first half of the twentieth century, or by the National Trust in the early days of its ownership, and the library busts are also a recent and perhaps unnecessary introduction), it is still possible to form some impression of how this room might once have been used. Through much of the nineteenth century, Florence Court was frequently packed with visitors. Some, indeed, visited to see the fossils, but more frequently the guests were friends and family. In February 1833 the *Belfast News-Letter* reported to its readers that the 2nd Earl was 'keeping up old Irish hospitality at his splendid mansion Florencecourt – the noble host being never so happy as when surrounded by his friends'.[44] The previous year, readers of another newspaper learned that the house was 'crowded with company' over the summer of 1832, while in 1835

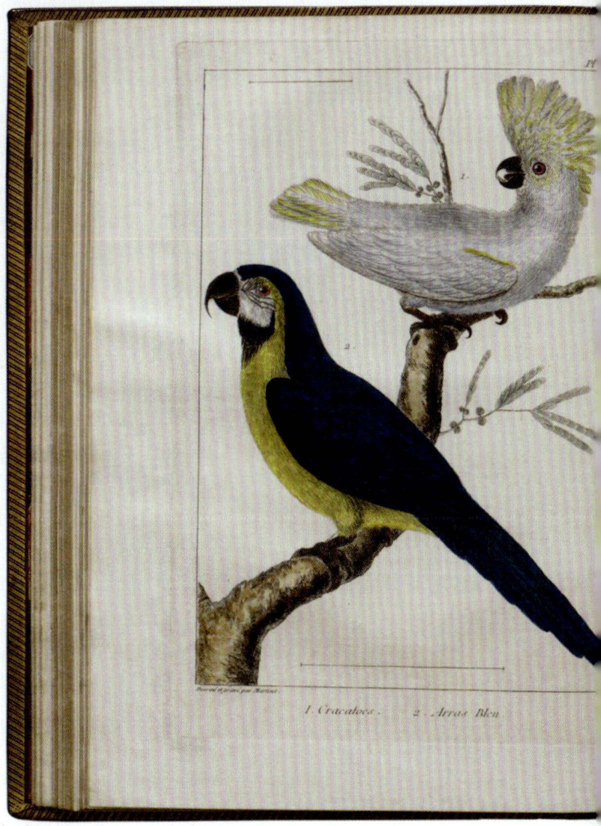

it was reported that 'a great number of distinguished visitors was expected at the house' for Christmas.[45] The more apparently mundane books – like the novels of Walter Scott, the poems of Tennyson, Sir Theodore Martin's biography of the Prince Consort – no doubt came into their own on such occasions, though in truth we do not really know whether the Library was open to all-comers, or whether is was essentially Lord Enniskillen's private study and work room. Nor do we know whether Richard Lovell Edgeworth's copy of the first edition of *Pride and Prejudice* (London, 1813), now at Cambridge, arrived at Florence Court as a collectable, or whether it was simply a secondhand reading copy whose provenance was of no particular interest. At the very least it seems possible that a man like the 3rd Earl's chaplain, the Revd Edward Labatt, might occasionally have ridden over from Manorhamilton, County Leitrim, to check a reference for a sermon.[46] Even the rows of the *Quarterly Review, Annals of Natural History,* or *The Numismatic Chronicle, The Dublin University Magazine* and *The Transactions of the Zoological Society of London* (too easily assumed to have been 'bought by the yard') hint clearly at the need to maintain contact with metropolitan culture and to keep abreast of current developments in the worlds of culture, high society and scholarship.

The geologist Earl was succeeded by his son and grandson, the 4th (1845–1924) and the 5th Earls. The family remained in Ireland after Partition in 1921, though the border was close at hand, and the future of Florence Court in Northern Ireland must have seemed in doubt during the deliberations of the Boundary Commission in 1924 and 1925. After the Second World War, Florence Court was given to the National Trust in 1954 by Michael, Lord Cole (1921–54), with the support and agreement of his father, the 5th Earl of Enniskillen (1877–1963). It was not a moment too soon, as much of the house was gutted by fire in 1955, and the Trust then commissioned Sir Albert Richardson to repair it.[47] Richardson's work now seems heavy-handed, with a large part of Florence Court's nineteenth-century history purged away in favour of a bland neo-Georgian which bears only a fairly superficial resemblance to what was there before, and several of the interiors restored on a cost-cutting basis. But the house did at least survive, and had it remained in private hands the family would surely have had little option but to call in the demolition squads. When the old Earl died eight years later, the title passed to his nephew, David Lowry Cole, 6th Earl of Enniskillen (1918–89), who grew up in Kenya, and spent much of his adult life there. From 1963, the 6th Earl and his 'somewhat formidable' American second wife Nancy MacLennan lived at Florence Court, though as the decade progressed, relations with the National Trust became increasingly strained. Books were one of many bones of contention. The Enniskillens expressed concern that the library – not originally intended to be accessible to the public – was not adequately protected from marauding Trust visitors; eventually some of the more valuable books were removed for safekeeping to the nearby Killymanawley House. Reading the 40-year-old correspondence, once gets a definite sense that the Enniskillens valued their privacy – and understandably wanted post-war comforts like efficient central heating. National Trust officials, on the other hand, were understandably conscious that the Trust had recently rebuilt Florence Court at considerable cost, and that the demesne had been endowed by the Northern Ireland taxpayer, and had to be seen to be welcoming to visitors. The ongoing Troubles in a sensitive Border area probably did nothing to engender co-operative co-existence, and after ten years, the fragile accommodation broke down completely. When Trust officials visited Florence Court in the early 1970s, it is said that they were not offered sherry. In 1973 matters finally came to a head, and the Enniskillens left, taking almost all of the historic contents of the house with them.[48]

The National Trust did its best to furnish Florence Court with suitable contents, but for the next 25 years it remained a pale shadow of its former self. That is how it seemed certain that things would remain, but in 1997 there was an

Below
Florence Court, engraved in 1786 by Thomas Milton, from his *A Collection of Select Views from the Different Seats of the Nobility and Gentry in the Kingdom of Ireland* (Dublin, 1782-93)

unexpected rapprochement with Lady Enniskillen, who presented some of the principal historic contents in memory of her husband, who had died eight years previously. On her own death in 1999, the National Trust was able to purchase many more items from the executors. In a turn of events that might scarcely have been believed a few years earlier, these returned to Florence Court amid great rejoicing in the early years of the new millennium. The books, however, presented one of the most complex challenges. Some had already been sold in Edinburgh in 1986, but matters were complicated further because the principal legatee of the estate was Lord Enniskillen's *alma mater*, the University of Cambridge.[49] The Bradshaw collection in the University Library, originally the family collection of the incunabulist Henry Bradshaw, Librarian at Cambridge between 1867 and 1886, is often said to be the finest collection of Irish books in the world outside Ireland.[50] Unsurprisingly, therefore, Cambridge decided to retain many of the former Florence Court books, and has kept them together as a named collection. Many of the rest were purchased by the National Trust in 2000, where they now fill almost exactly half the nineteenth-century Library shelves. With the aid of various friends and benefactors (including the Northern Ireland Museums Council, the Friends of the National Libraries and the Fermanagh Association of the National Trust), further books continue to be added to the collection, ranging from geological and scientific offprints to books on travel and the Gothic revival, and most spectacularly of all the 3rd Earl's copy of the first French edition of John Ray's *Natural History* (Paris, 1767), in a splendid eighteenth-century red morocco binding and with 32 magnificent hand-coloured plates.

There are now some 1200 Florence Court books in public collections, of which half are in Cambridge and half at Florence Court itself. Though this does not represent all the books which were in the house in the nineteenth century, it certainly does appear to be a substantial proportion of the '3000 volumes' noted by the Ordnance Survey in the 1830s.

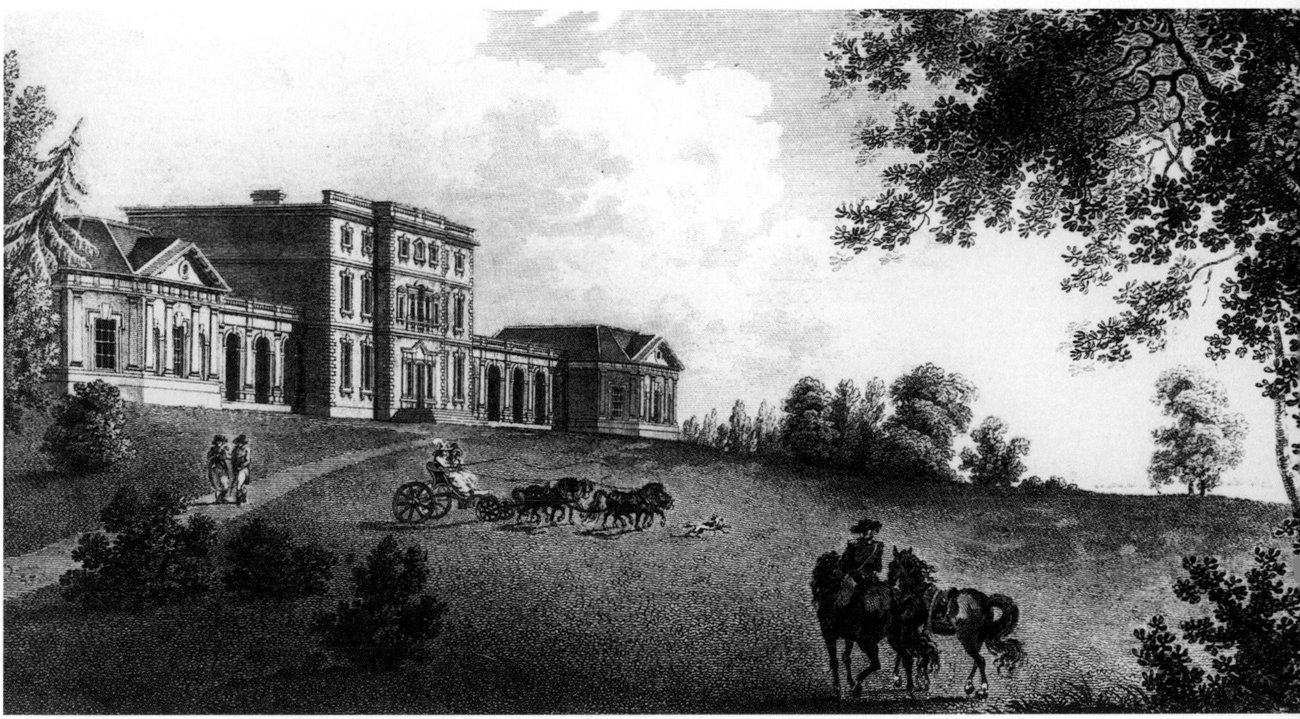

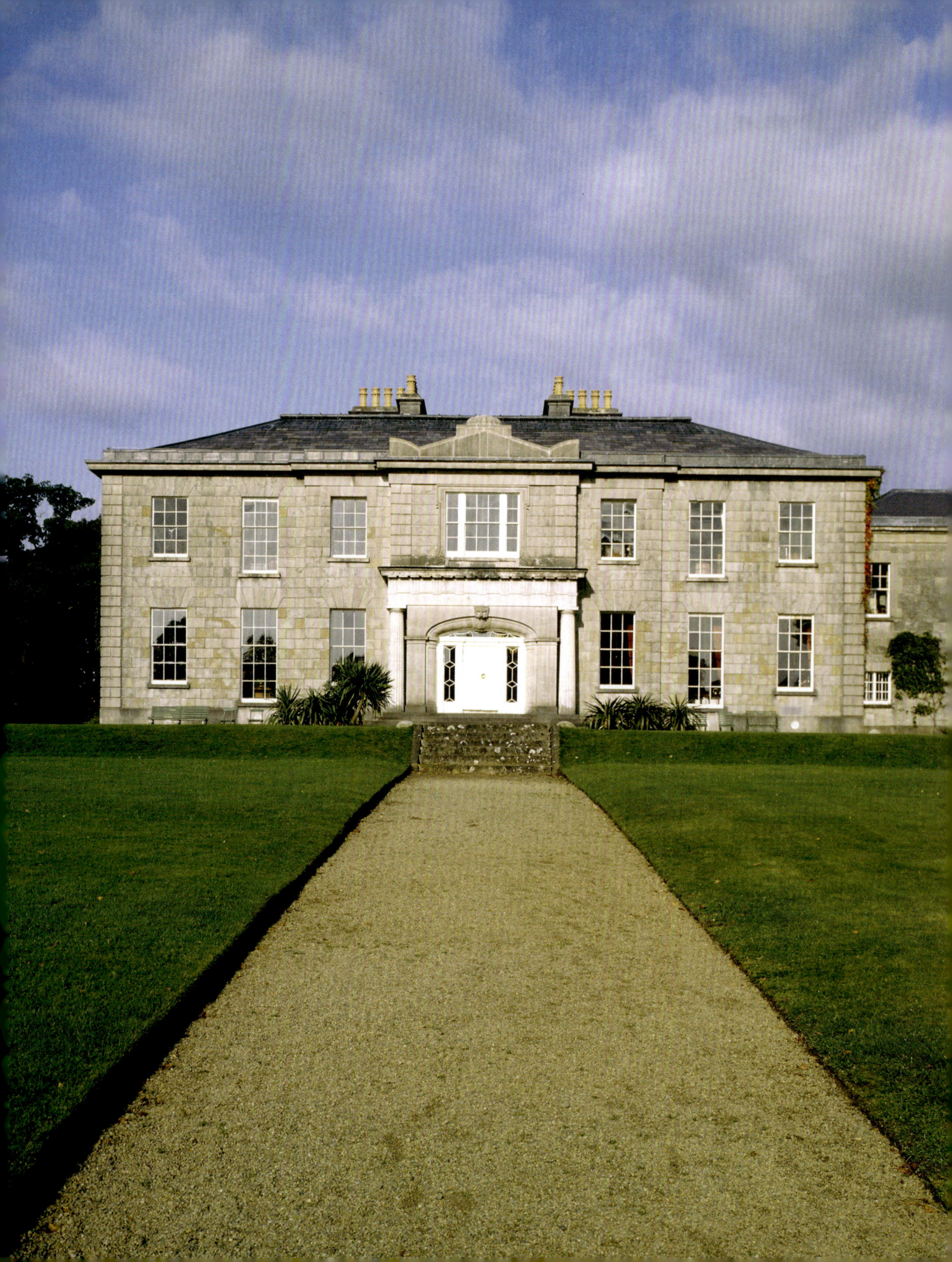

7 I Sent a Horseman to Dungannon for the Fire Brigade

The Argory, County Armagh, 1898

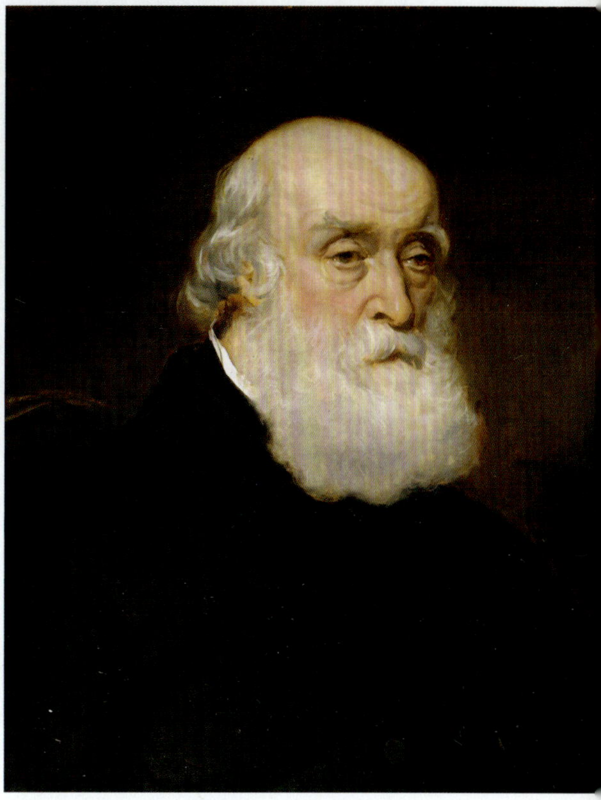

Right
Walter McGeough Bond (1790–1866), by Sir Francis Grant (The Argory)

On the morning of 3 June 1898, Henry Alexander penned an urgent letter to the County Armagh landowner Captain Ralph Shelton.[1] Captain Shelton's precise whereabouts being unknown, his agent's letter was forwarded to the Kildare Street Club, bastion of the Ascendancy in Dublin, in the hope that it would find its way to the intended recipient. Presumably it did, as the Captain was a resourceful man, whose chief claim to fame was surviving the wreck of the troop ship the *Birkenhead* by the simple expedient of 'keeping his trousers on (the sharks having first attacked those without protection)'.[2] Within a generation, gentry houses would be burning all over Ireland, but the house fire which Henry Alexander was writing to report was entirely accidental, originating, so he thought, 'from the kitchen flue in some way that I cannot clearly say.' A large part of The Argory had burned down.

The demesne at The Argory, once known as Derrycaw, was situated in the north of County Armagh, not far from the border with County Tyrone. It had belonged to Ralph Shelton's family since the 1740s, though the main family residence had long been at Drumsill, also in County Armagh. Only in the third decade of the nineteenth century had Shelton's father Walter McGeough[3] – prevented from living at Drumsill by a tiresome family will allocating the house there to his three unmarried sisters – constructed a sturdy Greek Revival house, designed in the most up-to-date taste by the Dublin architects Arthur and John Williamson.[4] This house was evidently not found substantial enough, and by 1834 a large north wing, complete with a substantial octagonal Library, had been grafted onto the original four-square main block, to which it was linked by a single-storey passage. It was this wing which was gutted in the 1898 fire. Nothing is known about the contents of its shelves, but the report which Henry Alexander sent to the Kildare Street Club the morning after its destruction provides a vivid description of its final hours.

Hurriedly scribbled in pencil ('I hope you can read it', as Alexander put it in the covering note), the agent's report

Opposite
The Argory, County Armagh

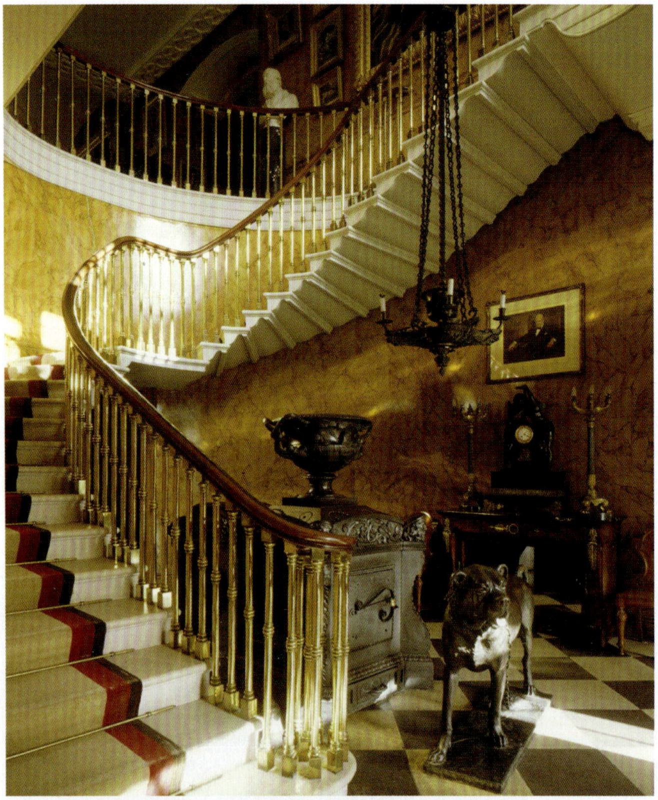

Above
The West Hall, The Argory

was based on a series of interviews with the resident staff: the steward Isaac Allen, a Miss Buchanan (evidently the housekeeper), the cook Ann Rafferty, an odd job man called Tommy Sloan, and 'two female servants', Annie Mulholland and Louisa Lee. The fire seems to have started in the small hours, and at about half past three the under-housemaid, Annie Mulholland, 'heard a crackling sound'. Alarmed, she immediately roused Ann Rafferty, and then dressed before going downstairs to alert Tommy Sloan, who usually slept in a room off the Pantry. It was Tommy who then roused the others, waking Miss Buchanan with a loud shout of 'House on fire'. He then attempted to turn a hose on the flames, but evidently without very much effect, as one of the other servants later observed, either because he was 'too nervous', or more likely because there was insufficient water pressure. By a quarter to four Isaac Allen had emerged and taken charge of proceedings, ordering the house bell to be rung, and mustering a group of 'about 10' men 'with buckets' to try to stem the blaze. By then the corridor linking the north wing to the main part of the house was burning, and two of its windows were broken in a frantic attempt to douse the flames. Under the steward's direction, water was thrown at the conflagration 'continuously from 4 till 8 o'clock', but it made little difference. He himself opened up the strong room to rescue the house silver, while at the time a team of around 40 men from the estate were set to work to clear from the house as many of the contents as could be rescued.

While all this was still going on, Allen somehow found time to send a man on horseback the five miles across country to Dungannon to call for the assistance of the local fire brigade. In the very same year an official report had heavily criticised the Belfast Fire Brigade for its inefficiency and poor organisation, and it seems unlikely that the men from Dungannon would have been any better.[5] They were certainly not fast in responding, and it was not until eight in the morning – four and a half hours after the fire had first been detected – that they finally arrived 'with their hand pump', accompanied by officers of the Royal Irish Constabulary.[6] The house water supply had long since failed, but the house pump was still working, and with the help of the Dungannon men the fire was finally brought under control. The main block of the house had survived, but the north wing, including the octagonal Library and its books, was destroyed. Subsequently generations of the McGeough Bond family succeeded in assembling a very large collection of mostly nineteenth- and twentieth-century books at The Argory, and some earlier books were transferred there from Drumsill – where there was certainly a library in 1817 – but there is no longer a proper Library room, and the books are scattered all over the house.[7]

Reading the accounts of the fire – and written as they were in such haste, it is clear that they are verbatim accounts, and it is almost possible to hear the voices of those involved – several things are immediately striking. In the first place, there is no mistaking the raw shock of the morning after a frightening night without sleep, with the various servants' accounts tumbling out in a stream of sometimes confused words. Then, in the confusion of the moment, there is the slowness of the initial reaction to the conflagration, with very nearly half an hour elapsing between Annie Mulholland hearing a crackling sound and the steward Allen taking command of the situation. Late Victorian standards of decorum and propriety clearly played a part, with Annie Mulholland – as under-housemaid at the bottom of the pecking order – evidently willing to wake the cook while still in her nightwear, but clearly deeming it essential that she put on proper clothes and make herself decent before going downstairs and going anywhere near the sleeping quarters of a more junior male servant like Tommy Sloan. In the rigidly hierarchical world of the servants' hall, segregated by sex to prevent impropriety and with the servants of house guests seated by precedence according to the rank of their employers, it seems unlikely that she was the only one who would have hesitated to disturb her betters or cause too much of a commotion without being absolutely sure what was going on. Equally, it is very striking that Allen and the other servants appear to have made no attempt to save books from the Library, or even to investigate their fate. In part, this may simply be a reflection of the fact that the flames took hold of the octagon so quickly that there was simply no opportunity to do anything else. The following day's press reports noted that 'while the valuable contents of the Library were destroyed', some of the Library furniture was apparently 'easily removed', and it seems curious that it was possible to extract bulky furniture but apparently none of the books.[8] This said, it seems clear that none of the servants was especially interested in the Library, each being very much more preoccupied with their own familiar provinces – the steward with his silver, while Ann Rafferty and her staff made shift to rescue china from the Pantry, even as 'timber was falling from the Library floor and the roof almost falling in'. In so doing, their reaction was broadly similar to that of their counterparts a generation later during the house burnings of the Irish Civil War.

At Spiddal, the County Mayo house of Lord Killanin, when the house was torched by Republican forces in 1923, the raiders gave the cook and Alice the housemaid precisely ten minutes to salvage what they could. The two servants naturally rescued the kitchen pots and pans and the contents of the linen cupboards, including covers for beds and other furniture which were about to go up in smoke. The owner's sister later recalled events with some

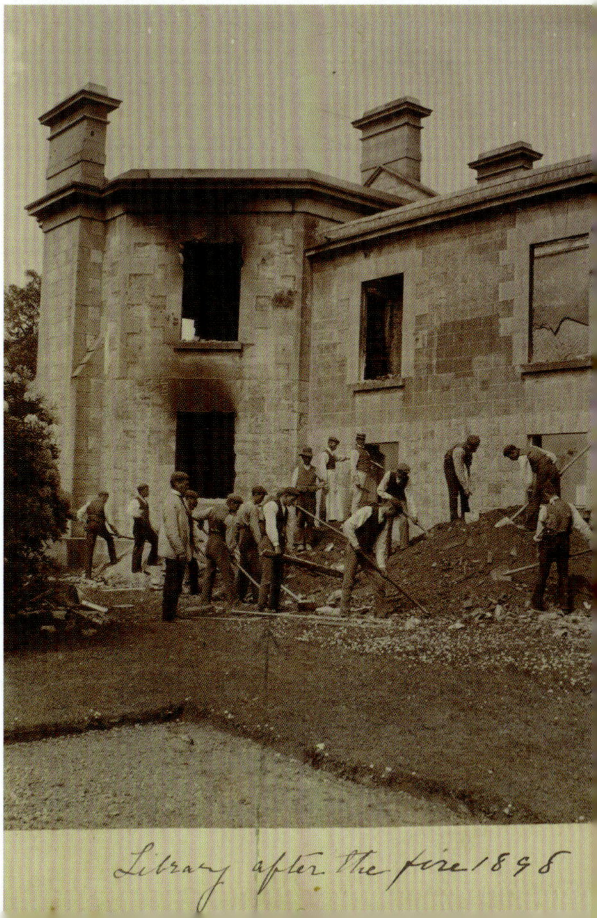

Right
Clearing the Library ruins after the 1898 fire (The Argory)

asperity, ruefully asking 'what was it to her that on the ground floor was a library full of valuable books and a collection of Irish works ancient and modern?'[9] In a sense, the question was an understandable one, but of course in the shock of the moment, country house servants could only do their best and hope that their decisions would eventually turn out well. Hardly surprisingly, their instincts could be to rescue what they knew and understood, so in another sense events at The Argory and at Spiddal are perhaps quite revealing. When Florence Court was badly damaged in an accidental fire in 1955, a neighbour, Viola, Duchess of Westminster arrived to help, and horrified to find the elderly butler rescuing Lord Enniskillen's socks, she took control of the situation and organised a human chain to evacuate the contents of the house.[10] By contrast, when Palmerstown, County Kildare, was burned in January 1923, Lord Mayo was in residence, and asked for, and was granted, time to remove the finest paintings in the house.[11]

The report on The Argory fire is an interesting document, and the most striking feature is the way that all concerned were anxious to clear their names and assert that the 'dreadful' fire was a terrible accident, an Act of God which no-one could have predicted, and which was no-one's fault. Such fires were, after all, not unknown in grand Irish houses, with the library at Westport, County Mayo, destroyed by a fire in a heating plant in 1826, and that at Birr Castle, County Offaly, by another in the 1920s.[12] At The Argory, for some of the servants – particularly perhaps the more junior ones – Henry Alexander's inquest the morning after the fire must have been a frightening experience, one which can only have been made more alarming by the presence of the officers of the Royal Irish Constabulary. Though nothing was said on the matter, it must surely have occurred to some of the servants that they might be accused of negligence and dismissed without a reference. Conceivably, in a period of widespread agrarian disturbances across Ireland, some might even have paused to consider whether accusations of a more sinister kind might be levelled at them. When Downhill had burned in 1851, Sir Henry Hervey Bruce had lost no time in asserting that his house had been 'maliciously set fire to', and at least one of the servants had immediately been prevailed on to sign an affidavit confirming that belief.[13] The Argory was a strongly Protestant household, the year after the fire hosting the annual demonstration of the County Armagh Royal Black Preceptory, and the senior house staff are likely to have been Protestants – either northern Protestants, or people brought over from England or Scotland, a common practice in nineteenth-century Ireland.[14] For the most part, their names strongly suggest that they were, and the locally-born Isaac Allen described himself as a Methodist in the 1901 Irish Census, and had arranged for the Portadown Methodists to hold their Sunday School outing at The Argory in 1896.[15] But this may not have been true of all the rest, and especially not the more junior house staff, or those working on the wider demesne. On the face of things, it is easy enough to interpret this as naked sectarianism, but in reality nineteenth-century landlords tended to consider themselves as honour-bound to see to their servants' moral and religious welfare, and in these circumstances it is not difficult to see why this naturally inclined them to employ co-religionists, or indeed why it might mean that good Irish Catholics might be reluctant to see their children exposed to the alien virtues of a Protestant household. All this goes some way to explain the existence in nineteenth-century Dublin of bodies like the Protestant Registration Office and the Protestant Servants' Registration Office, designed to find employment for prospective servants of the right sort; and in this context it seems unlikely that staff at The Argory in 1898 would have been wholly unaware that some Irish landlords had in the recent past been all too keen to take advantage of any pretext to replace unreliable – which in practice often meant Catholic – staff. The year before the fire at The Argory, Captain Blackley, agent to Lord Farnham in nearby County Cavan, had been encouraging his employer to do just this. He was later burned out and he and his family fled to England in 1922.[16] A generation earlier, Lord Cole, the heir to Florence Court, had been similarly inflammatory, in 1886 urging his neighbours at a public meeting in the Post Office School Room in Florencecourt village 'to employ more Protestants and don't employ Roman Catholics', while when Castle Ward was looking for a dairymaid in 1858, a Protestant was specified.[17] In the event, Henry Alexander was completely satisfied, the report forwarded to the Kildare Street Club not only blaming the fire on the kitchen flue, but praising the hard work of all concerned. Expressing his condolences to Captain Shelton, he assured his employer that 'it might have been worse & that's the only comfort'.

Below
The Billiard Room bookcase (The Argory)

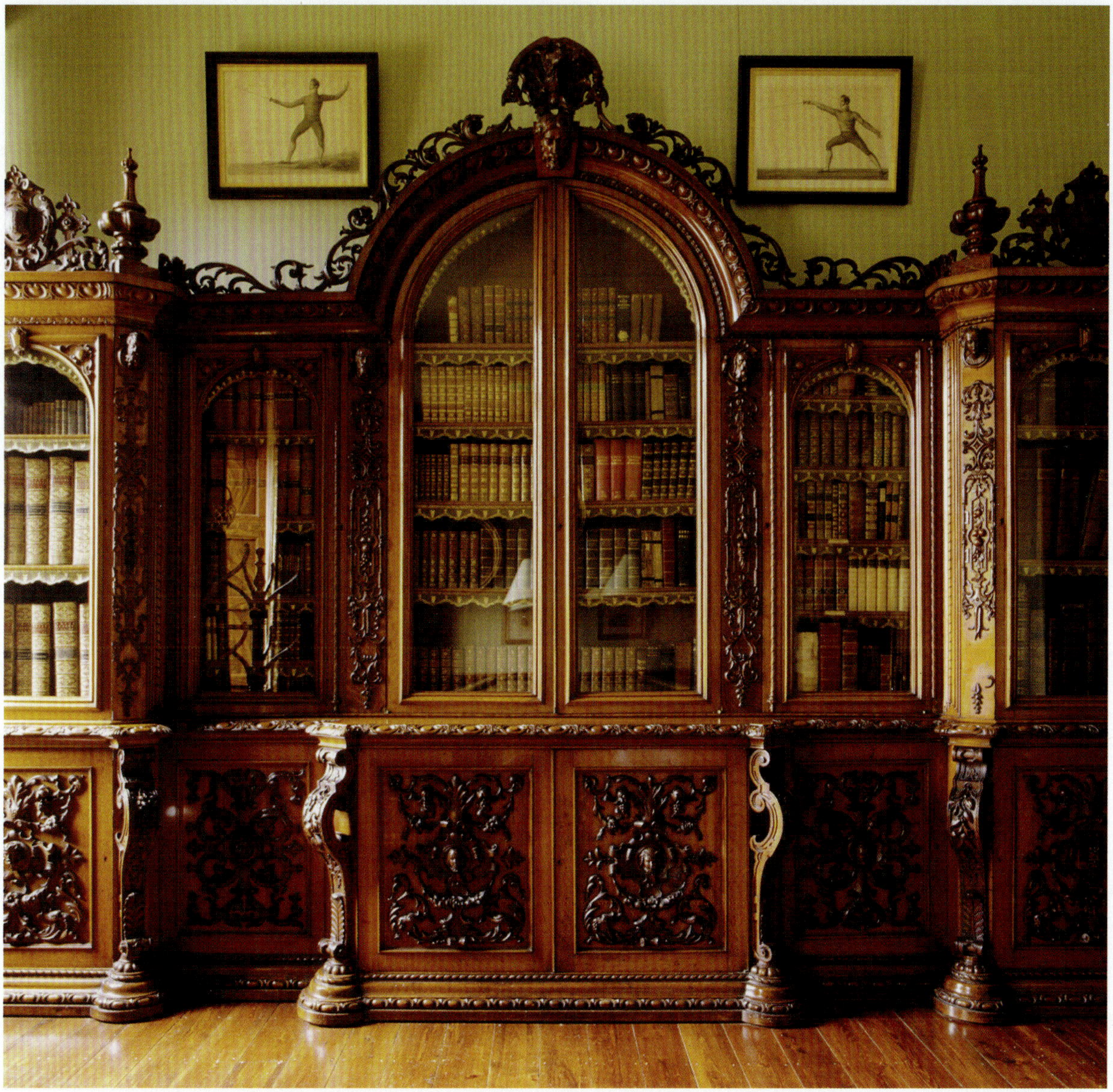

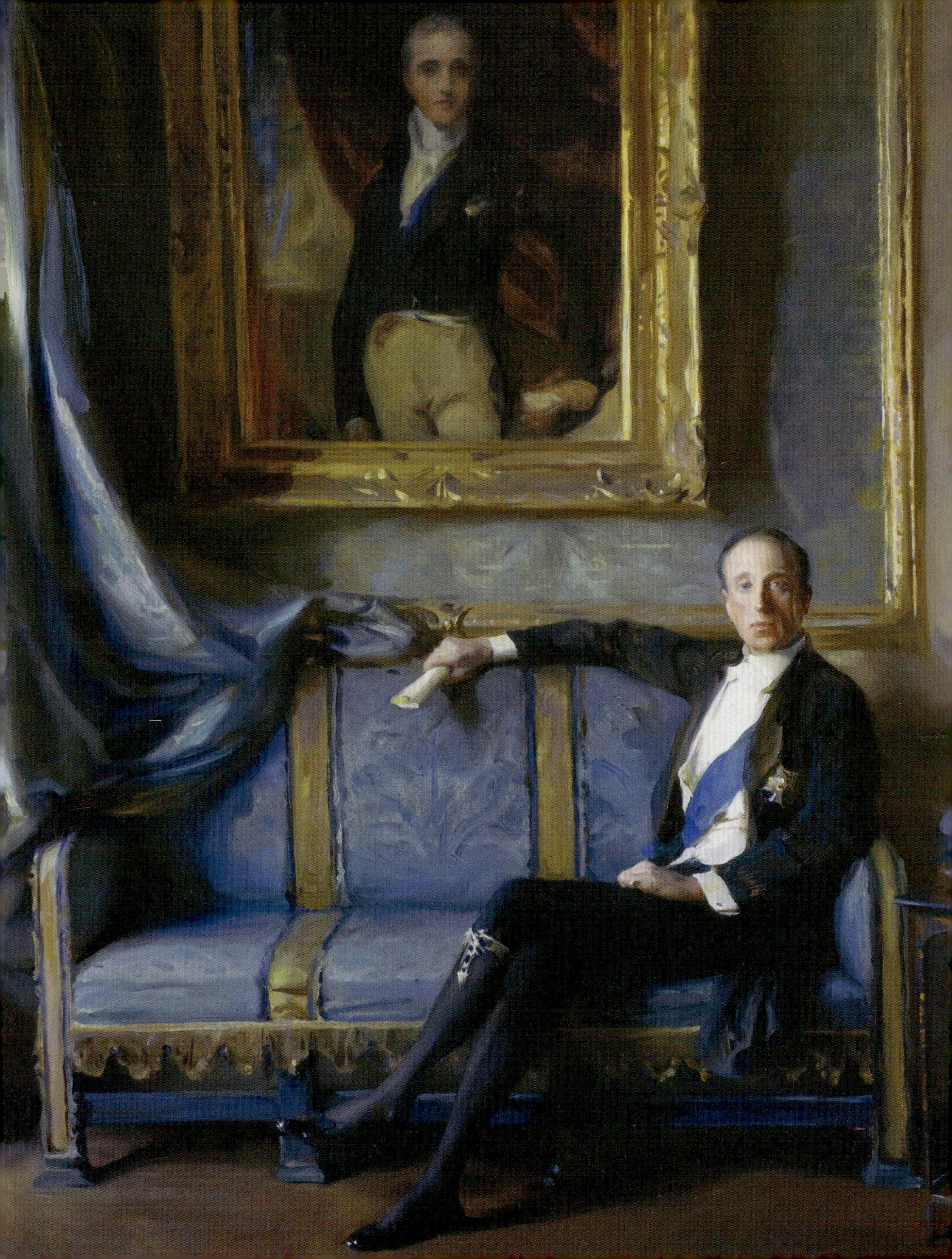

8 What a Splendid Binding to my Little Book

Mount Stewart, County Down, 1885–1962

Right
Edith, Marchioness of Londonderry (1879–1959); painted by Philip de Laszlo (Mount Stewart)

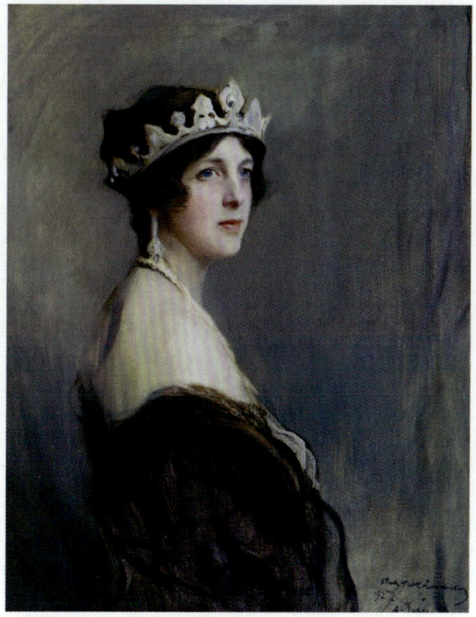

Opposite
Charles Stewart, 7th Marquess of Londonderry (1878–1949); painted by Philip de Laszlo (Mount Stewart)

At the time of Partition in 1921, Charles Stewart, 7th Marquess of Londonderry (1878–1949) was 43 years old. With a 'deep, rather careless voice', he was tall and slender, effortlessly patrician, and to his adoring wife's irritation something of a philanderer.[1] A veteran of the Great War and Tory MP for Maidstone since 1906, he had served as *aide-de-camp* to General William Pulteney ('Putty') on the Western Front, and had been a junior minister at the Air Ministry since 1919, an appointment secured for him by his cousin Winston Churchill. Between July 1917 and March 1918 he had also been secretary to the Ulster Unionist delegation at the Irish Convention, the government-sponsored forum, boycotted by Sinn Féin, which under the chairmanship of the centrist politician Sir Horace Plunkett strove in vain to forge a compromise between Nationalist and Unionist opinion.[2] In 1899 he had married Edith Chaplin (1879–1959), a celebrated beauty, daughter of the Tory MP and sportsman Henry Chaplin (1841–1923) and granddaughter of the 3rd Duke of Sutherland, the owner of some 1,358,546 acres, mostly in the Scottish Highlands.[3] Edie herself was brought up mostly by her mother's family, at Dunrobin Castle in Sutherland, and at Stafford House – now Lancaster House – the Sutherlands' palatial London house just yards from St James's Palace. Charley's father, Charles Vane-Tempest-Stewart, 6th Marquess of Londonderry (1852–1915), had been Lord Lieutenant of Ireland between 1886 and 1889, while his ancestor the 2nd Marquess (1769–1822) – better known to history as Lord Castlereagh – was the arbiter of the Congress of Vienna in 1815, and the architect of the 1801 Act of Union. Charley Londonderry was acutely conscious of his lineage, his friend Lady Spender noting with amusement, 'he wears a high black stock over his collar and a very tightly fitting frock coat, and doesn't look as if he belongs to this century at all.'[4] Sir Horace Plunkett, on the other hand, caught more than a whiff of the modern world, thinking he 'seemed to belong a little more to the later nineteenth and earlier twentieth century than either of his parents', and this was borne out when in middle age he developed an enthusiasm for flying.[5]

Charley's father, the 6th Marquess, had been a key figure in the Ulster Protestant revolt against Asquith's plans for Irish Home Rule, and when he happened on the Prime Minister at a formal dinner at the German embassy not long before the First World War, he was apoplectic with rage, and was barely restrained from walking out.[6] Though Lady Fingall thought him 'not very clever', from 1912 he served as Chairman of the Standing Committee of the Ulster Unionist Council, a body Churchill said was 'engaged in a treasonable conspiracy' by almost openly declaring its intention to set up a Provisional Government in Belfast if Home Rule was enacted.[7] But many thought that it was his formidable wife Theresa, Marchioness of Londonderry (1856–1919) who really wore the trousers. Born at Ingestre in Staffordshire, the daughter of the 19th Earl of Shrewsbury, Theresa claimed to have 'begun liking politics when I was only ten years old'.[8] The American-born Duchess of Marlborough thought she 'should have been born in the eighteenth century', and later recalled that Theresa was 'impressed by her splendid lineage' – her father was the premier earl of England – and 'she made great play of those rights which the governing classes still possessed, and sought to impress others with the importance of her position.' Theresa's 'frank materialism' and the way that 'to her, social and political power were all that mattered' shocked even a Vanderbilt, though she could also be kind and was a great dispenser of 'shrewd worldly wisdom'.[9] This worldliness was reflected in her own life. It was an almost open secret that Theresa's second son Reggie had been fathered by her brother-in-law Lord Helmsley, and there was talk of a seduction by the Prince of Wales, an affair with the notorious MP Harry Cust – as well as whispered rumours of a ground-floor window left open to facilitate nocturnal visits from the gamekeeper, Houliston. Daisy, Countess of Fingall later remembered Theresa – 'Nellie' to her friends – to be 'a most dominant personality'.[10] Mrs Carson, the wife of the Unionist leader Edward Carson, was blunter (in the privacy of her private diary), describing her as 'very bombastic. If she weren't Lady L. no-one would stand her for two minutes'.[11] Her husband had been appointed Lord Lieutenant of Ireland by Lord Salisbury and the Tories back in 1886 to provide a suitably ceremonious focus for British rule in Ireland after the collapse of Gladstone's 1885 Home Rule Bill, at a time when aristocratic circles were increasingly sniffy about the allegedly bourgeois atmosphere of the Viceregal Court in Dublin.[12] Lady Fingall remembered the Londonderrys' Viceroyalty as being of 'great magnificence', but though they were the first Viceregal couple to be in any sense Irish, they received a very cool reception on their State Entry into Dublin in September 1886. The 1886 general election had been a watershed in Irish politics, with changes to the franchise sweeping away the last remnants of the Ascendancy from elected office in the south, and, in a dramatic break with protocol, the city's Nationalist Lord Mayor and Corporation refused to greet the new Viceregal couple in the traditional way.[13] Londonderry's ancestry was as much an affront to Nationalists as his politics, one member of the Dublin Corporation angrily asserting that it would be 'the greatest insult that was ever offered to Irishmen if they were asked calmly to do honour to the descendant of the robber of Ireland's rights – bloody Castlereagh'.[14] It was rumoured that Londonderry owed his position mostly to Theresa's friendship with Lord Salisbury, though the *Irish Times* thought he had been 'selected in the first place because he is an Irishman, and in the second because he is a nobleman certain to maintain the tradition of the office with becoming splendour'.[15] Described by the Nationalist newspaper the *Irish People* as a 'diehard', who unlike lesser Ascendancy figures would never reconcile himself to a break in the Union because he, unlike them, had 'greater interests in England than in Ireland', the Lord Lieutenant was renowned in Dublin Castle for rushing formal Viceregal meals, to the consternation of less-exalted guests left with almost no dinner'.[16] Decades later, Edith Londonderry declared that her father-in-law had been Edward Carson's 'right-hand man', but it was Theresa who had originally introduced the young Dublin lawyer into aristocratic circles.[17] When Daisy Fingall met him at Mount Stewart, she was told by Theresa that she would be introduced to a fellow-guest, 'a clever lawyer' who 'may be useful', while Theresa herself – 'a personality born to rule' – addressed Unionist mass meetings during the Home Rule Crisis in 1914.[18]

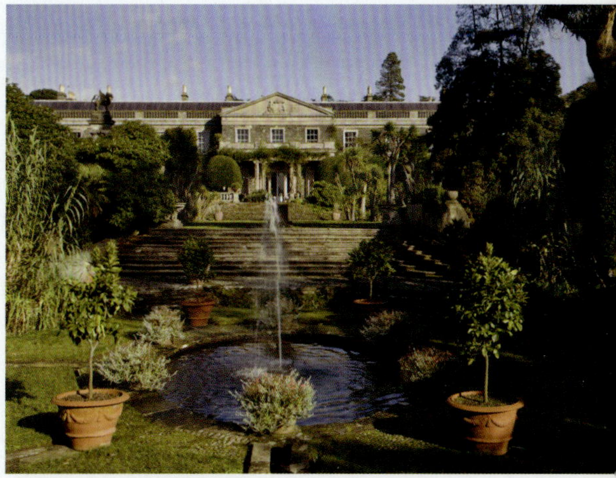

Right
The garden at Mount Stewart

Mount Stewart had been a political power house since the early nineteenth century, but contemporary accounts of it were often quite uncomplimentary. Visiting in the 1830s, Lieutenant Tucker of the Ordnance Survey was unimpressed. The gardens he acknowledged to be 'kept in good order and have hothouses and forcing houses', but the house was 'plain and small for a nobleman's residence', and there was 'not a library, nor any painting in the house'. All in all, it was very disappointing, and 'not as magnificent as might be expected as the residence of a noble marquess'.[19] Remodelled by George Dance between 1804 and 1805, and soon to be greatly enlarged by the Irish architect William Vitruvius Morrison (1794–1838), Mount Stewart in the 1830s was undoubtedly quite a modest house, but the comment that there was 'not a library' is slightly puzzling, as one was mentioned explicitly in an inventory compiled in 1821.[20] Clearly depicted in Dance's drawings in Sir John Soane's Museum, it measured 40 feet by 24 feet and was separated from a Study of similar dimensions by the small Music Room which stood at the centre of the main façade.[21] It remains an open question as to why the Ordnance Survey did not register the existence of any books. Had they, perhaps, been placed in temporary storage elsewhere prior to the proposed building works? Was it something to do with the dispute between

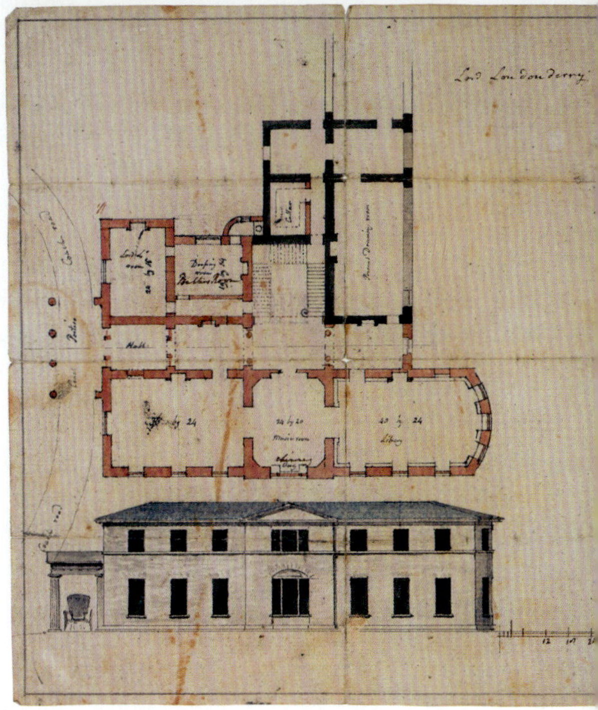

Right
George Dance's 1804 preliminary design for Mount Stewart, showing the Library in the bottom right-hand room (Sir John Soane's Museum)

the 3rd Marquess's wife and her relations about family chattels from England, which had ended up at Glenarm Castle, County Antrim, to be reacquired only in 1853?[22] If so, what had happened to the Londonderry family books from Mount Stewart, if indeed the books listed in a surviving late eighteenth-century booklist – shelved on eight bays of shelving, each bay between seven and nine shelves – had ever been at Mount Stewart?[23] Had the great Lord Castlereagh perhaps taken them to his house in England? Was it simply a clerical error on the part of the Ordnance Survey? Or was the Library regarded as part of the family's private apartment, and therefore inaccessible to visitors? In any event, the 3rd Marquess of Londonderry had clearly not succumbed to the fashionable vice of bibliomania. On a visit to Seville in the 1840s he grumbled that there was 'nothing remarkable' in the cathedral library 'except some curious missals'.[24] Perhaps the library at Mount Stewart was not drawn to Lieutenant Tucker's attention simply because – unlike the books on Irish history and topography shown to the Ordnance Survey at Florence Court – its contents were regarded as simply ordinary modern books, neither of any particular antiquarian interest, nor in any way relevant to the Survey's endeavours. We simply do not know, but some connection with Morrison's building works seems the most likely answer. However, in the course of the succeeding decades, the original Study was converted first into a Dining Room and then into a Library, and the splendid bookcases installed in the original Library by the master-carpenter John Ferguson were moved into it.[25] By 1921 both rooms – the Library by then known as 'Lady Londonderry's Sitting Room', and the Study either as the 'Castlereagh Room' or alternatively as 'Lord Londonderry's Study' – were both fitted out as libraries and packed with books of all kinds.

It was perhaps unsurprising that in 1921 Lord Londonderry felt compelled to accept Prime Minister Sir James Craig's offer of the post of Minister of Education in the new Northern Ireland cabinet, and it was this offer which had precipitated the move to Mount Stewart. He was descended in the male line from Alexander Stewart (1700–81), a country squire from Ballylawn, near Moville, County Donegal, who had purchased the demesne for £42,000 in 1744, so it was in a sense his family's original home.[26] Only one book survives which demonstrably belongs to Stewart's era, a copy of the anonymous *Letters from an Armenian in Ireland* (London, 1757), though there may well be other books lurking on the shelves unsigned. However by 1921, the Londonderrys had long since ceased to be a purely Irish family. Despite their Irish Marquessate, the marriage of Castlereagh's brother Lord Charles Stewart (1778–1854) to the nineteen-year-old coal heiress Frances Ann Vane-Tempest (1800–65) had brought them fabulous wealth. Miss Vane-Tempest was the only child of Sir Henry Vane-Tempest, who had inherited the County Durham estates of his uncle John Tempest in 1794. At the time of the marriage her husband was worth £18,000 a year, but Frances Anne's coal mines brought in a further £60,000, as well as the great house at Wynyard, near Stockton-on-Tees.[27] The young heiress inherited a taste for display along with her millions, and twenty years later and grown rather stout she was spotted by Disraeli at a costumed ball, her dress 'literally embroidered with emeralds and diamonds from top to toe. It looked like armour, and she like a rhinoceros'.[28] Already in 1821 the couple had spent £63,000 buying a second grand house in County Durham, Seaham Hall, and when on Castlereagh's suicide in 1822 his brother succeeded as 3rd Marquess of Londonderry, they spent a further £43,000 buying Holdernesse House (later renamed Londonderry House) in London's Park Lane. Within three years they laid out a further £200,000 commissioning Benjamin and Thomas Wyatt to remodel it in a suitably opulent *Louis Quinze* style. Shortly afterwards the same architects were also asked to remodel Wynyard as well.[29] The Londonderrys' fifth great estate was in Wales, Plâs Machynlleth, where an eighteenth-century house which had originally belonged to the wife of the 5th Marquess was inherited by Charley Londonderry on the death of an uncle in the notorious Abermule train crash in mid-Wales in 1921. And finally there were two hunting boxes, Springfield in Rutland, relinquished in 1924, and its subsequent replacement, Ranksborough.[30]

Mount Stewart was by the early years of the twentieth century well down the pecking order, useful as a holiday home, and as a *pied-à-terre* in Ireland, but no longer the centre of family life. For long periods it had remained more-or-less unused, and when the 4th Marquess of Londonderry had succeeded in 1853, he found the house so run down that he was forced to spend large sums on making it habitable.[31] Theresa was not especially fond of it, and 'regarded Wynyard as peculiarly her home'.[32] She and her husband visited Mount Stewart from time to time, but except during the run-up to the third Home Rule Bill of 1914 they were usually only there at Christmas, Easter and Whitsun.[33] By 1921, when Charley began his career as Minister for Education – introducing proposals for integrated education which were anathema to Catholics and Protestants alike – it was rather shabby and old-fashioned, bearing the stamp of Theresa's very Victorian tastes, 'with antimacassars on the chairs' and 'tall screens and palms and chairs arranged tête-à-tête, or in groups, so you could talk intimately and have good conversation'.[34] Edith's attempts to rectify the situation horrified her mother-in-law, who thought that Mount Stewart without its *bric-à-brac* and pot plants looked just like a barracks.[35] There were also changes of a more practical kind, including central heating brought in to overcome the damp which Queen Alexandra had complained about in the Mount Stewart visitors' book in 1903.[36]

Mount Stewart already had a substantial library in 1921, on the evidence of the catalogue probably commissioned by Edie, an equally superannuated mid-Victorian fossil, consisting mostly of books printed between about 1780 and 1850. Whether it had been much used is perhaps open to question. Theresa Londonderry was said to have 'loved books and flowers, and there were always masses of them in her rooms'. By her own admission she was poorly educated at home by 'decayed' governesses and her handwriting was a 'scrawl', but equally she was well-known as a skilled conversationalist, and was reputed to be well-read; she also numbered such luminaries as Thomas Hardy and Edmund Gosse among her friends.[37]

Whatever the situation in Victorian times, by the interwar period books were an important part of life for the Londonderrys.[38] There were libraries in all the houses, though Lord Londonderry's political books, in particular, were mostly at Londonderry House. The Library there was dominated by Stubbs's great picture of *Hambletonian*, originally belonging to the Vane-Tempests of Wynyard, though it also contained the 'manuscript collection … [of] about 10,000 documents' consisting of 'the political and private papers of Robert Stewart, Viscount Castlereagh and second Marquess of Londonderry'.[39] Both the Stubbs and the papers, magnificently rebound for Lord Londonderry as a present from the eccentric American socialite Laura Corrigan (1879–1948), were removed to Mount Stewart for safekeeping on the outbreak of war in 1939, and the papers are now in Belfast, though their boxes are

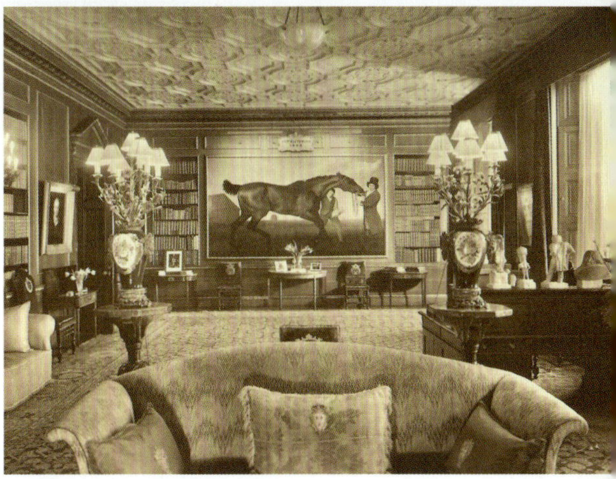

Right Stubbs's *Hambletonian* in the library of Londonderry House (Mount Stewart)

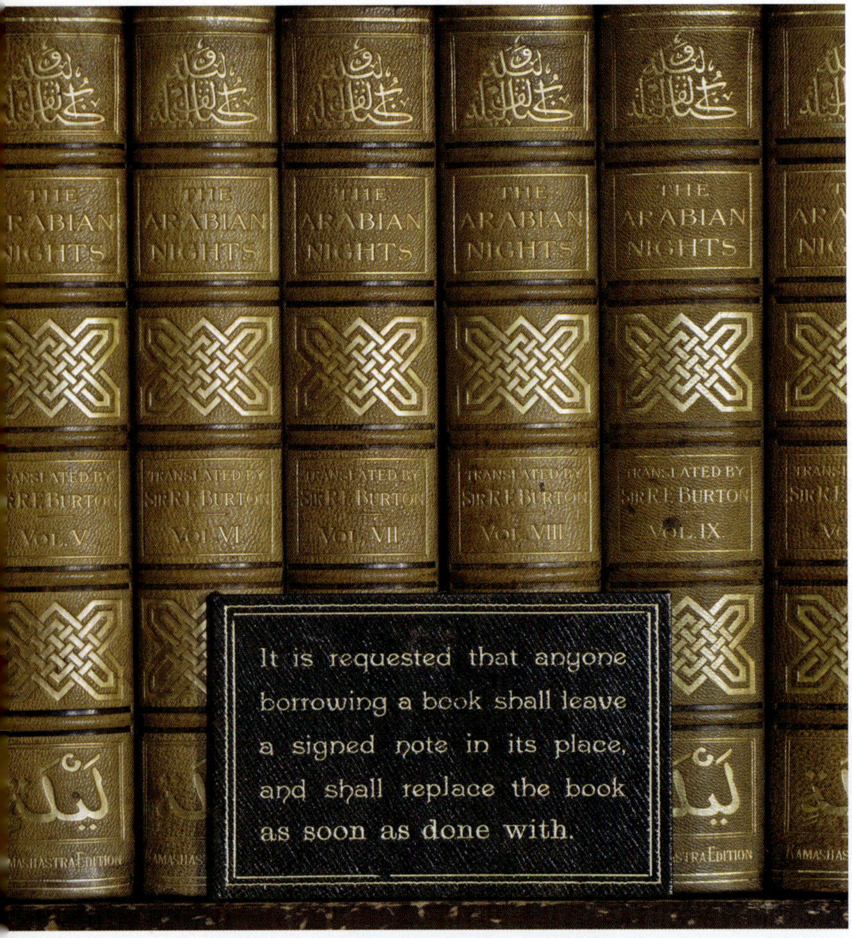

Above
A notice in the Study requests borrowers of books to mark their position on the shelf and replace them properly (Mount Stewart)

still on the shelves at Mount Stewart.[40] The rest of the Londonderry House books subsequently came to Mount Stewart as well, where, though not visible to visitors, they are mostly still shelved together. After desultory discussions in the 1940s with the National Trust (whose chairman Lord Esher thought Benjamin Wyatt 'a mightily indifferent architect'), Londonderry House itself was sold in 1962 to the property developer Isaac King for a reported £500,000.[41] The other major family library was at Wynyard, the grandest nineteenth-century house in County Durham, where the splendid room designed by the Wyatts was fitted with ebony, ormolu and tortoiseshell bookshelves.[42] Photographs taken in Theresa's time show an opulent carpeted interior, the books dimly visible amidst masses of flowers and huge tropical plants, but by 1978 the Wynyard Library was 'bare and desolate', the books scattered and dispersed, and in 1987 the house and estate were also sold to a property developer.[43]

At Mount Stewart books were divided, as they still are, between Lord Londonderry's Study (otherwise known as the 'Castlereagh Room') and Lady Londonderry's Sitting Room. Each of these rooms was the particular preserve of its owner, and though the Study contained many inherited books, the books on the shelves were substantially the personal books of Charley and Edith respectively. Both were enthusiastic readers, sitting quietly with a book in their own rooms; both were also constant travellers, and habitually took books with them as they moved around.[44] Edith was later to claim that her husband scarcely spent ten days in the same place during their whole married life, and the couple were frequently apart, absences brought about by politics, war and periods of *froideur* after Charley's latest infidelity.[45] They also travelled together, not only doing the rounds of the Londonderry houses, but frequently going further afield, with trips to Canada and India in their youth, and regular travel for both business and pleasure across Continental Europe. When they were at home, Mount Stewart was often full of visitors, but house parties were usually held in the summer and were dominated by outdoor pursuits that usually left little time for books: sailing was a particular favourite. Visitors would sometimes stay for a considerable time, the writer and politician Oliver St John Gogarty (1878–1957), a regular visitor between the wars, later recalling Mount Stewart as 'a house so hospitable that after a few days you wouldn't know which of you owned the place'.[46] But despite the gold-tooled leather signs on the shelves enjoining borrowers to put volumes back where they found them, the Study and the Sitting Room were essentially private rooms, and house guests did not have the run of

Right
Dummy books on the shutters in the Study, Mount Stewart

their well-stocked shelves. Visitors were certainly invited into them, and would undoubtedly have been allowed to borrow books if they asked, but not even Lord and Lady Londonderry's children would have helped themselves to the books without permission. The communal rooms were the nearby Drawing Room and Smoking Room, and suitable books were also put out in the guest bedrooms, just as they had been when Daisy Fingall had stayed at Mount Stewart and at the Viceregal Lodge in Dublin in the nineteenth and early twentieth centuries.[47] When Ramsay MacDonald came to stay, he found a copy of *Did She*? (London, 1934) by the racy romantic novelist Elinor Glyn, a particular favourite of Lady Londonderry. Asked next morning whether he had read it, he replied (according to gossip circulated by Sir John Leslie of Glaslough) 'about fifteen pages. In fact, until she did'.[48]

The books in the Study belonged mostly to Lord Londonderry, though it also contained family books inherited from as far back as the end of the eighteenth century; for the most part it is impossible to say who precisely they belonged to, as many contain a standard nineteenth-century family bookplate – often printed on pink paper – with a Londonderry 'L' cipher. Whether Charley was aware of them or not, a handful of these earlier books had belonged to his hero Lord Castlereagh, including an 1818 *Gentleman's and Citizen's Almanack*, and a couple of presentation copies, most notably the *Histoire du Canal du Midi* (Paris, 1799), inscribed to him by the author, the French general François Andréossy. Several other rather unusual books look suspiciously as if they might have been his as well, or at least belonged to someone preoccupied by fear of revolution, most notably a set of three pamphlets, namely a Parisian-printed copy of the French Revolutionary constitution of 1791, an English translation of the same text published in the same year, and a 1791

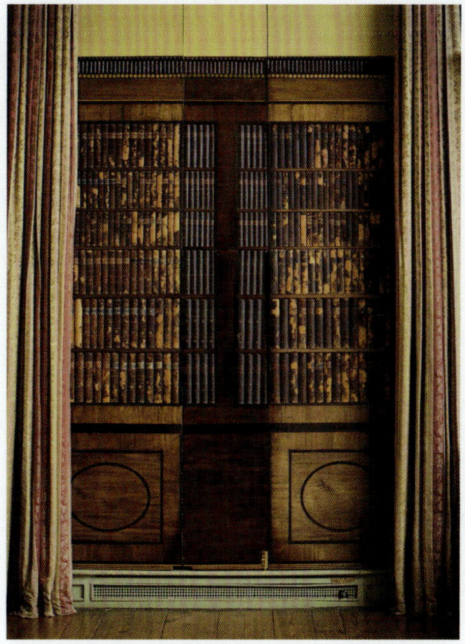

Polish constitution, again in English translation. But Lord Londonderry's own books, embellished with his own pictorial bookplate, were very much a working collection of modern publications, and the surviving catalogue – probably compiled for Edith shortly after 1921 – shows that a large set of the Badminton Library of Sports and Pastimes was early on moved from the Study to the upstairs Schoolroom, presumably to make space for more useful material.[49] These include many political books, though many more were generally at Londonderry House, where he spent more time than Edith, who frequently remained at Mount Stewart when he was in England.

Right
The Study, Mount Stewart

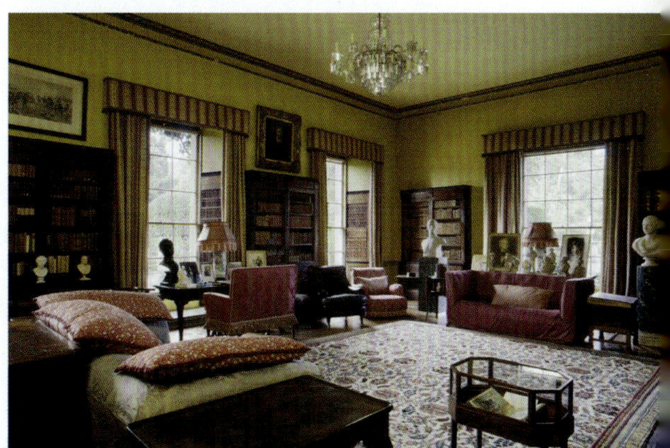

The shelves of Lady Londonderry's Sitting Room contain more varied fare, ranging from books on gardening – indispensable for Edith's great gardening campaign at Mount Stewart – through to general reading, a grand set of John Gould's *Birds of Great Britain* (1873), literary presentation copies, and in particular books on Irish and Scottish topics. Since neither Londonderry generally wrote in their books, it would be easy to infer that they remained unread on the shelves, but this seems to have been far from the case. Like many book-owners, the Londonderrys 'did not approve' of writing in books, feeling that it 'spoiled them for others', and that scribbling in their margins showed a lack of respect for both the book and for future readers.[50] A rare exception is Edith's copy of the Duke of Argyll's *Scotland as it Was* (Edinburgh, 1887), perhaps a youthful acquisition, with pencil notes in the margin. But the disadvantage of the generally clean copies is that while anecdotal evidence shows quite clearly that the Londonderrys did read their books, their libraries, unlike those of inveterate scribblers like the Trevelyns of Wallington (by the 1930s increasingly strident supporters of the Left), rarely provide any firm evidence as to precisely what they were reading and when, and what they thought of it.[51]

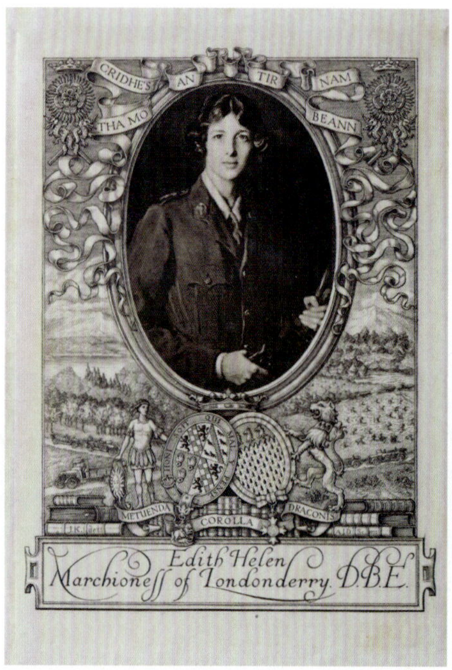

Right
Lady Londonderry's bookplate, after the portrait by Philip de Laszlo in the Imperial War Museum, London (Mount Stewart)

Until the 1930s there was also some sort of servants' library at Mount Stewart. Later converted into a Gun Room, by the late twentieth century it had been transformed again, this time into a photographic dark room.[52] Most of Mount Stewart's many distinguished visitors would no doubt have remained entirely unaware of its existence. In the 6th Marquess's day there was an awesome complement of staff at Mount Stewart, and while it is not clear who exactly used the servants' library – or even what it contained – potentially it might have served a considerable number of people. Lady Fingall's maid later recalled that the Londonderrys lived 'like royalty', their servants ruled over by the House Steward and by a 'stately Housekeeper, who wore grey alpaca in the morning and black silk in the evening'. The housemaids were kept 'like novices in a convent', and not allowed to go out alone, while below stairs strict etiquette prevailed, with visitors' servants seated in order of precedence and waited on by a footman.[53] By the 30s, when most Irish Big Houses were falling into decay, there were 44 indoor staff at Londonderry House alone, and the usual complement included a comptroller, a groom of the chambers, a butler and under-butler, four footmen, a piper, a nursery footman, odd job man, night watchman, head housekeeper and housekeeper, four chauffeurs, numerous maids and daily helps, as well as a telephonist and a nurse, two secretaries, a valet and ladies maids, and, of course, a governess for the youngest daughter Mairi.[54] Even in the straightened circumstances of the post-war era, the widowed Edith Londonderry still had 35 staff at Mount Stewart.[55]

There were further books in the house for children – they include Irish classics like Patricia Lynch's *The Turf-Cutter's*

Donkey (1934), the story of Seumas and Eileen and Long Ears, as well as books by the likes of Enid Blyton and Arthur Ransome – particularly for the Londonderrys' daughter Lady Mairi Stewart, who was born at Mount Stewart in 1921, and usually spent the whole summer there, even if her parents were away. One of Edith Londonderry's earliest memories was of her sporting father Henry Chaplin reading *Jorrocks* to her as a small girl, 'so overcome with laughter that his voice was half-choked with emotion and the tears trickled down his face'.[56] Lady Mairi also remembered being read to as a child, not just by her governess, but by both her parents as well. Her mother's book *The Magic Ink-Pot*, published by Macmillan in 1928, originated in a rather similar way, Lady Londonderry setting out its genesis in conversation with an *Irish Times* columnist: 'I always make a habit of telling stories [to] my youngest daughter Mary [*sic*], and when I was going to Spain some months ago she was disconsolate at the thought of missing her bedtime story.'[57] Deriving much of its imagery from Ella Young's *Celtic Wonder Tales* (Dublin, 1910), published with illustrations by the nationalist activist Maud Gonne, the Ink-Pot takes the Londonderry children on a series of adventures, including an encounter with a witch from nearby Scrabo and a boarhunt with the Ulster hero Cúchulain. Two inscribed copies remain in the library at Mount Stewart, one in a smart morocco binding, and the other with additional material by the book's illustrators Edmond Brock and Lady Margaret Stewart. There were other bookish entertainments laid on for the younger generation, and if learning Shakespeare by heart might have seemed like a chore, amateur theatricals at Christmas, from 1934 sometimes celebrated at Mount Stewart, were no doubt more amusing. In other ways, however, the twentieth century made itself felt. Her grandmother's friend Daisy Fingall recalled family readings of Dickens on winter afternoons in the dining room at Danesfield, County Galway in the 1870s – with alarming sanctions for the child who did not pay attention – but the young Mairi Stewart was brought up in the age of the wireless, and there was nothing similar at Mount Stewart in the 20s and 30s.[58]

Books in all the Londonderry houses were nominally under the charge of the historian and Unionist politician H. Montgomery Hyde (1907–89). Sometimes described as Lord Londonderry's secretary, from 1935 he was the Londonderrys' librarian, and he also assisted Lady Londonderry with several of her books, notably her 1938 edition of the letters written by Disraeli to Frances Anne, Marchioness of Londonderry.[59] Despite the almost regal grandeur of the Londonderry household, Hyde's role was confined to keeping an eye on the older books, and he was not much involved in selecting current reading matter, as royal librarians of the era certainly were. New books were mostly personally selected by the Londonderrys, who both read the *Times Literary Supplement*, and ordered those that took their fancy, usually from Bumpus in Oxford Street, though both browsed the shelves of London bookshops when the fancy took them, and Lady Londonderry also had dealings with the north-east dealer Steadman, who specialised in Scottish and Irish books. Books were expected to look smart, and binding was arranged by G. T. Bagguley of Newcastle-under-Lyme, a favourite with aristocratic customers, with many of the books in Lady Londonderry's favourite polished sponged calf. Others seem to have been bound up for Bumpus by top London binders like Zaehnsdorf or Sangorski and Sutcliffe. Many of the authors' presentation copies sent to Edith Londonderry were rebound in a similar style.

Described in her obituary as 'for years one of England's leading political hostesses', Lady Londonderry held eve-of-session receptions at Londonderry House which were one of the highlights of the

Parliamentary year.[60] Standing at the head of the stairs with the Prime Minister of the day, she would receive her guests – 1100 in 1924, rising to 1500 by 1933 – in what was already one of the last surviving great houses in London, a spectacle so brilliant that Lord Birkenhead sneered that Edie had catered her husband's way into the cabinet when he became Air Minister in 1931.[61] Her own political views were in some ways a curious combination of the radical and the very conservative, an old-fashioned Tory who had a snake tattoo on her left leg and was a vocal campaigner for women's suffrage, but grumbled when Bonar Law became Prime Minister in 1922 because he was not a landed magnate.[62] She held predictably strong views on the Irish question, writing to *The Times* in the aftermath of the 1916 Easter Rising to condemn the fact that 'ten years of Radical rule in Ireland have culminated in the tragedy of a fortnight ago'.[63] She was perhaps never entirely reconciled to Irish independence after 1922, asserting in her memoirs that 'most of the best things in Southern Ireland' now belonged 'to past history', and that 'Democracy as the British know it is not for Southern Ireland. They are a different race. They want firm, wise but powerful control, to prevent them from trying to eat one another up.'[64] Predictably this control was to be supplied by 'the ruling race from which the bulk of the Northerners have sprung'.[65] Nor did she think much of Irish land reform, complaining of the 'efforts of the Radicals to set up peasant proprietors in place of landlords'.[66] Her husband echoed her views in equally trenchant form, writing to the Prime Minister while briefly chairing the Northern Ireland cabinet during the illness of Sir James Craig in 1924:

> The Southern Irish can be very charming but they are certainly an inconsequent race – in fact very like children, and when given too much latitude, they get out of hand.[67]

As early as 1924 a Dublin gossip columnist reckoned Edith Londonderry 'a brilliant conversationalist', and on her death in 1959 her obituarist remembered her talent for making 'numerous and life-long friends', 'who she retained in spite of her sometimes disconcerting frankness'.[68] One of the most unlikely and far-reaching of these friendships was with Ramsay MacDonald (1866–1937), who headed the first Labour government from January to November 1924, returned to office again in 1929, and subsequently defected from his party at the height of the Depression in 1931 to lead a National Government consisting largely of Tories. MacDonald had been a firm opponent of the Great War, and Lady Londonderry had 'always disliked what she had heard' of him, but when they first met at Buckingham Palace in 1924 at a dinner hosted by George V for members of the new Labour cabinet, they rapidly discovered that they had interests in common.[69] Their implausible friendship deepened as the years went on; by 1929 his correspondence to her was addressed to 'My dearest Ladye', and soon after he was writing poetry to her.[70] By 1931 many thought that Ramsay MacDonald, an elderly and lonely widower, was in love, and there was much scurrilous gossip.[71] Edith Londonderry could find him tiresome, referring to him in private as 'that old fool', but MacDonald's Cabinet Secretary Sir Maurice Hankey was in no doubt that the Londonderrys were 'now the best friends of that rather lonely man, and have shown him innumerable kindnesses', the Prime Minister travelling to Mount Stewart by seaplane in August 1932.[72]

Beatrice Webb was baffled by MacDonald's association with those she regarded to be 'the wealthiest, most aristocratic, most reactionary and by no means the most intellectual of the Conservative Party', and she thought that his 'friendship with the Londonderrys almost amounts to a public scandal'.[73] Her views were echoed in the depths of the great Depression by an anonymous correspondent from his Seaham constituency, dominated by the Londonderrys' mines, who bluntly said of the owner: 'He is not our friend', adding more ominously 'when the next election comes you will get a great surprise'.[74] But Edith and MacDonald had a surprising amount in common. He a lonely widower, and she the devoted wife of an habitual philanderer, both were – for completely different reasons – well-read, but essentially self-educated, and both had been brought up in the Scottish Highlands, sharing an enthusiasm for Highland history, folklore and mythology.[75] In 1935 she was reportedly learning Scots Gaelic – she owned a copy of Neil McAlpine's *A Pronouncing Gaelic Dictionary* (Edinburgh, 1833) – and she continued to think of Dunrobin Castle as her real home for at least twenty years after her marriage.[76] By 1937 the *Irish Times's* 'Irishman's Diary' could report that Edith had set out 'about four years ago to reintroduce the harp into the *haut monde* and it has always been played since at her Gaelic entertainments', and it is intriguing that Edith's copy of Joseph Walker's *Historical Memoirs of the Irish Bards* (Dublin, 1818) should contain not only a note about the 'famous blind harper of Portadown', but an annotated photograph of an ancient Irish harp. Another favoured member of the Londonderry entourage was the Hebridean musician Duncan Morrison, who would attend house parties at Mount Stewart kilted, play Scots songs on the piano, and teach fellow-guests jigs and reels.[77] All of these enthusiasms are reflected on the shelves of Lady Londonderry's Sitting Room, packed with books of Celtic – and particularly Highland – interest, volumes like *Carmina Gadelica* (Edinburgh, 1900–), alongside several with very obvious connections to her Sutherland ancestors, notably George Eyre-Todd's *Highland Clans of Scotland* (London, 1923), with manuscript notes on the family, and Hector Munro Mackay's *Old Dornoch* (Dingwall, 1920), with a preface by Edith's aunt Millicent, Duchess of Sutherland, and based on a set of lectures given in the town before the Great War. Edith and MacDonald exchanged books, he presenting her with a copy of his *Wanderings and Excursions* when she visited him in Hampstead in April 1926, while in return she gave him a copy of her biography of her father, and asked for his advice on her edition of Disraeli's letters.[78]

Books of Irish, and specifically Ulster, interest are equally noticeable on the shelves. Some of these books were comparatively new at the time – in addition to monographs like Elizabeth Andrews's *Ulster Folklore* (London, 1913), and even a few periodicals like the complete run of the first series of *The Ulster Journal of Archæology*

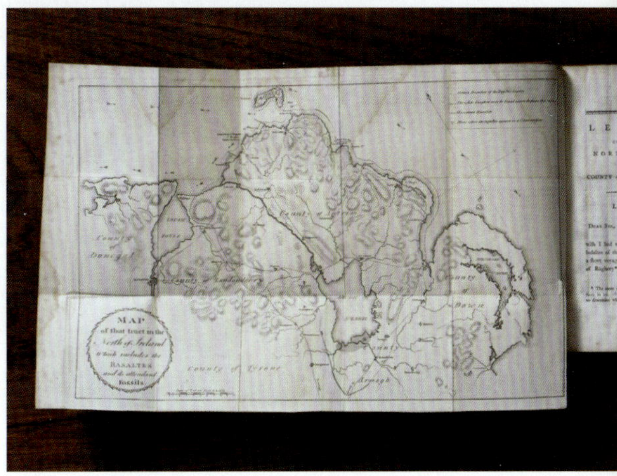

Right
William Hamilton, *Letters Concerning the Northern Coast of the County of Antrim* (Dublin, 1790), ESTC T146986 (Mount Stewart)

(1853–62), all potent symbols of the Ulster particularism that was emerging among the Protestants of north-east Ireland in the late nineteenth and early twentieth centuries. The earlier books – Henry O'Brien's *The Round Towers of Ireland* (London, 1834) or William Reeves's *Ecclesiastical Antiquities of Down, Connor and Dromore* (Dublin, 1847), for example – Edith generally had smartly rebound. One of the most attractive of all these is her copy of William Hamilton's *Letters Concerning the Northern Coast of Antrim* (Dublin, 1790), but of even more local interest at Mount Stewart is a book like Charles Smith's *Topographical and Chronographical Survey of the County of Down* (Dublin, 1740), one of the founding texts of Irish local history, and interesting because the bookplate suggests that it came from the library at Hillsborough Castle, sold in 1924. Whether Edith bought it locally or from a dealer further afield is now impossible to say.

Despite quips from the wags that MacDonald had changed his tune from the Red Flag to the Londonderry Air, the friendship between Edith and the Prime Minister was clearly a critical factor in Charley Londonderry's appointment as Air Minister in 1931.[79] Even with his impeccable connections at the very heart of the Establishment – Lord Halifax had been his fag at Eton – Londonderry was thought by some not really to be Cabinet material, and his ministerial career was short, controversial and ultimately ended in bitter disappointment.[80] In correspondence with Londonderry's son Robin Castlereagh, Stanley Baldwin later spoke for many in brutally asserting 'He owed his preferment really to the fact that Ramsay MacDonald greatly enjoyed standing at the top of the staircase in Londonderry House as the first Minister of the Crown.'[81] Admittedly, Londonderry could hardly have become Air Minister at a more challenging time, with the Nazis taking power in Berlin early in 1933, and much of the Left was still viscerally opposed to rearmament of any kind; the *Manchester Guardian* led the way by accusing Londonderry of wanting more planes, 'because a big Air Force is a pretty plaything to have'.[82] His successor Sir Philip Cunliffe-Lister acknowledged that Londonderry had been given 'a thankless and impossible task', but Baldwin was not alone in detecting 'a certain lack of drive at the Air Ministry', and despite Londonderry's defence of RAF budgets in 1932 and 1933, when Baldwin succeeded MacDonald as Prime Minister in 1935, Londonderry's days as Minister were clearly numbered.[83]

Having been sacked as Air Minister in May 1935, Londonderry limped on in the Cabinet as Lord Privy Seal until the following November, before losing that consolation prize in turn. The twin humiliation left him reeling, and he never forgave Baldwin.[84] His response to his dismissal was to seek to carve out a new role appropriate to his own evaluation of his political experience and social status. Inevitably this led him in the direction of Germany. Like many politicians of his era, Charley Londonderry shared the widespread sentiment that the Versailles settlement had not been entirely fair to the Germans, as well as an acute fear of Soviet Communism. Already in 1924 he was writing to his nemesis, Stanley Baldwin, expressing his concerns about the political situation in County Durham, telling him that he was 'proposing to devote a great deal of time in defeating the Socialist menace in one of the reddest portions of the kingdom'; two years later he was equally clear that fighting the General Strike was a crucial part of 'opposing Socialism'.[85] The press baron Lord Rothermere thought that 'sturdy young Nazis' were 'Europe's guardians against the Communist danger', and, like many others on the right, it seems clear that Charley Londonderry may initially have assumed the Hitler regime would provide a strong bulwark against Bolshevism.[86] Speaking shortly after his first visit to Germany early in 1936, he told the *Manchester Guardian* that Hitler bore no ill-feeling to Britain 'but certainly fears the Russian political system and its policy of world revolution'.[87] The seven-week visit itself was hosted by Goering, and included an audience with the Führer; generally speaking, the Londonderrys were impressed with all that they saw. Edith described Hitler as 'a man with wonderful, far-seeing eyes. I felt I was in the presence of one truly great. He is simple, dignified, humble. He is a leader of men.'[88]

This first visit, together with two subsequent forays in 1937 and 1938 provoked considerable criticism. The Conservative MP Harold Nicolson – who liked Charley Londonderry and thought him 'a real gent' – was horrified, confiding to his diary in 1936 that 'I do deeply disapprove of ex-Cabinet ministers trotting round Germany at the moment.'[89] Londonderry defended himself, saying 'my attitude has been misinterpreted and my motives misunderstood in various quarters', but the Left, predictably, was strongly critical.[90] In a column entitled 'Innocent Abroad', the *Manchester Guardian's* leader writer ridiculed Londonderry, suggesting that his conduct would make 'most people more grateful than ever to Mr. Baldwin for having pushed him out of the National Government'.[91] It was not necessarily a view which everyone would have endorsed, with Appeasement still enjoying widespread support from a public which had yet to learn of the worst enormities of the Nazi regime, and did not have the benefit of hindsight in knowing that the policy of conciliation was doomed to failure.

Nevertheless by 1937 the Nazis' initial attempts to woo the British Establishment were flagging, Londonderry noting in that year that he was finding Goering 'far less conciliatory' than previously.[92] In December 1938 the Foreign Office mandarin Sir Horace Rumbold – no friend of the Londonderrys – noted 'there is a growing conviction there is nothing to be done with the Nazis. Even the pro-Germans like Londonderry are turning against them.'[93] When Edith and Charley entertained Ribbentrop at Mount Stewart in 1938, the German Ambassador told the press that he had 'enjoyed the visit immensely … of course this is a purely personal visit, Lord Londonderry and I are close friends'.[94] By then it was clear that Londonderry was beginning to find the former Sekt salesman (a figure so poisonous that even the other Nazi leaders detested him) increasingly wearing, and after his visit to Wynyard in November 1936 he had grumbled to Montgomery Hyde that 'a few years ago this man was touting champagne round Europe.… Now everyone is fawning on him, myself included.'[95] Ribbentrop's notorious Nazi salute in Durham Cathedral may have contributed to this obvious asperity, but others took a yet stronger view, Chips Channon quipping in his diary in May 1936 'The Ribbentrops are intimate with the Londonderrys and he is known as the Londonderry Herr'.[96]

When war came in 1939, Lord Londonderry was swift to assert that 'he sincerely hoped that no doctrines would be put forward for making terms with Germany. There were no terms to be made', but by then the damage had already been done and his reputation was ruined.[97] But a sympathetic reviewer looking back on his career in 1943 could still write:

> Lord Londonderry, in the middle thirties, held that an understanding was then possible with Germany. He had met and talked with Hitler and Goering. For that reason, and because he was opposed to Communism, he was charged with being a Nazi. He repeatedly warned the British authorities of German rearmament and of the need of expediting our own preparations.[98]

The surviving parts of Lord Londonderry's library – the portions which were kept at Mount Stewart and at Londonderry House – certainly contain many twentieth-century books addressing the burning political issues of the day. Ranging from the mundane but useful – a set of the *Dictionary of National Biography* – through to the personal and rather intriguing – the author's presentation copy of Sir Keith Feiling's 1946 biography of Neville Chamberlain, they give a real feel for the preoccupations of the era. That these books were read, and influenced Charley Londonderry in some way seems almost beyond doubt, and some seem

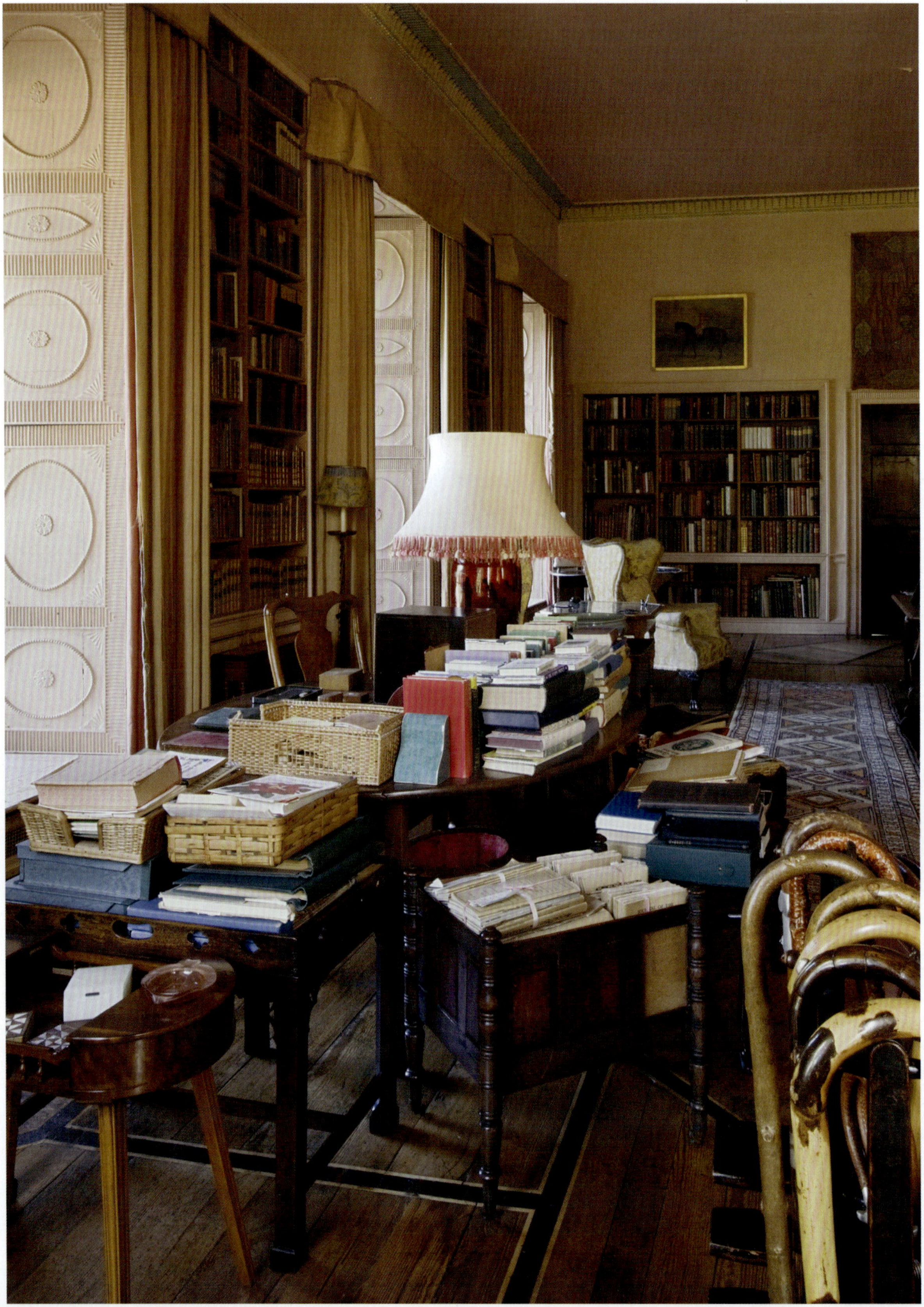

Opposite
Lady Londonderry's Sitting Room, Mount Stewart

likely to have been used by Montgomery Hyde, who helped prepare the raw materials for Londonderry's apologia, *Ourselves and Germany*, published in 1938.[99] But once again, the Londonderrys' reluctance to write in their books means that much of this can proceed little further than conjecture. Apart from the odd exception – Henry Wickham Steed's *The Fifth Arm* (London, 1940), a discussion of propaganda and psychological warfare, annotated in red ink, is one – we neither know which books were being read when, or much about what Edith and Charley Londonderry thought of what they did read. What, for example, did they make of two books by Hermann Rauschning (1887–1982) – leader of the Nazi party in the Free City of Danzig, who subsequently rejected National Socialism and fled to America – whose *Germany's Revolution of Destruction* (London, 1939) and *Hitler Speaks* (London, 1939) were much read at the time, but are regarded by contemporary historians to be little more than Allied propaganda?[100] For that matter, what did Charley think about the discussion of the nature of liberty and freedom in *Modern Democracies* (London, 1923), the last major work of the Belfast-born Liberal politician James Bryce (1838–1922) – and what did Edith, in particular, make of its critique of votes for women? Again, we can only guess.

There was, however, more to Edith's life than politics. A published author in her own right, at Mount Stewart she usually worked at a vast desk in her bedroom rather than surrounded by all the books in her Sitting Room.[101] She seems to have had some awareness of the history of the Mount Stewart library, and was apparently familiar with the various strata within the collection, including books which had once belonged to the Edwards family at Plâs Machynlleth, as well as the considerable number which had been inherited from Castlereagh's wife Amelia Ann Hobart (1772–1829) and from her parents John Hobart, 2nd Earl of Buckinghamshire (1723–93), Lord Lieutenant of Ireland from 1777 to 1780, and his second wife Caroline Conolly of Castletown.[102] Among the most remarkable of these books is a first edition of *Mansfield Park* (London, 1814): remarkable because Amelia Ann evidently shared the tastes of her half-sister Caroline, Lady Suffield, who also owned first editions of Jane Austen, including the 1813 *Pride and Prejudice*, which remains on the shelves of the Hobart family seat, at Blickling in Norfolk. But other books which have washed up at Mount Stewart clearly went back further still, inherited from George II's mistress Henrietta Howard, Countess of Suffolk (*c.*1688–1767), who was Buckinghamshire's aunt, and originally on the shelves of Marble Hill, the exquisite Thames-side villa built for her between 1724 and 1727. Intriguingly, one of this small group is a copy of volume four of *Vitruvius Brittanicus* [*sic*] (London, 1739), issued as an adjunct to the original publication of the same name by the Palladian architect Colen Campbell, who is believed to have been consulted on the design for Marble Hill.[103] Whether Lady Londonderry was aware of the connection with the Countess of Suffolk is unknown, but no doubt it would have intrigued and amused her.

Edith's artistic and cultural interests were most obviously expressed in her famous Ark Society, a literary and political salon which originated in informal entertainments at Londonderry House in 1915.[104] Its members took animal names which alliterated with their Christian names, and included politicians, artists and writers. Charley's cousin Winston Churchill was 'Winston the Warlock', while Charley himself was 'Charley the Cheetah'; Montgomery Hyde was 'Monty the Mole', while Ramsay MacDonald (who was invited to join in 1929) became 'Hamish the Hart'. Other members included the writers John Buchan, Osbert Sitwell, Oliver St John

Gogarty, Compton Mackenzie, Bernard Shaw, W. B. Yeats, Harold Nicolson and Vita Sackville-West, George Russell ('Æ'), politicians like Chamberlain (somewhat implausibly 'Neville the Devil') and Stanley Baldwin ('Bruin the Bear'), the artists Sir William Orpen and Sir John Lavery, and the Communist composer Rutland Boughton, who like Edith herself, was interested in the Celtic revival, and planned to turn Glastonbury into an English Bayreuth.[105] This extraordinary ensemble – the heart of the Establishment at play with the intelligentsia – was presided over by Edith as 'Circe the Sorceress' in what she later described as 'a salon where stage and star met statesmen, Liberals and Conservatives, writers and charmers, University dons, artists and playwrights', who 'all scratched, pinched or bit each other or argued fiercely together, but all answered to their names'. Not everyone approved – John Buchan was sceptical, and his wife thought 'the Ark business silly and vulgar', but one of its most striking features was the mix across the political –and particularly the Irish – divide, Edith taking the robust view 'where art is concerned politics really are quite secondary'.[106] One unlikely friend was the Belfast-born portraitist Sir John Lavery, a Catholic, who, together with his beautiful Irish-American wife, a Sinn Féin supporter ('Hazel the Hen'), became a fast friend, despite the poison pen letters sent to him when he visited Mount Stewart to paint the Church of Ireland Archbishop of Armagh in 1921 (in an eerie foretaste of the Nazis, the anonymous correspondent asking 'Do you have no sense of shame? Parasites like you should be exterminated').[107]

Other visitors to Mount Stewart included Sir John Pentland Mahaffy, Provost of Trinity College, Dublin, famed as one of the great wits of the day, Churchill (who visited with his wife in March 1926) and the deposed King Alfonso of Spain (July 1931).[108] Shane Leslie (1885–1971), aesthete, author and disinherited heir to Castle Leslie at Glaslough (he converted to Catholicism and espoused the Nationalist cause), was invited to see the library in 1933. He was suitably grateful, informing Lady Londonderry that 'I have been very fortunate of late amongst libraries': Edith probably did not know that this was because he had been using his Ascendancy contacts to help the Philadelphia book dealer Dr Rosenbach secure bargains from long-neglected Irish libraries owned by 'people who had no idea of the value of their books'.[109] Other visitors did not make it as far as Ireland, but paid court at Londonderry House, Bernard Shaw collapsing before lunch in December 1938, apparently the result of a bizarre hormone injection taken that morning. 'Transported to the library', he displayed the all-too-common anti-Semitism of the period (the Londonderrys themselves were not entirely guiltless of it either), by jokingly asking whether the footman who had looked after him was 'a non-Aryan refugee doctor in disguise'.[110] The friendship with Shaw is memorialised in slightly more tangible form in the large selection of early editions of his books on the shelves of Lady Londonderry's Sitting Room at Mount Stewart, most notably inscribed copies of *The Apple Cart* (London, 1930), as well as a large-paper copy of *St Joan* (London, 1924) with sketches and stage settings by Charles Ricketts (1866–1931), who also worked for the Abbey Theatre in Dublin, and for D'Oyly Carte in London.[111] Other 'animals' presented copies of their own books, the critic Edmund Gosse sending a copy of his *Father and Son*, inscribed 'to the divine Circe from her infatuated Gos-hawk'.[112] Another particular protégé was the radical Irish playwright Sean O'Casey, who first met Edith in 1926, in March of that year confiding to Lady Gregory, the *châtelaine* of Coole Park, County Galway, intimate friend of Yeats, and arguably the leading figure in the Irish literary revival, how much 'he had liked her'.[113] By the summer of that year, O'Casey's connection with Lady Londonderry was becoming a matter of common knowledge, the *Irish Times* reporting to its readers that:

Mr Sean O'Casey is the lion of the London season. Lady Londonderry, the leading hostess of the Conservative Party, was the first social leader to invite to dinner a man who still boasts his affection for the industrial workers of the world.… Mr O'Casey still refuses to buy a dress suit, and Lady Londonderry was tactful enough to allow him to dispense with the formality of evening clothes[114]

In 1935 Edith advanced £200 to underwrite his American tour, though O'Casey was able to write to her to inform her that 'you will be glad to hear that there was no need to touch it.'[115] Despite his left-wing beliefs, he had no hesitation in accepting, and presented her with a copy of *The Silver Tassie* (London, 1928), 'with warm regards & sincere wishes', perhaps by way of thanks. Decades later Lady Mairi Bury still remembered O'Casey as 'a communist' who 'never objected to being collected in my parents' Rolls', but far from being apologetic about this he actually wrote to her mother in 1936 offering to explain his politics to her: 'Some day when I have the pleasure of seeing you I will tell you why.'[116] Equally, O'Casey betrayed something of the caution surely felt by other friends in danger of being beguiled by Circe, on more than one occasion declining hospitality both at Mount Stewart and in London, perhaps in part because he saw the sense in keeping the Londonderrys just slightly at arms' length, and writing in 1926: 'I hesitate to make visits, for I am reluctant to become entangled in the elaborate mysteries that the English people seem to associate with a meal.'[117]

Another and less surprising literary friend, the poet and translator Helen Waddell (1889–1965), born in Tokyo but educated in Belfast, showed no such restraint, in her letters addressing Edith as 'Circe', 'beloved and fair' or even as 'darling', and presenting copies of her own books, with similarly gushing inscriptions.[118] Cultural patronage on this sort of scale might have been common enough from an eighteenth-century aristocrat, but in the changed world of the 1930s was decidedly unusual, as too was a Big House library packed with important twentieth-century books and association copies, rather than one gradually emptied of the treasures of an earlier era to pay the bills. The only obvious Irish parallel was also in the North, at nearby Clandeboye, the home of the Marquesses of Dufferin, who were, like the Londonderrys, Irish proconsuls and plutocrats, with connections at the summit of the British state, as well as secure sources of income largely unaffected by the Land Acts. The original library at Clandeboye would probably have been in the early nineteenth-century Study, which was combined with the adjoining Entrance Hall to form the present Library room in the 1880s. But in addition there was a separate library shelved in three rooms in the nearby 'Helen's Tower' – named after Helen, Marchioness of Dufferin (d. 1867) – completed in 1850, though the interior was not fitted up until 1861. Removed to the main house in the twentieth century, the Helen's Tower library is still packed with presentation copies of all kinds, with a gold stamp of the Tower on each binding.[119]

Despite her literary interests, Edith's principal pastime at Mount Stewart was her famous garden. Again, the contents of the shelves reflect what was going on out in the demesne, and since the garden was largely Edith Londonderry's own creation, she naturally owned many practical and reference books, including a long run of the *Journal of the Royal Horticultural Society*. There are surprisingly few antiquarian gardening books – one might perhaps have expected Lady Londonderry to assemble a substantial collection – but in fact there is barely a handful, of which much the most splendid is *La Théorie et la Pratique du Jardinage* (Paris, 1709), the seminal work on French formal gardening, the text by the royal secretary and garden connoisseur Antoine-Joseph Dézallier d'Argenville (1680–1765), and the magnificent plates by Jean-Baptiste-Alexandre le Blond (1679–1719), the French-born architect who became the chief designer of St Petersburg. More mundane books published in Edith's own era seem all the more interesting because the garden, despite its own fame, was essentially her own concept and creation. Books like Gertrude Clarke Nuttall's *Beautiful Flowering Shrubs* (London, 1920), William Rickatson Dykes's *A Handbook of Garden Irises* (London, 1924) or – more famously – Gertrude Jekyll's *Some English Gardens* (London, 1910) all presumably acted in some measure as factual guides to what was possible and what other gardeners were doing at the time. Others date from much later in Edith Londonderry's life, during her ten-year widowhood at Mount Stewart, when the garden was already well established, and range from William Jackson Bean's *Trees and Shrubs Hardy in the British Isles* (London, 1950), which Edith seems either to have bought or read in the August of its year of publication, to well-known trophy books of the era like Sacheverell Sitwell and Wilfrid Blunt's *Great Flower Books* (London, 1956).

Quite apart from being a great personal pleasure, the garden served a variety of practical purposes. Before the war it was often used for entertainments and garden parties, again underlining the Londonderrys' almost regal status in pre-war Northern Ireland.[120] It was also frequently open to the public for charitable purposes, Edith, like many aristocratic women of her day taking her charities very seriously, and organising numerous sales and bazaars to raise money for them. Certainly she had no qualms in taking advantage of her many literary friendships when it suited her, hosting a charity auction of literary manuscripts and signed first editions at Londonderry House in May 1933, with contributions from John Galsworthy and A. A. Milne, as well as signed copies of Bernard Shaw's *St Joan* and *The Apple Cart*, together with a letter from GBS. The last may not have sold, and if Edith bought them herself, they could quite conceivably be the very same copies which are today at Mount Stewart.[121] But the friendship could also work in reverse, and while Edith's literary illuminati may have seen her as a fellow enthusiast, and certainly enjoyed her hospitality, she was also recognised to be a powerful women with friends in high places. This seems to have been the starting point of her friendship with both W. B. Yeats and Augusta Gregory. In November 1924 – two years after the establishment of the Free State, and shortly after the end of the Civil War – Lady Gregory noted in her diary that Lady Londonderry had recently written to Yeats to ask 'where she can get "an authentic portrait of Cuchulain" as she wants to put up a statue of him in her garden'.[122] The request presumably came to her because Edith owned a copy of the version of the text that Augusta Gregory had herself published in 1902. If she and Yeats thought it strange or amusing from an arch-Unionist, neither showed it, either out of natural politeness, or because they had already cottoned onto the fact that she might be a powerful ally in one of their pet causes.

Hugh Lane (1875–1915) had been a nephew of Lady Gregory, an aesthete, and a great mover and shaker on the Irish arts scene. He more than anyone was behind proposals for a National Gallery of Modern Art in Dublin, a favourite project of Yeats, Lady Gregory, the Abbey Players and the Gaelic League. The gallery finally opened in 1908, but the project was mired in dispute and delay, and proposals for a magnificent new building by Lutyens on a bridge over the Liffey never came to fruition. Lane was more than irritated by this, and having initially promised his great collection of French Impressionist pictures to Dublin, struck the Corporation out of his will in 1913, instead stipulating that the works should all go to the National Gallery in London. He subsequently relented, but the revised will was never properly witnessed, and when Lane himself went down on the *Lusitania* in 1915 the pictures were still in London, and the ensuing dispute blossomed into a full-scale Anglo-Irish *cause célèbre*.[123] Matters were all the more fraught because the dispute coincided almost exactly with the Free State gaining its independence from Britain, and the future of the collection was perceived by many to have wider ramifications for the constitutional relationship between the two states, and between both and the British Crown, Yeats querying in a letter to Lady Londonderry 'whether the King has the right to act on the advice of his English ministers alone in a matter which concerns the vital interests of a Dominion'.[124] The cudgels were taken up by Lady Gregory, and Edith was carefully cultivated as a 'welcome helper' who might be able to pull strings with the great and good in England, though in the event the pictures remained in London until a deal was eventually brokered between the two governments in 1959.[125] Presents and blandishments passed back and forth between North and South, with Yeats sending an inscribed copy of the programme for the Abbey Theatre's 25th anniversary performance to Mount Stewart in 1925, with additional portraits of himself, Lady Gregory and J. M. Synge, and trying to entice Edith to a performance at the Abbey in 1926.[126] In the same year Lady Gregory presented a copy of her Dun Emer Press *Book of Saints and Wonders* (Dundrum, 1906), presented by the author 'gratefully', presumably for help with the pictures, while a little earlier Yeats had visited Mount Stewart, and towards the end of her life Lady Mairi Bury still recalled sitting on the great man's knee at the age of three or four ('I should think he must have hated it').[127] Edith could be equally fulsome in return, writing to Lady Gregory in January 1929 to inform her that 'I do adore all your long Irish books and read and re-read them', and with this appetite for the literary revival, it was perhaps unsurprising that her library should include a very attractive collection of the private press books issued by the Cuala Press, as well as its short-lived predecessor, the Dun Emer Press (both founded by the poet's sister Elizabeth Yeats), including works by Yeats, Sean O'Faolain, Æ, Oliver St John Gogarty and Elizabeth Bowen.

In January 1932 Yeats wrote to Edith Londonderry to let her know that Lady Gregory was 'now bed-ridden', though still 'vigorous in thought', and strong enough to read Trollope to him.[128] But a little later she died, and not long afterwards her house, Coole Park, County Galway, was demolished. Lady Gregory's published elegy for the library at Coole, which she knew would shortly be lost for ever, remains one of the most evocative descriptions of a Big House library, with its mixture of favourite books and seldom-touched heirlooms on the higher shelves, with 'walls of leather and vellum, mellowed by passing centuries', which might be admired 'even without knowledge of what their message is, as that of a traveller who is ignorant of astronomy may have its surface ruffled as he happens to journey under the stars'. But of course, she was also keen to emphasise to the sceptical that her library was more than simply wallpaper: 'I shall be sorry to leave all these volumes among which I have lived. They have felt the pressure of my fingers. They have been my friends.'[129] Edith, of course, owned a copy of *Coole*, issued by the Cuala Press in 1931, like most of her private press books smartly rebound in a half-marbled calf binding. Inserted

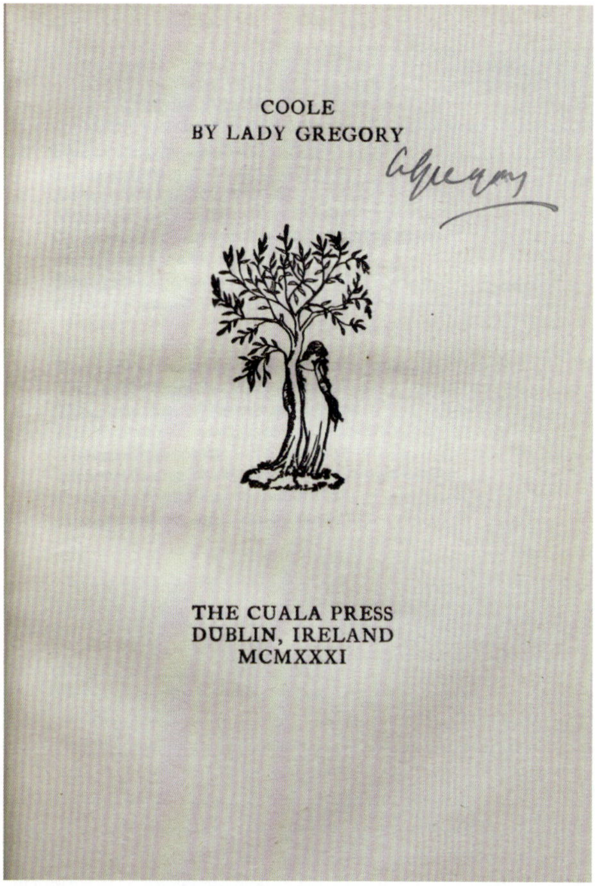
COOLE
BY LADY GREGORY

THE CUALA PRESS
DUBLIN, IRELAND
MCMXXXI

Above
Augusta, Lady Gregory, *Coole* ([Dublin], 1931), with letter from the author to Lady Londonderry tipped in (Mount Stewart)

inside is a short note written from Coole by Lady Gregory on 31 October 1931: 'Dear Lady Londonderry – What a splendid binding to my little book! It does it honour. Yours sincerely, A. Gregory'. Admittedly rather enigmatic, it may perhaps mean that Edith had sent a similarly-bound copy to Coole for the author in the last year of her life.

In a sense, too, the Londonderrys were also the last of their kind. Brought up in an era of imperial grandeur, the world changed rapidly around them, and when Charley died in 1949, the Attlee government was in power and his mines had been nationalised. Already in 1936, Chips Channon had thought that Edith was 'the only political hostess left', while her husband was one of the last great territorial magnates to harbour an aspiration to the sort of political career which his ancestors had taken for granted.[130] In an earlier era Lord Londonderry might, like his father, have occupied a viceregal throne, and it is probably no coincidence that he owned a copy of Lord Curzon's *Leaves from a Viceroy's Note-Book* (London, 1926), since he had hoped for India.[131] But his career ultimately ended in disappointment and, devastated by his ignominious dismissal by Stanley Baldwin, and his political reputation ruined by well-meaning if naïve attempts to negotiate with Hitler, Londonderry was brutal in his self-assessment, saying that 'he had had great chances and missed them by not being good enough'.[132]

As early as 1937, Charley had observed that Londonderry House was almost the last grand house left in London, its neighbours 'rapidly being converted into flats and other buildings which appear to be more in keeping with the spirit of the age'.[133] By 1940 he was toying with the idea of demolishing Wynyard and building a smaller house for his son Robin Castlereagh, and in 1948 he and Edith presented Plâs Machynlleth to the people of the town; the souvenir programme for the formal handover was specially printed at the Gregynog Press, and a copy bound for presentation to the Londonderrys by the National Library of Wales.[134] On Charley's death the following year, the remaining estates were divided, with Mount Stewart going first to Edith for the rest of her life, and then to their youngest daughter, Lady Mairi Bury. Edith spent most of the ten years of a lively and active widowhood at Mount Stewart, still enjoying her friends and her outdoor pursuits, working for the Red Cross, and busier than ever in her garden. Diagnosed with cancer in 1957, she died at Mount Stewart on 23 April 1959. She had already presented the garden to the National Trust in 1955, and Lady Mairi, who lived at Mount Stewart until her death in 2009, added the house and many of its contents in 1976. Edith's library, hardly altered, remains on the shelves.

Note on sources

This is a book about books viewed as material culture: a history of those who owned them, and the ways in which they were – or may have been – acquired and used by their owners. Most historic Irish private libraries have long since vanished, and what distinguishes the libraries in National Trust properties in Northern Ireland is precisely that the collections still exist, and that their books have remained together in an intelligible historical context. It should therefore be no surprise that the principal sources for much of what I have written were the books themselves: not for the printed texts that they contain (though they too can be illuminating, resulting in occasional flashes of serendipity), but for the visible physical evidence which can be found on them. Most cultural commentators have no difficulty in recognising – when they think about it – that old books, like works of art, pieces of clothing, furniture or other artefacts are discrete physical objects, each with their own history, and capable in some measure of telling their own story, quite independently of the texts that they contain. But books are so familiar and ubiquitous that many people simply do not pause to think about the issue at all.[1]

None of this evidence is acquired lightly. Ten years ago – with the exception of the splendid work done for STC- and Wing-period books by Gordon Wheeler at Castle Ward – none of the Trust's books in Northern Ireland was recorded in anything more than basic shelf-lists. Sometimes bibliographically pretty garbled, even when businesslike, none of these lists revealed anything at all about the history of the individual copies which they attempted to describe. In every case that history has emerged slowly, as the result first of collection-level surveys based on examining each single physical volume on the shelves of each library (a task which I myself mostly carried out, though Yvonne Lewis went through the books at The Argory, and Peter Hoare through the even larger library at Mount Stewart). The next stage was book-by-book cataloguing, a task now well-advanced across the National Trust's 250,000 books, with well over 7,000 now recorded in Northern Ireland alone – a task shared between me, Ed Potten, John Gandy, William Hale, Peter Hoare and Felicity Stimpson. Many authors very properly acknowledge the staff in the reading rooms of libraries and archives, but as both a user and a compiler of library catalogues, I am perhaps unusually well-placed to appreciate the intellectual and physical labour involved in work behind-the-scenes, without which any meaningful discussion of a group of historic libraries is all but impossible. Collating books and counting gatherings is time-consuming work, but it provides the raw materials of scholarship. When done for hours on end at levels of light and temperature more suited to paper and leather than to frail human frames, it can be exhausting. Title-pages must be transcribed with care and accuracy and unfamiliar languages (and alphabets) must be tackled. Collational formulae must be constructed, and made to add up. Bibliographical reference sources must be checked, perhaps online – not always easy in a Big House deep in the countryside, and less easy a decade ago than today; if on paper, then probably back at base, from hopefully well-structured notes. For evidence specific to individual copies of books, the guidebooks to the various National Trust houses, and in particular David Pearson's now-classic *Provenance Research in Book History* (London: British Library, 1994), between them provide indispensable assistance, backed up by reference sources ranging from nineteenth-century peerages and indexes of university *alumni*, through to directories of country houses, and of course the staggering riches of the recent online *Oxford Dictionary of National Biography*.

The physical evidence on books takes many forms. Bookplates and ownership stamps are two obvious instances, easy to find, relatively easy to identify, but often more difficult to interpret. What, for example, can be inferred from the bookplates put into books at Castle Ward in the time of the 3rd Lord Bangor in the 1830s? The answer is probably almost nothing, as they were clearly applied retrospectively to books of all kinds, some of which had already been on the estate for a century and a half. Bookplates in National Trust houses present special problems, precisely because the collections within which they are found have not been scattered, and consequently the bookplates within them eluded the clutches of the nineteenth-century *ex libris* hunters on whose collections the reference sources are based. Ownership inscriptions, too, can present their problems: in the first place sometimes simply in reading them, especially if they are early, or in unusual languages or scripts. One seventeenth-century book at Castle Ward, for example, is inscribed in Greek. It is a critical inscription because it establishes that a book which was clearly in Ireland by the middle of the seventeenth century had been in France in 1614, and so helps to date the formation of Lord Claneboye's library. With the help of a digital camera – a now indispensable tool for the nomadic bibliographer – Francesca Galligan at the Bodleian Library kindly read it for me; Stephen Massil was similarly helpful with Hebrew. Marks of other kinds can be more problematic. It took a degree of luck and patience – building on an initial hunch from Nicolas Barker – to identify Michael Ward's cipher on many of the books at Castle Ward, for example. Bindings, too, present their problems. For many, simply a convenient enclosure for a printed text and alarmingly vulnerable to well-meaning repairs intended to make a book 'fit for use', in reality they have the potential to tell us a great deal about the history and use of the book contained within. The deep expertise of my colleague Nicholas Pickwoad is beyond most, but a simple awareness that the physical structure of a book may have its own story to tell is a good start. Made from leather of one kind or another, unbound and stabbed through with thread, in paper wrappers, in plain sheepskin or embellished with gold-tooling, plain and simple or nicely decorated but actually cheaply made and flimsy, a binding can give away a good deal about both its intended place in the market, and the uses which its owner intended to make of it – or could afford to pay for. Handbooks exist which in some measure allow plain and everyday English bindings to be dated with reasonable accuracy, though if used in Ireland they may perhaps need to be deployed with care.[2]

All these apparently trivial signs nonetheless need to be set in a broader context if they are not simply to provide an agglomeration of meaningless antiquarian jottings. In Ireland the fundamental bibliographical apparatus is well established, from the pioneering work of Belfast-born E. R. McClintock Dix (1857–1936) through to the remarkable contribution of Mary 'Paul' Pollard (1922–2005), bibliographer, librarian, and meticulous cataloguer of the workings of the Dublin booktrade.[3] The development of the – in Ireland – unfortunately named *English Short Title Catalogue* has revolutionised bibliographical studies in these islands, and all the relevant material so far catalogued in National Trust libraries in Northern Ireland has been added to the file, and can be checked there.

Building on this impressive inheritance, and on theoretical concepts developed further afield, the comparatively new discipline of the history of the book is flourishing in Ireland. A series of pioneering studies have been published in the last ten years which have examined the history of books and reading in Ireland in a much broader historical context than has ever previously been attempted. With the almost total destruction of the Public Record Office in Dublin during the Civil War in 1922, they have perforce drawn on a varied and multifarious range of sources. My debt to the published work of Raymond Gilliespie and Toby Barnard and the other contributors to the third volume of *The Oxford History of the Irish Book* (2006), in particular, will be evident from the footnotes. Toby Barnard's 'heroic' *Making the Grand Figure*, an indispensable and microscopic discussion of a huge and complex subject, has been a particular inspiration. It is one thing to know that there were books in a house in County Londonderry or County Fermanagh in the 1750s. It is quite another to be able to begin to set those books in a broader context, not just of the history of books across eighteenth-century Ireland, but the wider history of the locality, of the people who owned them, and the social and political networks to which they belonged. Only then can we start to understand them as 'tools for living rather than inert curiosities'.[4]

And then there is the extensive literature on the history of the Big House in Ireland, ranging from traditional descriptions of architecture and high society, to more recent studies which have investigated everything from furniture to the technical operation of the various Land Acts. Much of this is well known, and the extensive footnotes in the text point out where I have used it, but two recent and essential guides are worth mentioning, both published in the *Maynooth Research Guides for Irish Local History* series: Toby Barnard's *A Guide to Sources for the History of Material Culture in Ireland* (Dublin: Four Courts Press, 2005), and Terence Dooley's *The Big Houses and Landed Estates of Ireland: a Research Guide* (Dublin: Four Courts Press, 2007).

Finally, some might wish to know about access to the libraries described in this book. With the growing availability of digital facsimiles of early books, the days when vast numbers of people will wish to read fragile originals in remote country houses are probably numbered. Nonetheless most of the Trust's libraries in Northern Ireland contain appreciable numbers of books which are not yet digitised and which are not readily available anywhere else in Ireland (in some cases not readily available anywhere at all). All of them contain books which are of interest for other reasons. Any and all of these books can be made available for researchers, given reasonable notice, and researchers should consult the Trust's web pages before making contact. Information about all of the books so far catalogued by the Trust – about two-thirds of the total – can be accessed online via *Copac* (www.copac.ac.uk).

References

Prologue: The Big House Library

1 Terence Dooley, *The Decline of the Big House in Ireland: A Study of Irish Landed Families 1860–1960* (Dublin: Wolfhound Press, 2001), pp. 27–28.
2 Tighearnan Mooney and Fiona White, 'The Gentry's Winter Season' in David Dickson (ed.), *The Gorgeous Mask: Dublin 1700–1850* (Dublin: Trinity History Workship, 1987), pp. 1–16.
3 Quoted in Valerie Pakenham, *The Big House in Ireland* (London: Cassell, 2000), p. 21.
4 *Seventy Years Young: Memories of Elizabeth Countess of Fingall told to Pamela Hinkson* (Dublin: Lilliput Press, 2005), p. 37.
5 Elizabeth Bowen, *Bowen's Court* (London: Longman, 1942), p. 132.
6 John Clarke, *An Essay upon Study. Wherein Directions are Given for the Due Conduct Thereof, and the Collection of a Library, Proper for the Purpose* (Dublin: printed by S. Powell for Edward Exshaw, 1736), pp. 223–6, 235, 244, 261. For Clarke himself, see Howard D. Weinbrot, 'John Clarke's "Essay on Study" and Samuel Johnson on "Paradise Lost"', *Journal of Philology*, lxxii, 4 (May 1975), pp. 404–7 (p. 404).
7 Seán O'Reilly, *Irish Houses and Gardens from the Archives of Country Life* (London: Aurum Press, 1998), p. 72.
8 *Catalogue of the Law and Miscellaneous Library of the late Daniel O'Connell, Esq., M.P. which will be Sold by Auction, by Order of the Executors, by John F. Jones, at his Literary Sale Room, 9, D'Olier Street on Tuesday, May 22nd, and Following Days, Commencing at One o'clock* (Dublin: J. M. O'Toole, 1849) [copy in the National Library of Ireland, J 018].
9 I am very grateful to Valerie Ingram, Librarian of the Office of Public Works, for her file notes (29 January 2009) on books at Castletown and in other properties in the care of the OPW. For Ormonde books see: HMC, Ormonde, n.s. 7, pp. 514–5.
10 It was a privilege to have been allowed to examine the books in each of them, and I am suitably grateful to their respective owners, Thomas and Valerie Pakenham, and Pyers O'Conor-Nash, for welcoming me so kindly.
11 Denis Edward Browne, 10th Marquess of Sligo, *Westport House and the Brownes* (Westport: Westport House, 1981). When Thomas De Quincey visited Westport in 1800, he thought the library 'the worst I ever saw.… Almost all the books are about farriery and draining.' (Pakenham, *The Big House in Ireland*, p. 47).
12 Christine Casey, *North Leinster: The Counties of Longford, Louth, Meath and Westmeath* (London: Penguin, 2002), p. 505; the books themselves can be traced via Trinity's online catalogue.
13 William Reeves, *Catalogue of the Library at Lough Fea in Illustration of the History and Antiquities of Ireland* (London: Privately Printed at the Chiswick Press, 1872), p. v; Shane Leslie, 'The Shirley Library at Lough Fea, Carrickmacross in Co. Monoghan, Ireland', the *Book Collectors' Quarterly*, ii, 6, 1932, pp. 1–9; Noel Kissane (ed.), *Treasures from the National Library of Ireland* (Dublin: National Library of Ireland, 1994), pp. 11–12.
14 Illustrated (as it was before 1956) in O'Reilly, *Irish Houses and Gardens from the Archives of Country Life*, p. 72.
15 Quoted by Dooley, *The Decline of the Big House in Ireland*, p. 143.
16 Peter Mandler, *The Fall and Rise of the Stately Home* (New Haven: Yale, 1994), p. 4.
17 For a glimpse into several historic private libraries in the North (and to a lesser extent in the Republic), see Hugh Montgomery-Massingberd, *Great Houses of Ireland* (London: Laurence King, 1999). Though it rarely says much about books, it contains many tantalising photographs.
18 *The Library of Thomas Percy, 1729–1811, Bishop of Dromore, Removed to Caledon House, Co. Tyrone, in 1812, and now sold by the Trustees of the Caledon Estate and the Right Honourable the Earl of Caledon* (London: Sotheby's, 23 June, 1969). For Rosenbach, see Leslie A. Morris, *Rosenbach Abroad: In Pursuit of Books in Private Collections* (Philadelphia: Rosenbach Museum & Library, 1988) and the same author's *Rosenbach Redux: Further Book Adventures in England and Ireland* (Philadelphia: Rosenbach Museum & Library, 1989).
19 Robert S. Matteson, *A Large Private Park: The Collection of Archbishop William King* (1650–1729) (Cambridge: LP Publications, 2002); Davis Coakley, *Doctor Steevens' Hospital* (Dublin: Dr Steevens' Hospital Historical Centre, 1992), pp. 19–21.
20 Margaret Connolly, 'A Plague of Books: The Dispersal and Disappearance of the Diocesan Libraries of the Church of Ireland' in James Raven (ed.), *Lost Libraries: The Destruction of Great Book Collections since Antiquity* (London: Palgrave Macmillan, 2004), pp. 197–218.
21 Clarke, *An Essay upon Study*, p. 264.
22 Roy Foster, *Modern Ireland*, 1660-1972 (London: Allen Lane, 1988), p. 3.
23 The two catalogues, now London, British Library, Harleian MS 3756, were dated to 1518 in Sears Jayne, *Library Catalogues of the English Renaissance* (Berkeley: University of California Press, 1956), p. 97; the second is actually dated 1526 and continued to be used for new accessions until at least 1529. This second catalogue contains over 100 books, but omits the Irish titles of the first catalogue. I am grateful to Gordon Wheeler for this reference.
24 R. J. Hunter, 'Sir William Cole, the Town of Enniskillen and Plantation County Fermanagh', in Eileen M. Murphy and William J. Roulston (ed.), *Fermanagh: History and Society: Interdisciplinary Essays on the History of an Irish County* (Dublin: Geography Publications, 2004), pp. 105–45 (p. 110); *Duannaire Mhéig Uidhir: The Poembook of Cú Chonnacht Mág Uidhir, Lord of Fermanagh, edited from the Copenhagen Manuscript by David Greene* (Dublin: Institute for Advanced Studies, 1972).
25 Raymond Gillespie, *Reading Ireland: Print, Reading, and Social Change in Early Modern Ireland* (Manchester: Manchester University Press, 2005), p. 41.
26 Patrick F. Wallace and Raghnall Ó Floinn, *Treasures of the National Museum of Ireland: Irish Antiquities* (Dublin: Gill & Macmillan, 2002), p. 233.
27 Gillian M. Doherty, *The Irish Ordnance Survey: History, Culture and Memory* (Dublin: Four Courts Press, 2004), p. 165; *Irish Penny Journal*, 1841, p. 227; the manuscripts section of the O'Reilly sale catalogue, interleaved and priced (202 lots), is Dubin, Royal Irish Academy, C.19.3.A.
28 Hugh Fenning, 'Dublin Imprints of Catholic Interest, 1701–1739', *Collectanea Hibernica*, xxxix/xl (1998), pp. 106–54 (p.107).
29 Terence Dooley, *The Big House and Landed Estates of Ireland: A Research Guide* (Dublin: Four Courts Press, 2007), p. 9.
30 Foster, *Modern Ireland*, 1600–1972, p. 7.
31 For which, see The Knight of Glin, *Irish Furniture: Woodwork and Carving in Ireland from the Earliest Times to the Act of Union* (New Haven: Yale, 2007).
32 Alistair Rowan, 'The Irishness of Irish Architecture', *Architectural History*, xl (1997), pp. 1–23 (p. 12).
33 Lyn Gallagher, *Castle, Coast and Cottage: The National Trust in Northern Ireland* (Belfast: Blackstaff Press, 1992); Anthony Malcomson, 'Archives and Aedicules: PRONI and the Northern Ireland Region of the National Trust', *Statutory Report 1997–98 of the Public Record Office of Northern Ireland* (Belfast: Public Record Office of Northern Ireland, 1998), pp. 103–14 (pp. 103–4).
34 The books at Castle Coole are shelved in the magnificent room designed for them by James Wyatt. Of the older books, the most interesting are perhaps those which belonged to a late seventeenth-century churchman, William Armar, a graduate of Trinity College, Dublin, who became Archdeacon of Connor in 1694. But the thousands of ordinary nineteenth- and twentieth-century books in the attic stores are equally fascinating, recording as they do something of everyday life during one of the most turbulent periods of Irish history.
35 William Fordyce Mavor, *The British Tourists; or Traveller's Pocket Companion through England, Wales, Scotland, and Ireland* (London: Printed for E. Newberry, 1798), iii, p. 192.
36 I am grateful to Brian Jenkins and William Hale at Cambridge

University Library for their help in extracting descriptions of the Enniskillen books from the Cambridge online catalogue.

37 Plutarch, *Lives* (Dublin: J. Williams, [1769]) ESTC N20527, vols. ii, iii and vi only.

38 Though for designs of about 1850 for bookcases at Downhill, see Belfast, PRONI, D/1514/2/7/15A-B.

39 G. Vaughan Sampson, *Statistical Survey of the County of Londonderry* (Dublin: Graisberry and Campbell, 1802), pp. 419–20.

40 *An Introduction to the Abercorn Letters* (Omagh: Strule Press, 1972), p. 135.

41 *Belfast News-Letter*, 13 September 1850 (issue 11686). The sale, scheduled for January 1851, was deferred and the estate then sold by private contract – *Belfast News-Letter*, 8 January 1851 (issue 11719).

42 Malcomson, 'Archives and Aedicules', in *Statutory Report 1997–98 of the Public Record Office of Northern Ireland*, p. 107.

43 I am grateful to Peter Marlow, formerly the Trust's Historic Buildings Representative in Northern Ireland and (through him) to the late Sir Charles Brett for their recollections of this.

44 Dooley, *The Decline of the Big House in Ireland*, pp. 286–87.

45 Pakenham, *The Big House in Ireland*, p. 171. Gordon Wheeler tells me of a leaflet (no copy traced) offered for sale by Kenny's of Galway (list 42, part 1, item), *Notes on the Defence of Irish Country Houses*, with the suggested date of *c.*1900, but probably in fact from the 1880s, which suggested that for barricading doors and windows 'heavy library books, particularly bound newspapers, are good'.

46 Dooley, *The Decline of the Big House in Ireland*, p. 193; Terence Dooley, 'The Burning of Ballynastragh, 9 March 1923', *Journal of the Wexford Historical Society*, xix (2003), pp. 42–54.

47 Frank Thompson, 'The Land War in County Fermanagh', in Murphy and Roulston (ed.), *Fermanagh: History and Society*, pp. 287-305 (p. 293).

48 Mark Bence-Jones, *The Twilight of the Ascendancy* (London: Constable, 1987), pp. 90–2.

49 Dooley, *The Decline of the Big House in Ireland*, p. 144.

50 Henry Cole Bowen, *Statutory Land Purchases in Ireland Prior to 1923 and Land Acts Saorstát Éireann* (Dublin: Falconer, 1928).

51 Terence Reeves-Smyth, *Florence Court Demesne* [unpublished typescript] ([Rowallane]: National Trust, 1990), i, p. 45.

52 Anthony Malcomson, 'The Erne Family, Estate and Archive, *c.*1610–1950', in Murphy and Roulston, *Fermanagh: History and Society*, pp. 203–239 (pp. 223–24).

53 J. P. Mahaffy, 'Irish Landlords', *The Contemporary Review* (1882), cited in Dooley, *The Decline of the Big House in Ireland*, p. 110. I am grateful to Gordon Wheeler for drawing this quotation to my attention.

54 3 Edw. VII, chapter 37, pp. 202, 207; Fingall, *Seventy Years Young*, p. 384.

55 Olwen Purdue, *The Big House in the North of Ireland: Land, Power and Social Elites*, 1878-1960 (Dublin: University College Press, 2009), pp. 92–118.

56 H. V. Morton, *In Search of Ireland* (London: Methuen, 1930), pp. 172-92.

57 Mina Lenox-Conyngham, *An Old Ulster House and the People who lived in It* (Dundalk: W. Tempest, 1946), p. 209.

58 Dooley, *The Decline of the Big House in Ireland*, p. 135; Paul M. Canning, 'The Impact of Eamon De Valera: Domestic Causes of the Anglo-Irish Economic War', *Albion, A Quarterly Journal of British Studies*, xv, 3 (autumn 1983), pp. 179–205.

59 *Catalogue of the Fine, Extensive and Valuable Library of the Rt. Hon. The Earl of Gosford, K.P. … (Removed from Gosford Castle, Armagh, Ireland) … To be Sold … on Monday, April 21, 1884* (London: Puttick and Simpson, [1884]); the total realised is marked in manuscript in the copy at Oxford, Bodleian Library, Hanson 121(3).

60 Dooley, *The Decline of the Big House in Ireland*, p. 140; *'Kilkenny Castle', Kilkenny, Ireland. Messieurs Battersby & Co. are Favoured with Instruction from the Right Hon. the Earl of Ossory to Sell by Auction at "Kilkenny Castle" the Valuable Furnishings and Appointments of the Historic Mansion, Together with the Library, Outdoor Effects, etc.* (Dublin: Battersby & Co., 1935); *A Catalogue of the Hillsborough Castle Library, Co. Down, Sold by Order of the Marquess of Downshire, … Which will be Sold by Auction by Messrs Hodgson & Co. … on Wednesday, November 26th, 1924* (London: Hodgson, 1924); Dooley, *The Big House and Landed Estates of Ireland*, p. 160.

61 *Catalogue of Valuable Printed Books in Fine Condition from the Library of the Most Honourable the Marquess of Sligo … Monday, June 27, 1955* (London: Christie, Manson & Woods, 1955); *Catalogue of the Fine and Valuable Contents of Gloster, Brosna, Birr, Co. Offaly, the Property of Major E. T. T. Lloyd … Which will be sold by Town and County Estates (Ireland) … on Tuesday, 28 October, 1958, and Three Following Days* ([Naas?]: [Town And Country Estates], [1956]); Sotheby's, *The Library of Malahide Castle … May 12 1976* (Dublin: Keane, Mahony and Smith, 1976); 'Bibliophile's Diary', *Long Room*, xxxviii (1993), p. 13.

62 Brendán MacAodha, 'The Big House in Western Ireland', in Jacqueline Genet (ed.), *The Big House in Ireland: Reality and Representation* (Dingle: Brandon, 1991), pp. 19–29 (p. 25).

Chapter 1: Plantation

1 Edward Miller, 'Library Report, Castle Ward, November 1978' (unpublished typescript in files of National Trust Libraries Curator).

2 The most helpful published source for the history of Castle Ward is undoubtedly Anthony Malcomson's description of the Ward papers, printed as Appendix 1 to the *Statutory Report of the Public Record Office of Northern Ireland, 1998–1999* (Belfast: Department of the Environment for Northern Ireland, 1999), pp. 63–6. See too: Mark Girouard, 'Castleward, County Down: A Property of the National Trust', *Country Life*, 23 November 1961, pp. 1260–63; 30 November, 1961, pp. 1320–23.

3 John Stevenson, *Two Centuries of Life in County Down* (Belfast: McCaw, Stevenson Orr, 1920), p. 283.

4 Walter Harris, *The Antient and Present State of the County of Down* (Dublin: A Reilly, 1744), pp. 60–61; Belfast, PRONI, D.2092/1/3/142; Francis Joseph Biggar and Herbert Hughes, 'Some Notes on the Architecture and Monumental Remains of the Old Abbey Church of Bangor in the County of Down', *Ulster Journal of Archaeology*, vi, 4 (October 1900), pp. 191–203 (p. 203); Ingrid Roscoe, 'Peter Scheemakers', *Walpole Society*, lxi (1999), p. 243, cat. 91, figs.71, 73; *An Archaeological Survey of County Down* (Belfast: HMSO, 1966), p. 26; Homan Potterton, *Irish Church Monuments, 1570–1880* (Belfast: Ulster Architectural Heritage Society, 1975), pp. 59, 76–77.

5 For the Hamiltons, see: *The Hamilton Manuscripts* (Belfast: Archer & Sons, [1867]), especially the fearsomely complex pedigree (pp. 158–166) and pp. 4–5, 10–12 and 31–33, on which the account which follows is based. See too material in *The Oxford Dictionary of National Biography*.

6 *Dictionary of National Biography* (London: Smith, Elder, 1908–9), xiii, p. 854.

7 The title-page of the Castle Ward copy of the Wechel Press's Xenophon, *Quae Exstant Opera* (Frankfurt, 1596), in Greek and Latin, Adams X16, is inscribed: 'Claneboye'; the text is copiously annotated in what is probably his hand, though he cannot have owned it much earlier than the second decade of the seventeenth century, as it also bears a date inscription of 1614 in Greek by one Sebastian Galland.

8 *Oxford Dictionary of National Biography*; The Hamilton Manuscripts, p. 31.

9 Gillespie, *Reading Ireland*, p. 64.

10 Cicero, *Opera Omnia Quae Exstant* ([Geneva], 1594), inscribed: 'Lord Clanebrasill eius sanguine scriptum'. I am grateful to David Adshead for spotting the possible allusion to Cicero.

11 Emily Georgiana Susanna Reilly, *Historical Anecdotes of the Families of the Boleynes, Careys, Mordaunts, Hamiltons and Jocelyns* ([Newry]: [Printed by J. Henderson], 1839), p. 52.

12 Polydore Vergil, *Angliae Historiae Libri* (Basel, 1570), inscribed by Clanbrasil in 1570, an interesting copy, with seventeenth-century marginal annotations including translations of Irish place names on pp. 221–22.

Chapter 2: This Book is Mr Justice Ward's

1 Raymond Gillespie, 'Print Culture, 1550–1700, in Raymond Gillespie and Andrew Hadfield (ed)., *The Oxford History of the*

Irish Book, iii. *The Irish Book in English 1550–1800* (Oxford: Oxford University Press, 2006), pp. 17–33 (p. 25). Bishop Ward's book list is Dublin, Trinity College Library, MS. 865, fols. 295v–86v.

2 Toby Barnard, *Making the Grand Figure: Lives and Possessions in Ireland, 1641–1770* (New Haven: Yale, 2004), p. 182.

3 *ODNB*; Edith Mary Johnston-Liik, *History of the Irish Parliament* (Belfast: Ulster Historical Foundation, 2002), vi, pp. 497–9.

4 *The Founders of the Royal Dublin Society: With Illustrations of their Houses and a List of Members who joined the Dublin Society between 1731 and 1800* (Dublin: Royal Dublin Society, 2005), pp. 42–5.

5 Toby Barnard, 'Lawyers and the Law in Later Seventeenth-Century Ireland', *Irish Historical Studies*, xxvii, 111 (May 1993), pp. 256–82 (p. 260).

6 For 1741, 1751, 1753, 1756 and 1760.

7 Belfast, PRONI, D.2092/1/5/20.

8 Raymond Gillespie, *Reading Ireland*, p. 16.

9 Belfast, PRONI, D.2092/1/12.

10 Harris, *The Antient and Present State of the County of Down*, p. 41; Belfast, PRONI, D.2092/1/2/24.

11 *Calendar of Home Office Papers of the Reign of George III, 1760–1775* (London: HMSO, 1878–99), iii, p. 381.

12 Johnston-Liik, *History of the Irish Parliament*, vi, p. 495.

13 S. J. Connolly, 'A Woman's Life in mid-eighteenth-century Ireland: The Case of Letitia Bushe', *Historical Journal*, xliii, 2 (2000), pp. 433–51 (pp. 436, 445–51).

14 Belfast, PRONI, D.2092/1/6/158–9; Belfast, PRONI D.2092/1/6/59; Belfast, PRONI, D.2092.1/6/4.

15 Hugh Montgomery-Massingberd, *Great Houses of Ireland* (London: Laurence King, 1999), p. 155.

16 Barnard, *Making the Grand Figure*, p. 170.

17 Montgomery-Massingberd, *Great Houses of Ireland*, p. 132.

18 Barnard, *Making the Grand Figure*, pp. 29–34.

19 Johnston-Liik, *History of the Irish Parliament*, vi, p. 494–5.

20 Belfast, PRONI, D.2091/1/9/15.

21 Máire Kennedy, 'The Top 20 French Authors in Eighteenth-Century Irish Private Libraries', *Linen Hall Review*, xii, 1 (Spring 1995), pp. 4–8 (p. 4); Máire Kennedy, 'Foreign Language Books, 1700–1800', in Raymond Gillespie and Andrew Hadfield (ed.), *The Oxford History of the Irish Book*. iii. *The Irish Book in English, 1550–1800* (Oxford: Oxford University Press, 2006), pp. 368–82.

22 Bernard Burke, *Genealogical and Heraldic History of the Landed Gentry of Great Britain & Ireland* (London: Harrison, 1875), i, pp. 384–5.

23 M. Perceval-Maxwell, 'Stafford, the Ulster-Scots and the Covenanters, *Irish Historical Studies*, xviii, 72 (September 1973). pp. 524–51, (p. 525); *Archaeological Survey of County Down*, p. 295.

24 Stevenson, *Two Centuries of Life in Down*, pp. 288–92; *Archaeological Survey of County Down*, pp. 382–4, plates 159–160; Harris, *The Antient and Present State of the County of Down*, p. 64.

25 M. Pollard, *Dublin's Trade in Books*, 1550–1800 (Oxford: Clarendon Press, 1989), p. 215. Gordon Wheeler notes (personal correspondence, 14 December 2009) that his own analysis of book auction catalogues from 1695 to the 1830s confirms this broad pattern, but observes that the libraries of nobility and gentry may be under-represented simply because dynastic libraries kept in a great house were less liable to sale; other libraries were certainly transferred to English seats after the Union, with many peers abandoning their Dublin town houses in the early decades of the nineteenth century.

26 Edward Smyth, *An Account of the Trial of Edward Smyth, late Curator of Ballyculter, in the Diocese of Down* (Dublin: Printed by William Kidd, 1777), p. 12.

27 Angélique Day and Patrick McWilliams (ed.), *Ordnance Survey Memoirs of Ireland: Volume Seven: Parishes of County Down, II, 1832–4, 1837: North Down and the Ards* (Belfast: Institute of Irish Studies, 1991), p. 11; Angélique Day and Patrick McWilliams (ed.), *Ordnance Survey Memoirs of Ireland: Volume Seventeen: Parishes of County Down, IV, 1833–7: East Down and Lecale* (Belfast: Institute of Irish Studies, 1992), p. 27;

28 John Moore Johnston, *Heterogenea, or Medley* (Downpatrick: James Parks, 1803), pp. 69–70, 216.

29 Belfast, PRONI, D.2092/1/5/15.

30 Belfast, PRONI, D.2092/1/6/132; Belfast, PRONI, D.2092/1/8/80.

31 *ODNB*.

32 Stevenson, *Two Centuries of Life in Down*, p. 300.

33 Belfast, PRONI, D2092/1/4/91.

34 A. Riddell, 'The Dublin-Belfast Coach', *Ulster Journal of Archaeology* (1947), pp. 26–9 (p. 26).

35 Gordon Wheeler, 'Bishop Francis Hutchinson: His Irish Publications and his Library', in John Gray and Wesley McCann (ed.), *An Uncommon Bookman: Essays in Memory of J.R.R. Adams* (Belfast: Linen Hall Library, 1996), pp. 140–55 (p. 147).

36 For example Johan-Henricus Alsted, *Lexicon Theologicum* (Hanau, 1620), signed by both James and Archibald Hamilton (i.e. James Hamilton of Bangor, and his great-uncle, the former Writer to the Signet). Archibald Hamilton's name is also on Lambert Daneau's *Ethicae Christianae* (Geneva, 1588), carefully inscribed 'Archibaldus Hamiltonus, Mihi Satis in Coelis'. An imperfect Calvinist Bible of 1607, in Italian, lacking its title-page, but presumably printed in Geneva, is also highly suggestive. The first of these is illustrated in Nicolas Barker (ed.), *Treasures from the Libraries of National Trust Country Houses* (New York: Royal Oak Foundation, 1999), no. 43.

37 Charles Brett, *Long Shadows Cast Before: Nine Lives in Ulster, 1625–1977* (Edinburgh: J. Bartholomew, 1978), pp. xii, 22–3. I am grateful to Gordon Wheeler for identifying Jasper Brett.

38 M. Pollard, *Dictionary of Members of the Dublin Book Trade, 1550–1800* (London: Bibliographical Society, 2000), pp. 410–11.

39 Pollard, *A Dictionary of Members of the Dublin Book Trade, 1550–1800*, pp. 195–7.

40 Belfast, PRONI, D.2092/1/5/138.

41 Day and McWilliams (ed.), *Ordnance Survey Memoirs of Ireland: Volume Seventeen: Parishes of County Down, iv, 1833–7: East Down and Lecale*, p. 27;

42 Edward Ward, *Number One Boy* (London: Michael Joseph, 1969), p. 15. There are two catalogues from this era at Castle Ward today, neither of any great sophistication, one just possibly from the end of the eighteenth century (1353 titles), and the other dated 1813 (1507 titles); see too Thomas McErlean and Terence Reeves-Smyth, *Castle Ward Demesne* [unpublished typescript] ([Rowallane]: National Trust, 1990), ii, p. 70.

43 I am grateful to the present Lord Bangor for the information that he believes his late father sold books from the library before the National Trust acquired Castle Ward.

44 The other two books appear to have been Jean Bodin's *Les Six Livres de la République* (Geneva, 1629) and *Recueil de Diverses Pièces Servant à l'Histoire de Henry III* (Cologne [i.e. Amsterdam], 1666).

45 *ODNB*; Owen Harry, 'Mary Ward at Castle Ward: The Making of a Naturalist', *Apollo*, cxli, 398 (April 1995), pp. 37–41.

46 *Belfast News-Letter*, 19 August 1863 (issue 25634).

47 Anne de Courcy, *Society's Queen: The Life of Edith, Marchioness of Londonderry* (London: Phoenix, 1992), p. 286.

48 Edward Ward, *I've Lived like a Lord* (London: Michael Joseph, 1976), p. 161; *The Times*, 23 May 1953, p. 6.

Chapter 3: A Convenient Dwelling of Lime and Stone

1 Belfast, PRONI, D.1449/1/11.

2 Toby Barnard, *A Guide to Sources for the History of Material Culture in Ireland, 1500–2000* (Dublin: Four Courts Press, 2005), p. 40.

3 Barnard, *Making the Grand Figure*, pp. 188–91, 219–20; Good-Will Conyngham's will (1720), quoted at length in Lenox-Conyngham, *An Old Ulster House*, p. 21, suggests that the elderly testator took a special interest in his gardens and orchards.

4 Sampson, *A Statistical Survey of the County of Londonderry*, pp. 246–7. The classic account is T. W. Moody, *The Londonderry Plantation, 1609–41; the City of London and the Plantation of Ulster* (Belfast: William Mullan, 1939), helpfully read in conjunction with Raymond Gillespie, 'T. W. Moody, The Londonderry Plantation, 1609–41

(1939)', *Irish Historical Studies*, xxix, 113 (May 1994), pp. 109–13.

5 *Belfast News-Letter*, 8 July 1862.

6 Quoted by Jonathan Bardon, *A History of Ulster* (Belfast: Blackstaff Press, 2001), p. 131.

7 Lenox-Conyngham, *An Old Ulster House*, pp. 3, 5.

8 Lenox-Conyngham, *An Old Ulster House*, pp. 213–15, 223–6.

9 Sampson, *A Statistical Survey of the County of Londonderry*, pp. 246–7, 288, 296–7.

10 *Land Owners in Ireland. Return of Owners of Land of One Acre and Upwards, in the Several Counties, Counties of Cities, and Counties of Towns in Ireland* (Dublin: printed by Alexander Thom, 1876). pp. 256, 232; John Bateman, *The Great Landowners of Great Britain and Ireland* (London: Harrison, 1883). p. 277.

11 Lenox-Conyngham, *An Old Ulster House*, p. 233.

12 Jean Agnew, *Belfast Merchant Families in the Seventeenth Century* (Dublin: Four Courts Press, 1996), p. 39.

13 This complex network of intermarriage is not set out in the family tree given in Lenox-Conyngham, *An Old Ulster House*, pp. xx–xxi, but can in large measure be untangled by careful reading of the text in conjunction with that pedigree, and with occasional reference to standard genealogical sources; Johnston-Liik, *History of the Irish Parliament*, v, p. 84.

14 Lenox-Conyngham, *An Old Ulster House*, pp. 11, 16, 24.

15 Lenox-Conyngham, *An Old Ulster House*, pp. 23, 46.

16 Barnard, *Making the Grand Figure*, pp. 249, 295.

17 Lenox-Conyngham, *An Old Ulster House*, pp. 66, 77.

18 Agnew, *Belfast Merchant Families in the Seventeenth Century*, p. 93; Johnston-Liik, *History of the Irish Parliament*, v, p. 84.

19 Belfast, PRONI, D/1449/1/33. For Boyd, see Thomas Witherow, *Historical and Literary Memorials of Presbyterianism in Ireland*, 2nd series (London: Mullin, 1880), p. 1.

20 Belfast, PRONI, D.1449/1249; the papers taken from Fr. Fottrell are now Belfast, PRONI, D/1449/14; see Hugh Fenning, *The Fottrell Papers* 1721–1739 (Belfast: PRONI, 1980).

21 *The Matriculation Albums of the University of Glasgow from 1728 to 1858* (Glasgow: James Maclehose, 1913), p. 261; a dated ownership inscription of 1813 in his copy of *The Poetical Works of William Collins* (London, 1804).

22 Lenox-Conyngham, *An Old Ulster House*, p. 140.

23 Lenox-Conyngham, *An Old Ulster House*, p. 159. The precise identity of the books at Springhill in the early nineteenth century would presumably be identified by a library catalogue of 1808, noted (without a full reference) in the subject index of the PRONI, but not listed in any of the current finding aids, and consequently untraceable without searching the whole of the Springhill archive at PRONI.

24 Lenox-Conyngham, *An Old Ulster House*, p. 5

25 Lenox-Connygham, *An Old Ulster House*, p. 8.

26 Richard Baxter, *The Life of Faith* (London: printed by R. W. for Nevill Simmons, 1670), p. 2.

27 Toby Barnard, *A New Anatomy of Ireland: The Irish Protestants*, 1649–1770 (New Haven: Yale, 2003), p. 35.

28 There were evidently friendly relations between the Chichesters and the extended Lenox and Conyngham families, with Good Will Conyngham's brother-in-law, the merchant David Butle, importing claret into Belfast in partnership with Lord Donegall in 1701 (Belfast, PRONI, D.1449/13/1).

29 Fingall, *Seventy Years Young*, p. 265; the Library (no longer extant) is illustrated in Randal MacDonnell, *The Lost Houses of Ireland* (London: Weidenfeld & Nicolson, 2002), p. 130.

30 Numerous examples can be found on books in, for example, the contemporary library of Richard Allestree – no friend of Dissenters – who was Regius Professor of Divinity at Oxford, and Provost of Eton College, and died in 1681. See: Mark Purcell, 'Useful Weapons for the Defence of that Cause: Richard Allestree, John Fell, and the Foundation of the Allestree Library', *The Library*, 6th series, vi, 21 (June 1999), pp. 124–47.

31 Belfast, PRONI. D.1449/1/19A.

32 Ian Roy, 'The Libraries of Edward, 2nd Viscount Conway, and Others: An Inventory and Valuation of 1643', *Bulletin of the Institute of Historical Research*, xli, 103 (1968), pp. 35–46; more detailed information kindly supplied by Gordon Wheeler, based on unpublished research notes compiled at Robinson's and elsewhere in the late 1960s.

33 Lenox-Conyngham, *An Old Ulster House*, pp. 58-59.

34 Barnard, *Making the Grand Figure*, pp. 311, 321; Lenox-Conyngham, *An Old Ulster House*, p. 167.

35 Belfast, PRONI, D.1449/1/173.

36 Barnard, *Making the Grand Figure*, p. 256; John Stevenson, *Two Centuries of Life in Down, 1669–1800*, p. 255.

37 *The Several Acts for the Improvement of the Hempen and Flaxen Manufactures in this Kingdom* (Dublin: printed by Andrew Crooke, 1732 [i.e. 1735), ESTC N70554. Of the three copies known to the *English Short Title Catalogue* at the time of writing, the third copy is in the Senate House Library in London.

38 Belfast, PRONI, D2092/1/7/101.

39 Barnard, *Making the Grand Figure*, p. 227.

40 Lenox-Conyngham, *An Old Ulster House*, p. 84.

41 Illustrated in Lenox-Conyngham, *An Old Ulster House*, p. 19.

42 Gillespie, *Reading Ireland*, p. 89; Robert S. Matteson, 'Francis le Jau's Letters to William King, 1695–1704', *Long Room*, 16–17 (Spring–Autumn 1978), pp. 13–24; for William King's library, see also Robert S. Matteson, 'Archbishop William King and the Conception of his Library', *The Library*, 6th series, xiii, 3 (September 1991), pp. 238–54, and Matteson, *A Large Private Park: The Collection of Archbishop William King*.

43 Gillespie, *Reading Ireland*, p. 81.

44 Agnew, *Belfast Merchant Families in the Seventeenth Century*, p. 39.

45 Gillespie, *Reading Ireland*, p. 79; Johnston-Liik, *History of the Irish Parliament*, v, pp. 265–6.

46 cf. *Album Studiosorum Academiae Lugduno Batavae MDLXXV–MDCCCLXXV: Accedunt Nomina Curatorum et Professorum per Eadem Secula* (The Hague: M. Nijhoff, 1875); *Album Promotorum, qui inde ab anno MDCXXXVI usque ad annum MDCCCXV in Academia Rheno-Trajectina gradum doctoratus adepti sunt* (Utrecht: in aedibus Broekhoffi, 1936).

47 I am grateful to Professor William McCormack for showing me round Worth's Library in September 2008, and to him, Dr Elizabethanne Boran, Dr Danielle Westerhof and Simon McCormack for the thought-provoking discussions that followed.

48 Anthony S. Drennan, 'On the Identification of the First Belfast Printed Book', *The Library*, 7th ser., i, 2, (June 2000), pp. 193–6.

Chapter 4: The White Presses in the Library

1 Barnard, *Making the Grand Figure*, p. 202; The *Survey of London* (London: Athlone, 1980), xl, pp. 210–21.

2 Horace Walpole, *Horace Walpole's Correspondence with Sir Horace Mann* (London: Oxford University Press, 1954–1971), vi, pp. 138–41; Johnston-Liik, *History of the Irish Parliament*, v, p. 258. *Public Advertiser*, 15 December 1781.

3 Bence-Jones, *A Guide to Irish Country Houses*, p. 188; Johnston-Liik, *History of the Irish Parliament*, vi, pp. 322–3.

4 Lenox-Conyngham, *An Old Ulster House*, p. 166.

5 *An Introduction to the Abercorn Papers*, pp. 90–91.

6 Belfast, PRONI, D/671/D2/1/17A–B.

7 Barnard, *A Guide to Sources for the History of Material Culture in Ireland*, p. 33; Barnard, *Making the Grand Figure*, p. 120; Vaughan Sampson, *A Statistical Survey of the County of Londonderry*, pp. 246–7; 288; 296–7.

8 Mark Bence-Jones, *A Guide to Irish Country Houses* (London: Constable, 1988), p. 44; unattributed contemporary quotation given in E. Charles Nelson, 'The Dublin Florists' Club in the Mid Eighteenth Century', *Garden History*, x, 2 (autumn 1982), pp. 142–8 (p. 144); *ODNB*. For more details of Blessington House, see Kathy Trant, *The Blessington Estate* 1667–1908 (Dublin: Anvil, 2004).

9 Brian de Breffney, 'The Building of the Mansion at Blessington', *GPA Irish Arts Review* (1988), pp. 71–7 (p. 73).

10 Samuel Lewis, *A Topographical Dictionary of Ireland* (London: S. Lewis,

1837), i, p. 213.
11 The Knight of Glin and James Peill, *Irish Furniture: Woodwork and Carving in Ireland from the Earliest Times to the Act of Union* (New Haven: Yale University Press, 2007), p. 58.
12 *The Victoria History of Hampshire and the Isle of Wight* (Folkestone: Dawson, 1973), iv, p. 54; *The Victoria History of the County of Middlesex* (London: Oxford University Press for the Institute of Historical Research, 1989), ix, pp. 15–33; *Survey of London*, xl, pp. 117–66.
13 Nelson, 'The Dublin Florists' Club in the Mid Eighteenth Century', p. 143.
14 Foster, *Modern Ireland*, 1600–1972, p. 5.
15 Barnard, *Making the Grand Figure*, p. 253.
16 Toby Barnard, 'Learning, the learned and literary in Ireland. *c.*1660–1760', in Toby Barnard, Dáibhí Ó Cróinín and Katherine Sims, *A Miracle of Learning: Studies in Manuscripts and Irish Learning: Essays in Honour of William O'Sullivan* (Aldershot: Ashgate, 1998), pp. 209–35 (p. 215).
17 Elizabethanne Boran, 'Libraries and Collectors, 1550–1700', in Gillespie and Hadfield (ed.), *The Oxford History of the Irish Book*, iii, pp 91–110 (p. 107); Trant, *The Blessington Estate*, pp. 42–4.
18 Barnard, *Making the Grand Figure*, p. 333; Thomas Hayter, *A Sermon Preach'd before the Society Corresponding with the Incorporated Society in Dublin for Promoting English Protestant Working-Schools in Ireland* (London: Printed and Sold by J. Oliver, 1754), p. 60.
19 Barnard, *Making the Grand Figure*, pp. 15, 232.
20 ESTC T213588.
21 John Spitzer, 'Grammar of Improvised Ornamentation; Jean Rousseau's Viol Treatise of 1687', *Journal of Music Theory*, 33 (Fall 1989), pp. 299–332.
22 Trant, *The Blessington Estate*, pp. 60–1.
23 Vaughan Sampson, *Statistical Survey of the County of Londonderry*, p. 411.
24 Belfast, PRONI, D/1567/B/11.
25 Lenox-Conyngham, *An Old Ulster House*, p. 166.
26 Robert Welch (ed.), *The Oxford Companion to Irish Literature* (Oxford: Clarendon Press, 1996), p. 148
27 Sebastian P. Brock, *The Bible in the Syriac Tradition* (2nd ed. Piscataway, NJ: Gorgias Press, 2006), p. 126.
28 *ODNB*.
29 Raymond Gillespie, 'The Irish Protestants and James II, 1698–90', *Irish Historical Studies*, xxviii, 110 (1992), pp. 124–33 (p. 125).
30 Toby Barnard, 'Gathering Ideas: A Clerical Library in County Cork, 1774', in Martin Fanning and Raymond Gillespie (ed.), *Print Culture and Intellectual Life in Ireland, 1660–1941. Essays in Honour of Michael Adams* (Dublin: Woodfield Press, 2006), pp. 24–52.
31 Thomas D. Halsted, *Our Missions, a History of the Principal Missionary Transactions of the London Society for Promoting Christianity amongst the Jews* (London: William Mackintosh, 1866), p. 55; David S. Katz, *The Jews in the History of England, 1485–1850* (Oxford: Clarendon Press, 1996), p. 382. I am grateful to Stephen Massil both for these references, and for reading the manuscript.
32 Robin Fedden to the Earl of Antrim, 28 April 1959: Belfast, PRONI, D.3839/B/14.
33 Lenox-Conyngham, *An Old Ulster House*, pp. 175–229; Report of Kenneth Villiers, Charles Howard Interior Design, to the Earl of Antrim, 19 November 1959: Belfast, PRONI D.3839/B/14/.
34 Lenox-Conyngham, *An Old Ulster House*, p. 196.
35 *Belfast News-Letter*, 6 February 1854; Lenox-Conyngham, *An Old Ulster House*, p. 190.
36 Alistair Rowan, *The Buildings of Ireland: North West Ulster* (Harmondsworth: Penguin, 1979), p. 250.
37 Lenox-Conyngham, *An Old Ulster House*, pp. 190, 196; Bernard Burke, *A Genealogical and Heraldic History of the Landed Gentry of Ireland* (London: Harrison and Sons, 1904), p. 363. The crucial will which led to Marcus Gage inheriting Bellarena is Belfast, PRONI, T.1201/3.
38 Lenox-Conyngham, *An Old Ulster House*, p. 196.
39 *Belfast News-Letter*, 1 April 1859.
40 Rowan, *The Buildings of Ireland: North West Ulster*, p. 540; Lenox-Conyngham, *An Old Ulster House*, p. 196; Burke, *A Genealogical and Heraldic History of the Landed Gentry of Ireland*, p. 34.
41 Lenox-Conyngham, *An Old Ulster House*, pp. 196, 202–3, 209.
42 Lenox-Conyngham, *An Old Ulster House*, pp. 224–25.
43 Lenox-Conyngham, *An Old Ulster House*, pp. 235–6.
44 Lenox-Conyngham, *An Old Ulster House*, p. 236.

Chapter 5: The Exhilarating and Invigorating Air

1 John Wesley, *The Journal of the Rev. John Wesley* (London: Robert Culley, [1910–16], vi, pp. 65–6.
2 Arthur Young, *Autobiography* (London: Smith Elder, 1898), p. 106.
3 Young, *Autobiography*, p. 104.
4 *The Journal of Elizabeth Lady Holland (1791–1811)* (London: Longmans, Green & Co., 1908), i, p. 219.
5 Jan Eccles, *Downhill: A Scrapbook of People and Places from the Notebooks of Miss Jan Eccles* (London: Printing Ideas & Graphics, 1996), p. 71.
6 W. S. Childe-Pemberton, *The Earl Bishop: the Life of William Hervey, Bishop of Derry, Earl of Bristol* (London: Hurst & Blackett, 1925), i, p. 147.
7 Peter Rankin, *Irish Building Ventures of the Earl Bishop of Derry* (Belfast: Ulster Architectural Heritage Society, 1972), p. 12; Robert Slade, *Narrative of Journey to the North of Ireland in the Year 1802* (London: Printed by R. and H. Causton, 1803), p. 54.
8 Childe-Pemberton, *The Earl Bishop*, i, p. 12.
9 Belfast, PRONI, D2798/5/8; the relations of the Earl-Bishop with Irish Catholics are discussed in: John R. Walsh, *Frederick Augustus Hervey, 1730–1803, Fourth Earl of Bristol, Bishop of Derry: 'Le Bienfaiteur des Catholique'* (Maynooth: St Patrick's College, 1972).
10 Belfast, PRONI, D2798/5/6.
11 Childe-Pemberton, *The Earl Bishop*, i, p. 109.
12 *An Introduction to the Abercorn Letters*, p. 145.
13 Childe-Pemberton, *The Earl Bishop*, pp. 113–14.
14 Gillian Darley, *Sir John Soane: An Accidental Romantic* (New Haven: Yale, 1999), p. 59; the building campaign at Downhill is helpfully summarised in Rowan, *The Buildings of Ireland: North West Ulster*, pp. 244–8, drawing on the original research in Rankin, *Irish Building Ventures of the Earl Bishop of Derry*, p. 32.
15 Belfast, PRONI, D2798/2/23.
16 *The Journal of John Wesley*, vii, p. 286.
17 Young, *Autobiography*, p. 104; Rowan, *The Buildings of Ireland: North West Ulster*, p. 139.
18 Angélique Day and Patrick McWilliams (ed.), *Ordnance Survey Memoirs of Ireland: Volume Six: Parishes of County Londonderry I* (Belfast: Institute of Irish Studies, Queen's University, 1990), p. 48.
19 Brian Fothergill, *The Mitred Earl: An Eighteenth-Century Eccentric* (London: Century, 1988), p. 7.
20 Young, *Autobiography*, pp. 106, 113.
21 Slade, *Narrative of a Journey to the North of Ireland*, p. 56.
22 Young, *Autobiography*, pp.104–6.
23 M. de Lactonaye, *A Frenchman's Walk through Ireland 1796–7: translated from the French of De Lactonaye by John Stevenson* (Belfast: Blackstaff Press, 1984), p. 220.
24 Belfast, PRONI, D2798/4/34.
25 Fothergill, *The Mitred Earl*, p. 125.
26 Rankin, *Irish Building Ventures of the Earl Bishop of Derry*, p. 22
27 Rankin, *Irish Building Ventures of the Earl Bishop of Derry*, p. 52.
28 *A Frenchman's Walk Through Ireland 1796–7*, p. 203.
29 Raymond Keaveney, *Views of Rome* [from the Thomas Ashby Collection in the Vatican Library] (London: Scala Books, 1988), p. 250; Darley, *John Soane: An Accidental Romantic*, p. 56.
30 James Howley, *The Follies and Garden Buildings of Ireland* (New Haven: Yale, 1993), p. 153.
31 Sir Edward Newenham, quoted in C. Litton Faulkner, *Studies in Irish History and Biography, Mainly of the Eighteenth Century* (London: Longman, Green, 1902), pp. 78–9.
32 James Gibbs, *Bibliotheca Radcliviana: or, A Short Description of*

the Radcliffe Library, at Oxford (London: Printed for the Author, 1747); H. M. Colvin, *Unbuilt Oxford* (New Haven: Yale, 1983), pp. 64–71; H. M. Colvin, 'The Building' in David McKitterick (ed.), *The Making of the Wren Library, Trinity College, Cambridge* (Cambridge: Cambridge University Press, 1995), p. 32, plates 28–31.

33 Åke Setterwall, *The Chinese Pavillion at Drottningholm* (Malmö: Allhem, 1974).

34 Smyth, *An Account of the Trial of Edward Smyth*, p. 12

35 Thomas Milton, *A Collection of Select Views from the Different Seats of Nobility and Gentry in the Kingdom of Ireland* (London, [1793]), p. 9; I am grateful to Valerie Ingram of the Office of Public Works for the information that the books on show in the Casino today are not original to the house.

36 Belfast, PRONI, D2798/2/24.

37 Walsh, *Frederick Augustus Hervey*, p. 7.

38 Rankin, *Irish Building Ventures of the Earl Bishop of Derry*, p. 55.

39 Lucretius, *De Rerum Natura*, ii, 1–2.

40 Stuart Gillespie and Philip Hardie (ed.), *The Cambridge Companion to Lucretius* (Cambridge: Cambridge University Press, 2007), p. 14.

41 Robert Day, *Robert Day (1746–1841): The Diaries and Addresses to Grand Juries* (Tralee: Polymath Press, 2004), p. 59.

42 *Downhill: A Scrapbook of People and Places*, p. 147.

43 I am grateful to Dr Stephanie Coane, Librarian of Sir John Soane's Museum, for access to draft catalogue entries for these two books.

Chapter 6: Fossils and the Orange Order

1 The outline family history which follows is based (unless referenced to the contrary) on Anthony Malcomson, 'The Enniskillen Family, Estate and Archive', *Clogher Record*, xvi, 2 (1998), pp. 81–122.

2 R. J. Hunter, 'Sir William Cole, the Town of Enniskillen and Plantation County Fermanagh', in Eileen M. Murphy and William J. Roulston (ed.), *Fermanagh: History and Society* (Dublin: Geography Publications, 2004), pp. 105–45 (pp. 105–8).

3 Roulston, 'Castles, Churches and Country Houses: The Lost Architecture of County Fermanagh in an Age of Improvement, *c.*1700–*c.*1750', in Murphy and Roulston (ed.), *Fermanagh: History and Society*, pp. 171–202 (pp. 173, 184).

4 Roulston, 'Castles, Churches and County Houses', in Murphy and Roulston (ed.), *Fermanagh: History and Society*, p. 187.

5 William Wilson, *The Post-Chaise Companion: or, Travellers' Directory through Ireland* (London: Printed for W. Faden, 1784), col. 52.

6 For the architectural history of Florence Court, see Edward McParland, 'Florence Court, Co. Fermanagh', *Country Life* (7 May 1981), pp. 1242–5; *Country Life* (14 May 1981), pp. 1318–21.

7 Marianne Elliott, *The Catholics of Ulster* (London: Allen Lane, 2000), p. 118.

8 I am grateful to Alec Cobbe for this information.

9 Toby Barnard, 'Learning, the Learned and Literacy in Ireland. *c.*1660–1760', in Toby Barnard, Dáibhí Ó Cróinín and Katherine Sims, *A Miracle of Learning: Studies in Manuscripts and Irish Learning: Essays in Honour of William O'Sullivan* (Aldershot: Ashgate, 1998), pp. 209–35 (p. 214).

10 John Watson Stewart, *The Gentleman and Citizen's Almanack* (Dublin: Printed by Thomas Stewart and John Watson Stewart, 1799), p. 68; *Belfast News-Letter*, 26 March 1851.

11 Milton, *A Collection of Select Views from the Different Seats of Nobility and Gentry in the Kingdom of Ireland*, p. 229; Barnard, *Making the Grand Figure*, pp. 339. 229.

12 Elliott, *The Catholics of Ulster*, p. 171; *ODNB*.

13 Peter Marson, *Belmore: The Lowry Corrys of Castle Coole, 1946-1913* (Belfast: Ulster Historical Foundation, 2007), p. 7.

14 Muriel McCarthy, *Marsh's Library in Dublin: All Graduates and Gentlemen* (Dublin: Four Courts Press, 2003), p. 62; *ODNB*.

15 Belfast, PRONI, D.704/179.

16 *Robert Day (1746–1841): The Diaries and Addresses to Grand Juries* (Tralee: Polymath Press, 2004), p. 55; *Morning Chronicle*, 21 March 1829.

17 Belfast, PRONI, D552/A/8/4/97.

18 Angélique Day and Patrick McWilliams (ed.), *Ordnance Survey Memoirs of Ireland: Volume Fourteen: Parishes of Fermanagh, ii, 1834–5: Lower Lough Erne* (Belfast: Institute of Irish Studies, 1992) p. 85.

19 *Belfast News-Letter*, 18 January 1881.

20 Frank Thompson, 'The Land War in County Fermanagh', in Murphy and Roulston (ed.), *Fermanagh: History and Society*, pp. 287–305 (p. 287).

21 *Daily News*, 28 December 1880.

22 Francis Thompson, 'Attitudes to Reform: Political Parties in Ulster and the Irish Land Bill of 1881', *Irish Historical Studies*, xxiv, 95 (May, 1985), pp. 327–40 (p. 335); D. C. Savage, 'The Origins of the Ulster Unionist Party, 1885–6', *Irish Historical Studies*, xii, 47 (May 1961), pp. 185–208. (p. 202).

23 *Land Owners in Ireland. Return of Owners of Land of One Acre and Upwards, in the Several Counties, Counties of Cities, and Counties of Towns in Ireland* (Dublin: Printed by Alexander Thom, 1876).

24 *Belfast News-Letter*, 19 December 1883; *Freeman's Journal and Daily Commercial Advertiser*, 24 April 1845.

25 Bardon, *A History of Ulster*, pp. 302–4.

26 *Report of the Special Committee of the Grand Lodge of Ireland, appointed November 1849* (Dublin: Edward Bull, 1849), p. 32.

27 Mary D. Condon, 'The Irish Church and the Reform Ministries', *Journal of British Studies*, iii, 2 (May 1964), pp. 120–42.

28 Kenneth W. James, *Damned Nonsense!: The Geological Career of the Third Earl of Enniskillen* (Belfast: Ulster Museum, 1986); *ODNB*.

29 William Willoughby Cole, 3rd Earl of Enniskillen, 'Alphabetical Catalogue of Fossil Fishes in the Collection of the Earl of Enniskillen at Florence Court', *Geological Magazine*, vi (December 1869), pp. 556–60.

30 Day and McWilliams (ed.), *Ordnance Survey Memoirs of Ireland: Volume Fourteen: Parishes of Fermanagh II 1834–5: Lower Lough Erne*, p. 84.

31 *Belfast News-Letter*, 8 May 1835.

32 Day and McWilliams (ed.), *Ordnance Survey Memoirs of Ireland: Volume Fourteen: Parishes of Fermanagh II 1834–5: Lower Lough Erne*, p.3

33 R. A. Baker and R. A. Bayliss, 'Louis Compton Miall, F.R.S.: Scientist and Educator 1842–1921', *Notes and Records of the Royal Society of London*, xxxvii, 2 (March 1983), pp. 201–34 (p. 205).

34 Edward Lurie, *Nature and the American Mind: Louis Agassiz and the Culture of Science* (New York: Science History Publications, [1974]).

35 *ODNB*.

36 F. Chandler, *Photography in Ireland: The Nineteenth Century* (Dublin: Edmund Burke, 2001), p. 103.

37 *The Gentleman's Magazine*, July 1843, p. 77; for Lord Enniskillen's books on Irish history and topography see: Mark Purcell and William Hale, 'Hibernica from the Library at Florence Court', *National Trust Houses & Collections Annual, Published in Association with Apollo Magazine* (2008), pp. 30–35.

38 *The Gentleman's Magazine*, August 1864, p. 198; *Freeman's Journal and Daily Commercial Advertiser*, 18 February 1845; *The Gentleman's Magazine*, May 1850, p. 519; London, British Library, Add. MS 15240.

39 I am grateful to Mary Cahill, Assistant Keeper in the Irish Antiquities Division of the National Museum of Ireland, for access to transcripts of the register of the Royal Irish Academy now incorporated into the collections database of the National Museum.

40 Aideen M. Ireland, 'Colonel William Gregory Wood-Martin, 1847–1917', *Journal of Irish Archaeology*, x (2001), pp. 1–11; *The Gentleman's Magazine*, December 1851, p. 639.

41 Thomas Wright, *Arbours & Grottos* (London: Scolar Press, 1979), p. [27].

42 Jeanne Sheehy, *The Rediscovery of Ireland's Past: The Celtic Revival, 1830–1930* (London: Thames & Hudson, 1980), p. 23.

43 Day and McWilliams (ed.), *Ordnance Survey Memoirs of Ireland: Volume Fourteen: Parishes of Fermanagh II 1834-5: Lower Lough Erne* (Belfast: Institute of Irish Studies, 1992), p. 84.

44 *Belfast News-Letter*, 12 February 1833.

45 *Freeman's Journal and Daily Commercial Advertiser*, 23 June 1832; *Belfast News-Letter*, 22 December 1835.

46 *Belfast News-Letter*, 21 April 1840.
47 Francesca Scoones, 'The Professor at Florence Court', *Georgian Group Journal*, xiv (2004), pp. 75–88.
48 Something of the flavour of the period comes across in Nancy, Countess of Enniskillen, *Florence Court: My Irish Home* (Monaghan: R. & S. Printers, 1972); and the Trust perspective in Ian B. McQuiston, 'The Palingenesis of Florence Court', in Terence Reeves-Smyth and Richard Oram (ed.), *Avenues to the Past: Essays Presented to Sir Charles Brett in his 75th Year* (Belfast: Ulster Architectural Heritage Society, 2003), pp. 213–24.
49 *Good Printed Books Comprising the Early Medical, Natural History, Botanical, Fishing & Sporting Books from the Right Hon. the Earl of Enniskillen [and] Part 1 of the Library of the Late Dr Robert Mowbray of Penrith to be Sold by Auction on Wednesday 17th December 1986* (Edinburgh: Phillips, 1986).
50 David McKitterick, *Cambridge University Library: A History: The Eighteenth and Nineteenth Centuries* (Cambridge: CUP, 1986), pp. 684–7.

Chapter 7: I Sent a Horseman to Dungannon

1 I am extremely grateful to my colleague Edith Stafford, Conservation Assistant at The Argory, who very kindly provided me with transcripts of these key documents – unlike most of The Argory's archive, still in the house rather than in the Public Record Office in Belfast – as well as helpful advice on The Argory and its history.
2 *Introduction: MacGeough Bond Papers* ([Belfast: PRONI, 2007]), p. 4.
3 Ralph Shelton had, for reason unknown, reversed his names by deed poll in 1873, changing from Ralph Shelton McGeough to Ralph MeGeough Shelton.
4 Peter O. Marlow, *The Argory, Co. Armagh* (London: National Trust, 1992), pp. 22–7.
5 William Broadhurst and Henry Walsh, *The Flaming Truth: A History of the Belfast Fire Brigade* (Belfast: Flaming Publications, 2001), p. 117.
6 *Belfast News-Letter*, 4 June 1898.
7 Belfast, PRONI, D.254/61.
8 *Belfast News-Letter*, 4 June 1898.
9 Pakenham, *The Big House in Ireland*, p. 174.
10 Scoones, 'The Professor at Florence Court', p. 78.
11 Dooley, *The Decline of the Big House in Ireland*, p. 175.
12 Pakenham, *The Big House in Ireland*, p. 47.
13 Belfast, PRONI, D2798/9/1–2.
14 *Belfast News-Letter*, 14 August 1899.
15 Belfast, PRONI, MIC354/2/9; *Belfast News-Letter*, 17 August 1896.
16 Dooley, *The Decline of the Big House in Ireland*, pp. 161–5.
17 *Freeman's Journal and Daily Commercial Advertiser*, 16 January 1886; *Belfast News-Letter*, 8 July 1858.

Chapter 8: What a Splendid Binding

1 *The Irish Times*, 16 January, 1932, p. 4.
2 H. Montgomery Hyde, *The Londonderrys: A Family Portrait* (London: Hamish Hamilton, 1979), pp. 115, 129.
3 John Bateman, *The Great Landowners of Great Britain and Ireland* (New edn. London: Harrison, 1879), p. 424.
4 Bardon, *A History of Ulster*, p. 502.
5 Hyde, *The Londonderrys*, p. 130.
6 Consuelo Vanderbilt Balsan, *The Glitter & the Gold* (Maidstone: George Mann, 1973), p. 137.
7 Fingall, *Seventy Years Young*, p. 208; De Courcy, *Society's Queen*, p. 120; Hyde, *The Londonderrys*, p. 109
8 Hyde, *The Londonderrys*, p. 66.
9 Vanderbilt Balsan, *The Glitter & the Gold*, pp. 135–6.
10 Hyde, *The Londonderrys*, p. 77.
11 Diane Urquhart, *The Ladies of Londonderry: Women and Political Patronage* (London: I. B. Tauris, 2007), p. 78.
12 Joseph Robins, *Champagne & Silver Buckets: The Viceregal Court at Dublin Castle, 1700–1922* (Dublin: Lilliput Press, 2001), p. 136.
13 David Cannadine, *The Decline and Fall of the British Aristocracy* (London: Papermac, 1996), p. 169; Hyde, *The Londonderrys*, p. 75.
14 *The Irish Times*, 17 September 1886. p. 3.
15 Urquhart, *The Ladies of Londonderry*, p. 80; *The Irish Times*, 30 July 1886, p. 5.
16 Philip Bull, 'The Significance of the Nationalist Response to the Irish Land Act of 1903', *Irish Historical Studies*, xxviii, 111 (May, 1993), pp. 283–305 (p. 286); Fingall, *Seventy Years Young*, p. 162.
17 Edith, Marchioness of Londonderry, *Retrospect* (London: Frederick Muller, 1938), p. 218; Andrew Gailey, 'King Carson: an Essay on the Invention of Leadership', *Irish Historical Studies*, xxx, 117 (May 1996), pp. 66–87 (p. 68).
18 Fingall, *Seventy Years Young*, p. 206; *The Times*, 17 March 1919, p. 14; Urquhart, *The Ladies of Londonderry*, p. 105.
19 Angélique Day and Patrick McWilliams (ed.), *Ordnance Survey Memoirs of Ireland: Volume Seven: Parishes of County Down, ii, 1832–4, 1837: North Down & The Ards* (Belfast: Institute of Irish Studies, 1991), pp. 69–70.
20 Belfast, PRONI, D654/S/1/1.
21 London, Sir John Soane's Museum, D3/9/5.
22 Anne Casement, 'The Strange Sale of Pictures from Glenarm: Gibbs's "Hambletonian, Rubbing Down"', *National Trust Historic Houses & Collections Album, Published in Association with Apollo Magazine* (2007), pp. 57–61.
23 Belfast, PRONI, D654/S1/2.
24 3rd Marquess of Londonderry, *A Steam Voyage to Constantinople* (London: Henry Colburn, 1842), ii, p. 201.
25 Charles Brett, *Buildings of North County Down* (Belfast: Ulster Architectural Heritage Society, 2002), pp. 96–9.
26 Hyde, *The Londonderrys*, p. 1.
27 Hyde, *The Londonderrys*, pp. 23–4.
28 De Courcy, *Society's Queen*, pP. 177.
29 H. Montgomery Hyde, *Londonderry House and its Pictures* (London: Cresset Press, [1937]), p. 5; Hyde, *The Londonderrys*, p. 30.
30 De Courcy, *Society's Queen*, p. 236.
31 Bence-Jones, *Life in an Irish Country House*, p. 197.
32 *The Times*, 17 March 1919, p. 14.
33 Hyde, *The Londonderrys*, p. 111.
34 Bardon, *A History of Ulster*, pp. 502–3; Fingall, *Seventy Years Young*, p. 207.
35 Hyde, *The Londonderrys*, p. 132.
36 Bence-Jones, *Life in an Irish Country House*, p. 200; De Courcy, *Society's Queen*, p. 76.
37 Fingall, *Seventy Years Young*, p. 207; Urquhart, *The Ladies of Londonderry*, pp. 76–8; the autograph manuscript of her autobiography is Belfast, PRONI, D.3084.
38 Much of the material which follows is derived directly from the recollections of the Londonderrys' youngest daughter, Lady Mairi Bury, in conversation with the author at Mount Stewart in March 2009.
39 Hyde, *Londonderry House and its Pictures*, p. 17.
40 De Courcy, *Society's Queen*, p. 284; the associated statement that both *Hambletonian* and the Castlereagh papers were at Mount Stewart through the 1930s is incorrect.
41 James Lees-Milne, *Diaries, 1942–1954* (London: John Murray, 1995), pp. 360–72; *The Times*, 27 July 1962, p. 5.
42 Nikolas Pevsner, *The Buildings of England: County Durham* (2nd edn. London: Penguin, 1983), p. 515.
43 *The Londonderry Album: Portraits from a Great House* (London: Blond & Briggs, 1978), p. 86.
44 Interview with Lady Mairi Bury, 26 March 2009.
45 De Courcy, *Society's Queen*, pp. 60, 180–1.
46 Bence-Jones, *Life in an Irish Country House*, p. 203.
47 Interview with Lady Mairi Bury, 26 March 2009; Fingall, *Seventy Years Young*, p. 164.
48 Bence-Jones, *Life in an Irish Country House*, p. 201.
49 Belfast, PRONI, D654/51/15.
50 Interview with Lady Mairi Bury, 26 March 2009.
51 Felicity Stimpson, 'The Library at Wallington', *The Book Collector*, lviii, 1

(Spring 2009), pp. 45–71.

52 Interview with Lady Mairi Bury, 26 March 2009.

53 Fingall, *Seventy Years Young*, p. 208.

54 De Courcy, *Society's Queen*, p. 288.

55 Hyde, *The Londonderrys*, p. 258; Bence-Jones, *Life in an Irish County House*, p. 206.

56 Edith, Marchioness of Londonderry, *Henry Chaplin: A Memoir* (London: Macmillan, 1926), p. 123.

57 *The Irish Times*, 19 November 1928, p. 6.

58 Fingall, *Seventy Years Young*, pp. 29, 35.

59 Hyde is usually described in press articles (for example in *The Irish Times*, 30 April 1937) as Lord Londonderry's secretary, a designation which puzzled Lady Mairi Bury, who recalled (interview, 26 March 2009) that her father already had a secretary when Hyde first became acquainted with the Londonderry family. The *ODNB* – derived mostly from personal knowledge – implies that the appointment as Private Secretary may have followed that as Librarian; *The Irish Times*, 19 July 1956, p. 6.

60 *The Times*, 24 April 1959, p. 17.

61 Urquhart, *The Ladies of Londonderry*, p. 185; Cannadine, *The Decline and Fall of the British Aristocracy*, p. 344; *ODNB*.

62 Urquhart, *The Ladies of Londonderry*, p. 138; Cannadine, *The Decline and Fall of the British Aristocracy*, p. 228.

63 *The Times*, 16 May 1916.

64 Londonderry, *Retrospect*, pp. 189–90.

65 Londonderry, *Retrospect*, p. 222.

66 Londonderry, *Henry Chaplin: A Memoir*, p. 161.

67 Hyde, *The Londonderrys*, p. 160.

68 *The Irish Times*, 27 December 1924, p. 14; *The Times*, 24 April 1959, p. 17

69 David Marquand, *Ramsay MacDonald* (London: Cape, 1977), p. 405.

70 Marquand, *Ramsay MacDonald*, p. 182; Stephen R. Ward, *James Ramsay MacDonald: Low Born Among the High Brows* (New York: Peter Lang, 1990), p. 238.

71 De Courcy, *Society's Queen*, p. 271.

72 Marquand, *Ramsay MacDonald*, p. 200; *The Irish Times*, 6 August 1932, p. 9.

73 Urquhart, *The Ladies of Londonderry*, p. 168

74 David Marquand, *Ramsay MacDonald*, p. 187.

75 Londonderry, *Retrospect*, pp. 223-4; Hugh Dalton, *Call Back Yesterday* (London: Muller, 1953), pp. 175–6.

76 *The Irish Times*, 14 June 1935, p. 3; De Courcy, *Society's Queen*, p. 1.

77 Bence-Jones, *Life in an Irish Country House*, p. 204.

78 Hyde, *The Londonderrys*, p. 173.

79 Cannadine, *The Decline and Fall of the British Aristocracy*, p. 344.

80 Andrew Roberts, *'The Holy Fox': the Life of Lord Halifax* (London: Phoenix, 1997), p. 152.

81 J.C.C. Davidson, *Memoirs of a Conservative* (London: Weidenfeld & Nicolson, 1969), p. 405.

82 *The Manchester Guardian*, 24 February 1936.

83 Hyde, *The Londonderrys*, p. 221; *ODNB*.

84 Hyde, *The Londonderrys*, p. 226.

85 Hyde, *The Londonderrys*, p. 172; Ward, *James Ramsay MacDonald*, p. 234.

86 Ian Kershaw, *Making Friends with Hitler: Lord Londonderry and Britain's Road to War* (London: Penguin, 2005), p. 59.

87 *The Manchester Guardian*, 22 February 1936, p. 16.

88 Urquhart, *The Ladies of Londonderry*, p. 195.

89 Hyde, *The Londonderrys*, p. 230.

90 6th Marquess of Londonderry, *Ourselves and Germany* (London: Robert Hale, 1938), p 7.

91 *The Manchester Guardian*, 24 February 1936.

92 Urquhart, *The Ladies of Londonderry*, p. 200.

93 Martin Gilbert, *Sir Horace Rumbold: Portrait of a Diplomat, 1869–1941* (London: Heinemann, 1973), p. 440.

94 *The Irish Times*, 30 May 1938, p. 9.

95 Hyde, *The Londonderrys*, p. 240.

96 Kershaw, *Making Friends with Hitler*, p 182; Henry Channon, *Chips. The Diary of Sir Henry Channon* (London: Weidenfeld & Nicolson, 1993), p. 62.

97 *The Times*, 14 October 1939, p. 10.

98 *The Observer*, 2 May 1943, p. 3.

99 Londonderry, *Ourselves and Germany*, p. 10.

100 Ian Kershaw, *Hitler, 1889–1936: Hubris* (London: Penguin, 1999), p. xiv.

101 Interview with Lady Mairi Bury, 26 March 2009.

102 Interview with Lady Mairi Bury, 26 March 2009; *ODNB*.

103 *ODNB*.

104 The most detailed material on the Ark can be found in a dossier compiled by Lady Londonderry towards the end of her life, now Belfast, PRONI, D3099/3/12/1–39. Lady Londonderry appears to have been contemplating a book on the Ark shortly before her death in 1959.

105 *ODNB*.

106 Urquhart, *The Ladies of Londonderry*, p. 145; Londonderry, *Retrospect*, p. 197.

107 De Courcy, *Society's Queen*, p. 199.

108 Londonderry, *Retrospect*, p. 190; *The Irish Times*, 4 March 1926, p. 7; *The Irish Times*, 21 July 1931, p. 4.

109 Hyde, *The Londonderrys*, p. 244; Shane Leslie, *Long Shadows* (London: John Murray, 1966), p. 246.

110 Belfast, PRONI, D3099/3/16/222; for Lord Londonderry's own attitude, see *Londonderry, Ourselves and Germany*, pp. 170–1.

111 *The Times*, 5 January 1933, p. 8.

112 Londonderry, *Retrospect*, p. 205.

113 Augusta, Lady Gregory, *Lady Gregory's Journals* (Gerrard's Cross: Smythe, 1978), ii, p. 75.

114 *The Irish Times*, 12 June 1926, p. 4.

115 Belfast, PRONI, D3099/3/16/185.

116 Belfast, PRONI, D3099/3/16/171.

117 Belfast, PRONI, D3099/3/16/161; D3099/1/16/153.

118 Belfast, PRONI, D3099/3/16/229–238.

119 Harold Nicolson, *Helen's Tower* (London: Constable, 1937), p. 138; *Catalogue of the Library of Helen's Tower belonging to the Marquess of Dufferin and Ava* (Belfast: M'Caw, Stevenson & Orr, 1901); Peter Rankin (ed.), *Clandeboye* (Belfast: Ulster Architectural Heritage Society, 1985), pp. 19, 24. 29–30.

120 In June 1925, there was a garden party for 5000 at Mount Stewart, for example, with the RUC band and 'refreshments were provided on the lawn' (*The Irish Times*, 10 June 1925, p. 4).

121 *The Times*, 3 May 1933, p. 17.

122 Gregory, *Journals*, i, p. 603.

123 Sheehy, *The Rediscovery of Ireland's Past*, pp. 107, 111–12.

124 Belfast, PRONI, D3099/3/16/247.

125 Gregory, *Journals*, ii, p. 132; Sheehy, *The Rediscovery of Ireland's Past*, p. 119.

126 Belfast, PRONI, D3099/3/16/243.

127 Interview with Lady Mairi Bury, 26 March 2009.

128 Belfast, PRONI, D3099/3/16/251.

129 Augusta, Lady Gregory, *Coole* (Dublin: Cuala Press, 1931), pp. 1–2, 21.

130 Henry Channon, *Chips. The Diaries of Sir Henry Channon* (London: Weidenfeld, 1993), p. 35.

131 Hyde, *The Londonderrys*, p. 141.

132 Hyde, *The Londonderrys*, p. 260.

133 Hyde, *Londonderry House and Its Pictures*, p. v.

134 Hyde, *The Londonderrys*, p. 257.

Note on sources

1 The question, which with the increasingly availability of digital surrogates is becoming pressing, is very helpfully addressed by David Pearson in his recent *Books as History* (London: British Library, 2008).

2 David Pearson, *English Bookbinding Styles, English Bookbinding Styles, 1450–1800* (London: British Library, 2004).

3 M. Pollard, *Dublin Trade in Books, 1550–1800* (Oxford: Clarendon Press, 1989); M. Pollard, *A Dictionary of Members of the Dublin Book Trade, 1550–1800* (London: Bibliographical Society, 2000).

4 Toby Barnard, *A Guide to Sources for the History of Material Culture in Ireland, 1500–2000* (Dublin: Four Courts Press, 2005), p. 59.

Index

Page references in *italics* refer to illustrations